John VAHLSTROM

Christmas

from Ma...

Luther Englund

Charcoal portrait of C. V. Bowman by Warner Sallman

Son of the People

The Autobiography of C. V. Bowman

translated by Eric G. Hawkinson
edited by Lois Bowman Michaelson

Photos: We are indebted to the Covenant Archives and members of the Bowman family for the pictures that grace this book. The charcoal sketch by Warner Sallman is included by permission of C. V. Bowman's grandson Ted Bowman.

ISBN 0-910-452-68-7
Copyright © Covenant Publications
3200 W. Foster Avenue
Chicago, Illinois 60625
312-478-4676

Design: Mary M. Helfrich
Production assistants: Gregory Sager,
Jane K. Swanson-Nystrom, and Jill D. Taylor

Foreword

The soul of a religious movement is always more than the sum of those daily events by which its progress in history can be traced. Though bound like everything human to space and time and subject to the limitations of earthly life and death, the spirit of a people—especially a Christian people—is never entirely captive to those realities.

Sometimes that spirit or soul comes alive in one or another of its members, in this case a young lad who later became a pastor, historian, and president of what we now know as The Evangelical Covenant Church.

That is reason enough for publishing *Son of the People,* but sensitive and thoughtful readers will garner a good deal more as well. This is a truly human story, filled with the pathos and joy that belong to being human, and it is marked by that irenic spirit of good will for all of humankind that has characterized the Covenant Church at its best.

We are grateful, therefore, to all who have had a share in bringing the book to completion. And we send it forth in the same spirit that we believe generated it in the first place—not to call attention to itself but to laud the name of the sovereign God who has provided all that any of us needs to be fully human in the person of Jesus Christ and the ongoing work of his Church in the world.

James R. Hawkinson
Executive Secretary of Publications

Introduction

This publication culminates an effort begun in 1974, when Eric G. Hawkinson, then Covenant archivist, translated the book, *Allmogesonen,* by Carl Victor Bowman. Hawkinson then went on to do the same for an unpublished manuscript Bowman wrote in 1929 and intended as a sequel to the previously published volume. The second manuscript, found among Bowman's files after his death, was preserved by his son Malcolm.

In the late 1970s, informal discussion by members of the Bowman family laid the groundwork for a formal effort in 1983 to encourage the publication of the two translated manuscripts as a single volume. Affirmative interest by the Commission on Covenant History and Covenant Publications paved the way for development of a framework for editing and correcting the manuscript.

Two grandchildren of C. V. Bowman made major commitments to this task. Vernon B. Westburg carefully reviewed, clarified, and corrected the translation. Lois Bowman Michaelson edited the manuscript in consultation with Westburg.

Bowman himself commented in the preface to Volume One that he knew the manuscript needed further revision, but that he had neither the time nor desire to work on it. The fact that Volume Two was left incomplete implies that Bowman did not consider it ready for publication either.

Michaelson summarizes her thoughts on working with the project as follows:

"As I have worked on this manuscript and become acquainted for the first time with a grandfather I never knew, I've developed a feeling of loyalty to him. I must help convey his ideas as accurately and gracefully as possible, even if that means occasionally saying things more effectively than he said them originally. I hope he would approve of my completing what he began."

In her own fashion as a writer and teacher of English, Michaelson is following in the footsteps of her grandfather, who, according to Covenant historial Karl A. Olsson, was a "fair and able historian with a professional respect for sources and for responsible inferences from them."

Hence, Michaelson's priorities for the editorial task were: 1) faithfulness to the original meaning; 2) clarity and readability; and 3) enjoyment of the reader. As the reader may surmise, considerable debate and discussion among those working on this project transpired over issues of fidelity to form and substance.

The book itself is disarming in its forthright style, as Bowman writes with a gentle truthfulness about his life. To some extent he appears to feel his life was representative of a generation of people who, like himself, were products of social upheaval transformed by the clear grace and working of God over the years of their lives; hence, *Son of the People.* In choosing this title, he seemed to be saying that while family molds a life, so does the wider community, especially the community of faith. At the same time Bowman emerges as a thoughtful and insightful commentator on topics ranging from pastoral calls to parental discipline. Often his views bear a remarkable sense of contemporary application.

During my own education, I noticed that Bowman was somewhat of an unknown quantity. He was president of the Covenant during one of our most difficult periods. Yet few of his papers found their way into the Covenant Archives to become source material for subsequent historians. While this volume ends but midway through his career, a clearer picture of the man emerges, as well as of the influences and people who helped shape his life. We are indebted to Zenos E. Hawkinson for his epilogue to this volume, noting that life in context and indicating what later became of Bowman in the Covenant he loved and served.

Besides Westburg and Michaelson, others deserving credit for their roles in this publication are Doreen Olson for typing the original Hawkinson manuscripts, Merle Michaelson for typing the edited manuscript, and several members of the Bowman family for the funding to underwrite publication. Finally, I would like to thank the Commission on Covenant History, James Hawkinson, and the staff of Covenant Publications for their work and support of this publication.

Mark S. Olson, great-grandson
May 23, 1988, Aurora, Nebraska

Chronology of Carl Victor Bowman

June 13, 1868	Born, Småland, Sweden
Sept. 9, 1879	Left home for America
Oct. 3, 1879	Arrived in Chicago
1885	Converted under preaching of F. M. Johnson, Tabernacle Church, Chicago
Dec. 1889—May 1890	First return trip to Sweden
1892	Entered Covenant school in Minneapolis, 1 year
1894	Returned to Covenant school, now North Park in Chicago
1896	Graduated, North Park Seminary
	Intern pastor, Escanaba, Michigan
	Intern preaching, Blue Island, Illinois
Summer 1896	Pulpit supply, Mission Covenant Church, Rockford, Illinois, while F. M. Johnson was in Sweden
Oct. 1896—Oct. 1900	Pastor, Tabernacle Church, Chicago
March 10, 1897	Married to Julia Nelson, Chicago
June 3, 1897	Ordained at Annual Meeting at North Park
1900-1907	Pastor, Salem Covenant Church, Minneapolis
1904-1907	Part-time superintendent, Northwest Conference
Summer 1906	Second return trip to Sweden
1907-1910	First full-time superintendent, Northwest Conference
1910-1917	Pastor, Covenant Congregational Church, Boston, Massachusetts
1917-1920	Pastor, Edgewater Covenant Church, Chicago
1920-1927	First secretary of missions, Evangelical Covenant Church
1927-1933	President, Evangelical Covenant Church
August 4, 1937	Died, Chicago

Contents

Dates covered by the book
Volume One   1868-1889
Volume Two   1889-1912

Marbäck Parish, with church in background

Volume One

Preface to Volume One

When I began to write these chapters nearly thirty years ago I had no idea that they would become this long or that they would be published in book form. I wrote because I needed the practice and because I enjoyed it as a pastime; only after my notes grew did I begin to consider the possibility of sharing them with the public. A few years ago [1923] the first chapter was published in the Christmas annual *Aurora,* and now, at the suggestion of friends who have read the manuscript, I have decided to let the other chapters be published also.

During the last two years I have occasionally taken my old work out of the drawer and found a certain enjoyment in rereading it, making minor changes as I went along. I am well aware that many other improvements could be made in both form and content if the manuscript were revised further, but for that I have neither time nor desire right now. Therefore the book appears without pretense, like a child at play in a nursery. But just as a child often entertains us adults, this book may evoke a smile and awaken memories of a happy childhood long past, in readers who have become gray and grim in the struggle of life. It also invites us to be thankful to him who leads us all according to his eternally good plans.

C. V. Bowman
Chicago, Illinois
October 1, 1926

Chapter One

The Old Soldier Home

About fifty years ago [1870s]
in the parish of Marbäck stood a little cottage at the foot of a hill.
It was old but not dilapidated, and its red walls and tile roof, its
white doors and window frames, and its fieldstone foundation made
it look youthful.

It was surrounded by birches, aspens, and alders, and a little
farther away on one side was a thick pine forest. These trees were
like sentries posted by the Creator to guard the safety and comfort
of those who lived in the cottage: an efficient craftsman, his happy,
hardworking wife, and their rosy children, two boys and two girls
born under that roof.

The oldest of the children was Kalle.*

In the yard were a small flower bed, a winding footpath, some
meager currant and gooseberry bushes, and a cherry tree whose
patriarchal crown yielded a rich yearly harvest of tasty white-heart
fruit. On a stone pile a little ways off grew a couple of tall mountain ash whose red berries the children liked to fry on hot coals to
eat when they got hungry between meals.

Dug out of the hill near the ash trees was the cellar, with its

---

* Carl (Swedish *Kalle*) was the name Bowman went by as a child. As a young man
and seminarian he was called Victor. He was best known as C. V. Bowman, the name
he used as a minister. He took the name Bowman from his aunt and uncle in Chicago with whom he lived upon emigrating; his parents' surname was Skott.

roof of boards. All the boys in the neighborhood—and sometimes even the girls—were fascinated by it and would succumb to the temptation to climb to the ridge of the roof and then slide, with gathering speed, down the sloping boards. But their wild joy often changed to wailing when a knot or nail would tear their pants or carve even deeper wounds. They paid little attention to the latter, as young skin heals easily, but the pants were a different matter, for torn clothing awakened storms at home. Parents always assumed that it implied mischief to be cured with the whip. A few smarting birch-branch stripes on a boy's already scratched posterior was a sad conclusion to the fun of the cellar door. Yet the tempting roof with its slivers and nails remained a constant invitation to new adventures, mishaps, and stripes.

Near the cottage, on the left as one came out, lay a greyish barn roofed with straw made mossy by age. This was the main building in the complex, serving as haymow, threshing floor, hog pen, chicken coop, and woodshed. Here lived the useful cow, the shaggy sheep, the grubbing swine, and the cackling chickens, all with their own quarters furnished according to their needs.

In front of the cottage were pastures and meadows, open fields and fences. The rolling ground sloped away from the house to the slow stream, where it began to rise again until the pine forests finally obscured the view to the west.

On the incline of the hill behind the cottage was the "waterworks," never in human memory out of order, a spring with clear, murmuring water from which one scooped freely with dipper and bucket. When they became thirsty at play the children would drink without dippers, lying flat with their faces mirrored in the water. The stream wound its way through the meadow where the field creatures slaked their thirst both summer and winter.

The fields of the cottage were small and not very fertile, for the whole area was meager and stone-bound. In fact, one author suggests that heaven had given this area stones instead of bread. Nevertheless, the earth gave a moderate harvest, which was all the farmer expected as reward for his labor. Our contemporary inflated demand for comfort and luxury was then unknown in Marbäck Parish.

But if the Creator had not endowed the area with fertile fields, he had bestowed it with beautiful scenery. Here were hills and dales, forests and cultivated fields, brooks, streams, waterfalls, and lakes with idyllic shores, all artwork from the hand of God.

The cottage was called Smedhemmet, the Blacksmith Home. Perhaps a blacksmith had lived there at one time and the cottage derived its name from that. Since the chief tailor of the parish now had his shop and dwelling there a more appropriate name would have been the Tailor Home, yet no one considered a rechristening. A change of name per se does not ennoble a place or person anyway.

The house was built in the old-fashioned way, intended to withstand the tooth of centuries. Between the dressed logs was a mixture of plaster and moss which made the walls tight, and the rest was carefully paneled with boards.

The main entrance, on the long wall facing west, had white double doors that were, by present standards, low, like the cottage itself. In front of the high threshold lay a broad stone slab unshaped by chisel or sledgehammer but worn by footsteps through the passing years.

Above the entrance hung a blue and gold tablet inscribed with the Swedish arms and a notice that the building belonged to the Twenty-seventh Company of the North Vebbo Division of the Swedish army; it had once been a soldier's home. At that time the servant of the crown did not receive his pay in money but was given a place to live and a little land to use as he wished. The small farmers in the district, as a portion of their taxes for the defense of the kingdom, were obliged to help the soldier with his farming. Like so many other soldiers' homes in Sweden, this one was later sold at auction. It has since been torn down and the property added to the nearest farm.

Let us go back now as if we were visiting Marbäck. The white doors, which open inward, hang on heavy hinges, and the right-hand door has a heavy wooden handle below a large keyhole. Since the door stands ajar, we take the liberty of stepping into the entry. There on the wall hangs a key the size of a small pistol, and alongside it the scythe and sickle, hoe and rake. The key probably hasn't been used for years because in this region no one fears thieves. Only when going on a long journey does one lock the door and hide the key under the stone slab or hang it on the corner of the cottage almost in front of the eyes of anyone who comes. This beautiful trait of confidence in others has all but disappeared with our rising civilization; now one installs locks and bolts on doors in order to feel safe in one's own house. Small honor, you proud civilization!

To the right in the entry is a broad unpainted door with hand-forged hinges, handle, and latch. Since there is no lock we can, according to the custom of the area, open and enter without knocking. The high threshold, worn in the middle by children's feet, is a quiet protest against the entrance of unauthorized persons.

The cottage is filled with an absolute quiet, like the solemn stillness of a cathedral. Even the cat seems to have left; his empty milk saucer sits by the stove. No one is home. We hesitate at the door as we used to when we entered a strange home as children.

Respectfully we examine the cottage. The furnishings are simple, in keeping with the family's resources. All the furniture has been made by "Carpenter Johan," who has himself felled the pine and birch in the forest, sawed it into boards, formed each piece in the "carpenter-cottage," and finally delivered items to his customers. At this time home industry is in flower and one trades directly with one's fellow parishioners without the increase in cost brought about by a middleman.

Immediately to the right of the door stands a tall unpainted chest whose drawers and doors have handles of lathe-turned buttons. On top of it, near the ceiling, is the household's library: a Bible, a book of sermons, a hymnal, a biblical history, a catechism, and an ABC book. A good library, though hardly extensive. Next to the chest, hanging in broad home-woven bands, is a black serving tray, bumped and scratched from much use.

Under the window on the long wall is a variegated sofa with a pull-out bed in which a straw mattress, pillows, and blankets are hidden. This is the children's bed when they have outgrown the cradle, and since the bottom of it is only a few inches from the floor it is like a deep trough that they cannot fall out of no matter how restless their sleep. Beyond this on the same wall and on the opposite wall are similar beds, both made up.

On the wall nearest the front stands the most elegant piece of furniture in the house, a well-made and newly painted bureau, father's sacred place which the children are not allowed to touch. Drawers and flaps are kept locked, including the little drawer containing father's shaving equipment. On the bureau stands a pretty little mirror, the only one in the house.

Next to the bureau hangs an old-fashioned wall clock with pendulum and weight. Quietly and solemnly it ticks as if to extol the virtue of thankfulness and chase away complaint. The clock and the tray, both practical, are the only wall decorations in the house.

Just in front of the gable window with its four square panes is an unpainted drop-leaf table on which are two brass candlesticks, and beside the table is a Singer sewing machine, one of the first to find its way to this area from America. The room also contains a simple dining table, a few chairs, a spinning wheel, and a cradle.

Though there is a home-woven rag rug on the scrubbed floor one can still see that the broad floorboards are joined rather carelessly and that footsteps and scrub brush have worn them deeply. The hard, raised knots are like bunions or warts, and big nail heads stand out in rows crossways.

In the corner on the left as we enter the cottage we see the massive fireplace with its vaulted arch. Up by the ceiling is a shelf for matches and birch branches, the latter a quiet warning to the children in case they should be tempted to disobey. During winter, large logs burn on the hearth.

When winter winds invaded nook and corner,
From skates and ice to hearth we would retire.
I still recall the evening's joy and beauty—
How good to dream beside the birchwood fire!

Now, however, it is summer, and the fireplace has been whitewashed and decorated like a bride, with leafy branches on the hearth and a simple vase of meadow flowers on the mantle.

This is the most prominent room in the house and functions not only as dining room, bedroom, and parlor but as tailor shop. It is large enough for all this because demands are modest.

Out in the kitchen, which has only one small window and a door to the backyard, there is a water bucket, a washboard, and a simple table. On the unplastered walls are shelves for pots, kettles, and pans. The kitchen stove with its big baking oven takes up most of one wall, and the bread supply of the household hangs near the ceiling on a long pole—thin loaves with a hole in the middle so that they can be dried and kept. In these days one seldom eats fresh bread in Marbäck Parish.

Before we leave the cottage we take the liberty of climbing up to the attic by an open stairway leading from the entry. The stair lacks handrails so it is dangerous for children, who sometimes in their nightmares fall down and bruise themselves terribly. The single room has a little window at each gable and the ceiling is so low that at its apex a grown man has to bend so as not to bump his head.

Against one of the long walls rests the loom, like a bear in hibernation. In the spring when it was "taken down" it was really carried up to the attic until mother found more time to weave. In one corner is a pile of rubbish which will be kept for a while. Both special clothing and everyday dress hang on heavy pegs burrowed into the rafters. There is mother's bridal gown, which has been used only on a few festive occasions since the wedding day, and father's wedding coat, highly valued but seldom worn, a proud aristocrat in a simple setting. Peas, apples, and dried cherries are also stored in the attic, all under lock and key so that the children cannot sample them without permission.

Generations have gone in and out of this simple cottage, all with their reasons for joy and their moments of sorrow. Only a few individuals who have lived under its roof remain, but they remember with special fondness their old childhood home. New generations have pressed forward with greater demands. The old soldier's home is no more.

Life is eventful and changing. We grow up with cradle songs, prattle, and childhood joys, but then comes life's seriousness when the flow of events tears us away and casts us out on the great highroad where the weak are often trampled. In the haste and tumult we forget our childhoods and the bright world of youth for a time. But suddenly the old memories revive as if from the dead, some like angels of light and others like black demons. In memory we all return to our childhood homes.

Home, home, my dear home!
No other place on earth is
As beautiful as you, my home.

Chapter Two

Life of the People in the Parish

The soldier's home was far from the king's highway or any other public thoroughfare. The eastern railroad trunk line was being built, but it went through nearby parishes without disturbing the quietness and calm of Marbäck. The stream of inquisitive tourists and the aimless folk wanderers were as yet unknown, and telephones, automobiles, and airplanes had not yet begun to buzz in people's ears.

The people lived a simple and unpretentious life, diligently keeping up their homes, cultivating their fields, harvesting their crops, and caring for their livestock. They looked upon the long hours of hard work as nature's good order in an evil world and complained only modestly as they assumed their burdens of labor and responsibility. These were honorable people who saw virtue in honest living even though they were afflicted with the usual human weaknesses. Of course, it was more difficult for some than for others to resist temptations and walk straight ahead on the path of righteousness.

The comparatively poor soil and small fields produced no great harvests for the market but bore just enough for the people's needs, though there were times when they hardly did that. The industrious farmer would have a few eggs and some butter to sell and on market days would send them to town, or he or his wife would take them personally and then buy coffee, sugar, and other household supplies.

At times a farmer would have a horse, a cow, a steer, or a pair of oxen to sell. These also were brought to the nearest marketplace where buyer and seller met to trade. With all the ability at his command he would expound on the excellent qualities and ancestry of the animals. The purchasers would listen, make their sagacious objections, and bargain vehemently. Sometimes, under favorable circumstances, the purchasers would outbid each other, much to the satisfaction of the seller, but at other times buyers were few or less inclined to do business so that the seller had to take the animals home again. If he did succeed in making a transaction, the sale was solemnly concluded and confirmed with several drinks at the local tavern at the seller's expense. This time-honored custom brought embarrassment and harm to many farmers who tended toward excess. Liquor muddied the upper story and weakened the lower limbs so that the farmer was rather helpless for the next few hours. He would fall asleep in the wagon on the way home while the sober oxen plodded philosophically on. In more severe cases the inebriated farmer tumbled out of the wagon unconscious and lay by the wayside until he had sobered up.

Earlier, home distilleries had blossomed in Marbäck, but this illicit practice had finally been abolished. Instead, hard liquor was now sold in the store under protection of law and without limitation by authorities. Thirsty throats could easily obtain liquor, yet drinking was not a great weakness of the people; rather, it was a matter of good form to treat liberally on fair and market days, for baptisms, funerals, and weddings, and at Christmas and New Year's celebrations. It was considered manly to treat and manly to drink, but during this exchange of courtesies the participants at times became drunk as crows.

The women of Marbäck Parish kept themselves untainted by this defect. They prepared the food and other necessities of the home and took care of the children. During the summer they also shared the work in the field, meadow, and barn. During the winter they mended clothing, knit stockings and mittens, and spun and wove for the whole household. They taught the children to read, and later when the youngsters began to attend school, examined them in their lessons. The women's work was therefore extremely varied and claimed all their time. They contributed an unbelievable amount to the preservation, comfort, and prosperity of the home.

Children were not permitted to be idle or to waste their time in play, for the people believed that "work furthers health and success and hinders opportunities to sin." Boys and girls alike were put to work early, both inside and outside the home so that it became as natural for them to work as to eat. At sixteen many a boy was a fully qualified farmhand or servant and many a girl could take full responsibility for a household.

The inhabitants of the parish had, with few exceptions, lived there all their lives, and in most cases their parents and grandparents had too, often on the same farmstead and in the same house. Many a graying farmer had hardly visited the nearest city, for in those days it was considered good to be quiet on the land and not desire to search out the wide world. In keeping with this view, it was counted as an honor for a young man to seek his life's companion among the daughters of the parish. Why should he be so vain and proud as to look outside the parish for a fiancée while there were excellent marriageable daughters right there in Marbäck!

We restless children of the twentieth century who can hardly be still while we sleep have difficulty understanding how calmly people lived in our ancestral country a half century ago. Our parents did not worry about national politics; the king took care of that with our Lord's help. And the common person did not even know about the ferment taking place in world politics until the worst aspects had subsided. It was truly a calm age, especially in the more remote settlements.

Now conditions are entirely different. Railroads and steamboat lines have spun a net around the earth, making it possible to travel far and wide at low cost. The telegraph, the telephone, the newspaper, and most recently the radio have brought us into contact with the whole world and awakened our interest in what is distant. People have wider views and greater demands. The whole world has become their parish, and world events have become local news. The narrow world of our parents has disappeared forever.

At the time of our story the weekly newspaper and a few small monthly publications had seen the light of day in the cities, but very few of them had found their way to the common people in the countryside. The great modern daily papers, those giants of printer's ink that engage whole armies of newshounds, editors, typesetters, and readers, had not yet had time to grow up in the kingdom of Sweden.

The few newspapers available at that time were small and

expensive, so most of the people could not afford to buy one however much they may have wanted to do so. Fortunately this difficulty was overcome if several people bought a subscription together, each paying a part and each reading the paper in turn, one after the other. The one who had it first had a cleaner copy and fresher news than the other "partnership readers," but all were satisfied because in any case they owned a share in the paper and could, though somewhat late, follow developments out in the big wide world. In this regard modern people make far greater demands. They want the morning paper in bed so they will know the latest world events before they puts their feet in their slippers. The ink is hardly dry before the newspaper is delivered and the news-hungry reader devours its encyclopedic and often questionable content.

In Marbäck those who subscribed to a paper together usually met at the church on Sunday and there delivered the "wisdom sheet" to each other. In this way the churchyard became a kind of post office where people not only received the newspaper, but discussed the remarkable things they had read during the week. Those who had no paper listened with hungry ears for the news crumbs that the paper-reading farmer let fall from his sumptuously laden table. Those who had a share in a subscription felt a bit superior to their neighbors who could not afford such luxury and who therefore were less enlightened.

This is how the subscription sharing had started:

It had always been a significant moment when Anders-Peter, crammed full of world news and self-importance, would deliver the paper to Per-August. Inquisitive parishioners would gather round as Anders-Peter solemnly related what had happened out in the world most recently. Not even the rector's mighty explication of the day's appointed gospel made such a deep impression on the Marbäck people as Anders-Peter's news proclamation out there in front of the church.

Among his listeners were some who felt a twinge of jealousy and were highly annoyed that Anders-Peter, who, of course, was an ordinary person, should every Sunday orate like a rector in the pulpit. They feared that the heavy-set man would become puffed up; they had already noticed that he behaved quite ridiculously over his knowledge. In Anders-Peter they began to see a practical exposition of the Bible passage that says that "knowledge puffeth up."

"Each of us should have a paper so that Anders-Peter cannot

in his pride destroy the whole worship service for Christians every Sunday," Kalle-Blink burst out with a toss of his head.

"Well spoken, Kalle. We do not need to stand here Sunday after Sunday and listen to his eternal and empty words," Kvan-Gustav added.

"If you agree," chirped Görans-Lasse, pressing his stiff leg into the ground, "the three of us will subscribe to a paper for ourselves. Then Anders-Peter can spread himself out over the whole church-yard and not get a living soul to listen to his reverberations."

All three were enthusiastic about the idea, and Görans-Lasse, who had clothed their thoughts in words, was given the task of ordering the subscription. Thus he became the leading member of the "newspaper partnership" and, outside the church on Sundays, a powerful competitor of Anders-Peter.

The more people in the parish read newspapers the more people craved them and the news they brought. Several "news part-nerships" were organized, and soon every farmer and tenant read newspapers more diligently than he read sermons and the psalm-book. In time the newspapers lowered their subscription prices so that the common person could afford a paper, and partnership read-ing gradually ceased.

Among the shining lights in Marbäck Parish the rector naturally took first place, for in spite of the increasing enlightenment of the people, he continued to be superior to his parishioners in knowl-edge and culture. He had, of course, studied at Uppsala for many years and acquired a great deal of general knowledge as well as spe-cial training for his unique calling. He had rich life experience, many volumes in his library, and newspapers from the capital city itself, and because of his office he was in contact with the large landowners and other people of status in the kingdom. In addition, his office gave him special veneration because he was the representative of the Most High and his messenger to the people in Marbäck Parish. At least the old folks saw him this way. He was an honest man who conscientiously took care of his work and walked worthy of his office. The life of drunkenness and card playing, which some of the servants of the church were guilty of in the old days, was completely foreign to him.

Yet in spite of the rector's exemplary living, several people saw him as less warm religiously than some others of the cloth. The warmhearted "readers" thought they could detect that his spiritual

15

pulse was not strong enough and his message did not have the right ring, but whether this was actually true cannot easily be determined at this late date.

As a whole, the people of the parish respected their shepherd of souls and venerated his office; but when it came to following his example and heeding his exhortations, they exercised considerable freedom. They said that it was the preacher's job to warn and exhort, but that neither the rector nor our Lord ought to be strict with people if they showed proper respect for the church and her servant; a few offenses here and there were inevitable because of the weakness of the flesh.

Though High Mass was the only worship service during the week in the old church, it seldom attracted large crowds. Only on the greater church festivals was the attendance better. Nor did all who went to the temple in their Sunday best go to listen to the exposition of the day's text. Some farmers, tenants, and farmhands spent their time at the parish stables talking about horses, cattle, and the year's crops, while the rector stood before the altar or delivered his important message to souls from the pulpit. While this was not seen as sanctification or Christian virtue, no one seemed to suffer a bad conscience either for this disdain for or lack of interest in the worship service. However, there were also many old and pious pilgrims who faithfully attended worship and with warm prayers supported the rector in his responsible calling.

For many the most interesting part of the worship service was the announcements. If, in the stables, one had talked away the time of the sermon, one usually sneaked into the church when the announcements were to be made. These were of great practical value for the people because they dealt with all sorts of situations in the parish. For example, it might be announced that the king's highway needed repairs here and there and that certain farmers were to put it in order again. It was announced when the crown and community taxes should be paid and when the parish meeting would be held. Announcement was also made concerning public-assistance business, about the folk school, and about parish catechetical meetings. If a young man in the parish had fallen in love with a marriageable maid and the two had now decided to be wed, these plans were announced from the pulpit three Sundays before the solemn act could take place. To elope quietly into the longed-for harbor of marriage was, during the good old times in Sweden, completely impossible.

All deaths in the parish were also noted in the announcements. Solemnly the rector would state that it had pleased God in his perfect wisdom to call apart N. N.,* a reminder to us of our own mortality. Funeral services were announced, and when inventory had been taken and the deceased's property was to be sold at auction, this too was made known. With the greatest care it was specified how many calves, steers, oxen, sheep, fowl, hogs, plows, rollers, wagons, household items, and clothes were to go on the auction block.

The farmers and tenants of the parish were interested in these notices because they dealt with material things, so they listened with both ears even though they had neglected the rector's sermon about the great treasures of the kingdom.

On the way home from church in small groups, people exchanged thoughts about the service and about the weather, but by far the most popular topic was the announcements. Similar conversation continued after returning home. If the wedding banns had been announced for the first time for Pelle of Bo and Stina of By this became a special item of conversation and they made their prophetic comments about the couple's future happiness or unhappiness.

For church celebrations, particularly at Christmas, attendance at services was more general and people placed greater importance on spiritual interests. Especially at Christmas matins at five o'clock Christmas morning, the mood was attractive and inspiring and the building was crowded. The long trip to church in the cold sparkling snow did not frighten old or young but beckoned them to the Lord's house in the early morning. Inside, hundreds of candles twinkled in chandeliers and candelabras. The old-timers gathered in their pews, brought forth the psalmbook painstakingly wrapped in a handkerchief, and carefully readied their glasses. The young, with big eyes and rosy cheeks, gathered with the old, all dressed in their best and in a festive mood. When the organist began to play, young beautiful voices and old trembling voices joined together to sing Wallin's immortal psalm, "All Hail to Thee, O Blessed Morn!" The rector's message about the heavenly gift, the Son of man, God's Son

---

* This could stand for *någon nämde,* meaning "someone named."

17

and the Savior of the world, sounded forth, solemn and inspiring. Who could sit unmoved and indifferent in this festival worship service? In many arose thanksgiving and praise for the arrival of the Heavenly Prince to our low earth and to our hearts. No one's worship was disturbed by the sexton making his rounds in the aisles to snuff the candles or by some old gentleman who, in spite of the mood of celebration, nodded and slept.

The old church in Marbäck was not heated at Christmas or any other time during the winter, so those who attended had to warm up the pews and icy walls as best they could. They shivered and froze when it was crackling cold, and on account of this, one exercised Christian tolerance with the old men who, to honor the season and provide warmth for the body, took a swig from the brandy bottle they had brought. Surreptitiously the flask went from mouth to mouth and the snuff box from nose to nose. Later, through the temperance movement, the brandy bottle came to ill repute and dared not show itself in church at Christmas matins. The old men probably did not freeze any more after this misconduct had been abolished than they had before.

Christmas was the greatest festival of the year at home as well as in church. Children and older folks alike were glad when it came. For several weeks before Christmas great preparations were made so when Christmas Eve came everything was ready. Then one had to *doppa i grytan,* eat *julgröt, lutfisk, sylta, limpa,* * fresh wheat rolls, and twisted cookies. What was not on the table at Christmas! And there were presents and a Christmas tree and celebrations with relatives and friends! Everything combined to create a festive mood which lasted several weeks.

In Marbäck as in other parishes, the Swedish Church had great influence on people. It did much to instruct them in Christian truths and was therefore of greater importance than some of the church critics have been willing to admit. But its deficiencies were also conspicuous. Under the protection of the state it often settled into indolence, satisfied with a cold, stereotyped worship according to the prescription in the handbook. Besides the clearly spiritual tasks of his calling, the rector had to tend to many clerical duties for the

---

* Dip rye bread in the saucepan, eat rice pudding, preserved codfish, jellied veal loaf, rye bread.

state, and these could become the main business if he was comfortable and careless and not burning for the welfare of souls.

Eventually the people in these areas were influenced by the revivals that flowered in many places and gave new impulses not only to the laypeople but to many of the preachers in the Swedish church. The so-called "lay movement" worked toward renewal, awakening and recreating people in Marbäck also. Drunkenness and coarseness disappeared completely. Mission houses were built in which colporteurs from Jönköping's mission society and the National Evangelical Foundation came to preach. Evangelical songs were sung with life and delight in the mission houses and in homes. When a new song came out it was memorized because there were no songbooks, though they were soon to come.

As has been said, the people in Marbäck Parish were by and large honest but poor, though there were a few "better people," as they were called, who had somewhat greater wealth and therefore the right to vote on all important community questions, which the poor at that time could not do. Some had distinguished titles because of their standing in the community or in the Swedish army. Such people were highly esteemed in the parish, and they, together with the rector, constituted a kind of nobility whom those of the lower ranks looked up to.

It must be said to the credit of the Marbäck gentry that they were generally friendly and helpful and did not despise those of lower rank. And those in the lower ranks had not yet learned to call the gentry "bloodsuckers" and other ugly names that are often thoughtlessly used nowadays.

At the time of this story people seldom had leisure for social parties. From childhood all had accustomed themselves to work, which was, in fact, the people's main entertainment, but on the way to and from the church and in the churchyard on Sundays when they met as neighbors and parishioners they greatly appreciated the opportunity to speak at length. At Christmas, however, they took time for entertainment and parties, setting aside all unnecessary work for twenty days until Hilarymass,* when they once again put on workclothes and entered the wholesome struggle for existence.

At times the young people did have a bit more festivity. They

---

* January 13

gave little nameday or birthday parties for each other and usually had a May Day festival and a Midsummer festival. They also had a dance hall for Saturday nights where they danced to the lively music of the violin or accordion until they were almost sick with exhaustion; they could rest up a bit on Sunday after the pranks of the evening.

But not all the youth of the parish could be enticed to the dance hall because the name itself was an abomination to the more serious people, who thought such things were unchristian. They could relate how the devil himself had sometimes appeared unexpectedly at a dance there and how he had once gone after a musician to take him back alive to Blåkulla.* The musician had quickly called on Jesus so that the evil one hastily returned to his dark dwelling with his errand unfinished.

Such stories struck fear into the children and awakened a certain loathing both for the dance hall and for the violin and dance, a disgust that remained in many throughout their lives. During the revivals in the parish the dance hall and other light-hearted activities received a crushing setback because there were hardly any young people left who desired such a life. The impulse itself was missing.

---

* A reference to Walpurgis Night, the eve of May Day, believed in medieval Europe to be the occasion of a witches' sabbath.

Chapter Three

The Strangers

At the time of our story the love of travel had not yet gripped the gentry, much less the common people of Marbäck. Seldom did anyone journey to other parishes except on fair or market days and seldom did people from other parishes come to Marbäck, though occasionally some stranger would visit because of business interests.

The old rag-and-bone man was one of these. He usually came twice a year to cleanse the whole parish of junk: old iron, unused bottles and flasks, and dry bones that had had the marrow cooked out of them. He pulled a rattling cart upon which he loaded his purchases, taking them to some central place where he transferred them to a horse-drawn wagon. He always wore a leather jacket, leather-covered pants, and shoes with wooden soles worn down on one side. He was a heavyset old man with a wrinkled face, short nose, and screwed-up eyes, and he had small brass rings in his ears and a crescent beard sprinkled with gray under his chin. Since he was genial and talkative and knew the art of making himself well liked by young and old, he was a welcome guest at farmsteads and tenant cottages.

In his deep purse he always had plenty of small coins, but he preferred to pay for his purchases with a bar of soap, a packet of sewing needles, or some trinkets that especially fascinated the eyes of children. He understood how to awaken his customers' desire to buy at the same time as he purchased their junk, so he usually

21

came away not only with the rags and castoffs but with a few extra copper and silver coins besides. As a rule he sold far more than he bought; his ability to put people in a good frame of mind made him a great success at business.

Another visitor to Marbäck was a middle-aged bearded man who walked through the parish regularly but less frequently than the rag-and-bone man. Since no one knew either his first or last name, he was simply called *Knallen* or "Old Thunder," which suited him well because he thundered about from place to place carrying a large back packet of weavers' reeds and a box of small things to sell. Because he was from far down in the countryside far to the west the people regarded him almost as a traveler from a foreign country, and he did not object because it gave him a certain respect that he in no other way deserved. From his youth he had been walking in this way through many Swedish provinces, and his ready tongue could relate interesting experiences from near and far.

Old Thunder sold a variety of items, but his specialty was weavers' supplies. At that time each housewife wove during the winter and very early would initiate her daughters into the art as well. One heard the thump of the loom in the cottages early and late as they produced wools and linens for the whole household, and occasionally made an art piece. Since every well-appointed home had a loom, there was a good market for weavers' reeds, and Old Thunder was the only one at hand who could supply them.

Still another peddler, more shrewd than Old Thunder, used to make his rounds in the parish about once a year. This was one of Israel's dispersed children, a chubby little middle-aged man with a big nose. On his back he carried a large heavy packing case which contained a whole variety store.

Upon entering a house, he would approach the sofa or a chair, roll the broad leather straps off his shoulders, and lower his pack to the floor. With his dark and sure business eyes he scanned the household while he made his introductory remarks about weather and road conditions, seeking a suitable connection to the little business speech with which he would open his commerce. He was a businessman clear down to his fingertips.

When his remarks had awakened interest in the members of the household and put them in the right mood, he began to bring forth many useful and gaudy pieces for examination. Since the people in the parish could seldom feast their eyes on the new and the beautiful because they were so far from a store, they lent both eyes and ears to the salesman and were completely enamored with what he displayed. Usually they were gripped by the temptation to buy, and both wisdom and character were required to resist, so that they would not exceed their purse's ability to pay.

"Here is imported lace, fit for a bride," said the salesman, handing it to the eighteen-year-old daughter of the house. "And," he added, looking at the blushing girl, "I also have engagement rings. Or "Look here, good friends, I have first-class soap which I have imported from Paris myself. You can't even buy it in Stockholm. Just smell it. It doesn't cost anything to smell." So the members of the household filled their lungs with the soap's perfume. "Yes, that is good soap, no one can deny it," said the boy who walked about in his stocking feet. It had to be bought, if for nothing more than the perfume, though one must add in passing that it did not last many hours after the salesman had gone his way.

The peddler continued to bring forth thread, silk, sewing needles, pins, hooks, eyes, hairpins, combs, glasses, scissors, pocket knives, and razors. And there were red handkerchiefs bearing the pictures of the king and queen, so beautiful that one could hardly stand to use them. It almost bordered on treason and other unchristian behaviour to wipe your nose right in the eyes of His Majesty King Oscar II and his noble wife Queen Sophia. At least this is what the unspoiled people in Marbäck Parish thought. The peddler assured them that there were thousands of citizens in the kingdom who had no conscience about using such handkerchiefs, but if they did not want to buy them they could instead buy hair oil, shoe black, pocket watches, watch chains, clock keys, tobacco pipes, perfume bottles, mirrors, pocketbooks, Ljunglöven's snuff, or whatever else they might need.

The peddler also brought with him several kinds of cloth for the women, silk shawls for the mother of the house, and strong moleskin for the father and the boys. Thus he was prepared to satisfy every imaginable need that could occur on an ordinary farmstead.

As a good businessman he always pointed out the high quality of his merchandise and the golden opportunity he now offered them to buy necessities at bargain prices. Never were Marbäck's inhabitants so richly provided with eloquent boasting as when the peddler set up shop in their cottages. There was openmouthed astonishment over the merchandise and the merchant's flow of words.

Oh, if only they had plenty of coins in some hiding place! The eighteen-year-old would gladly have bought one half of the peddler's goods and the boy in stocking feet the other, because as the salesman said, everything was so unreasonably good and cheap that in all probability there would never be another opportunity to do business at such prices.

But now the father of the house must decide what was to be purchased because he controlled the exchequer, and he was not as easily carried away by eloquence as the children were. The merchant understood this and made a special effort to awaken the father's desire to buy. When he did become interested in some item the bargaining began, for there was a great difference between the peddler's price and customer's. In order to narrow this gulf they stretched and pulled long and powerfully until through mutual concessions they approached each other. Finally they agreed on an amount, but only under the peddler's protests that he would be completely ruined in less than a month if he always sold at such bargain prices. But in this case he would do so for the sake of good friendship, for he was, as an honorable man, glad that he was able to do something good once to those who were not of his faith. Meanwhile the merchant's packet became a little lighter and father was relieved of a good many hard-earned coins without receiving any unusual value for them.

The rag-and-bone man and the peddler traveled much the same roads and therefore arrived in Marbäck at regular intervals. In contrast, the man from the far west had a larger area to cover and came less often.

Besides these visitors, unexpected businessmen walked through the territory, some perhaps only once, their origin and merits unknown. One of these was the old "clockman" from Mora, whose visit to the parish was still talked about long afterwards. He was an honorable old gentleman dressed a little differently than the people of Marbäck. He had a strange accent and a unique song that pleased the people's ears and hearts. He told of his home by Lake Siljan and his extensive journeys through the provinces, but his real errand was to speak about the clocks he tried to sell. As an expert he would tell how they were manufactured in Dalarna, his native area, and how customers everywhere were satisfied. Here and there at the farms he succeeded in his business, but more often he spoke in vain and had to continue his journey without a sale. But the old clockman left behind him nothing but good memories. Through his visits the people of Marbäck had higher regard for the honorable people of Dalarna who at one time had gathered around King Gösta to save Sweden from a foreign yoke.

But the most remarkable man who had visited Marbäck up to that time was one of the sons of the parish who in his youth had traveled abroad and lived in America for a while. Now after a long absence he came home to visit. At that time it was very unusual for anyone who had lived in America to return for a visit; he was the first of his kind in the whole parish, an extraordinary phenomenon. After a twenty-year absence the "American" was now completely unrecognizable to the friends of his youth and other old acquaintances. Consequently he could, without the least difficulty, play the part of a stranger even to his nearest relatives. This he did in cold blood as if his nerves had been of steel.

He came home without previously notifying his relatives. He walked up into the parish from the railroad station, deliberately arriving at his old parental home in the twilight. There as a stranger he asked for shelter for the night. The old folks, who had carefully considered the biblical word, "Forget not to be hospitable," had more than once gladly opened their home to traveling strangers. But here before them stood a traveler who was clearly a foreigner and, judging from his clothing, some kind of gentleman. The old folks could not see themselves opening their lowly cottage to such a distinguished visitor as this. No pleas from the stranger could induce them to change their decision. They just could not accommodate him.

When he was unsuccessful in staying overnight there he went to a nearby farm and made the same request. After several objections from the housewife she finally consented and promised the stranger shelter. He made himself at home, very talkative and inquisitive but very secretive and inaccessible. His name, his home, and the reason for his visit in the area he kept to himself. The following morning, after sleeping on a hard sofa, he asked his hostess about a certain person from the parish who had gone abroad as a youth. He maintained that he had met him both in Sweden and America and wanted to bring greetings to his parents and sister.

The conversation warmed considerably. It turned out that the housewife was the sister who was to have the greetings. As the conversation wore on the stranger had to confess that he himself was the person they were talking about, and thus the woman's own brother. One can easily imagine the sister's surprise. When she had gathered her thoughts, her joy at seeing her brother again was almost overwhelming. The brother himself, proud of having been able to play such a trick on his sister, thought this lark was worthy of a real American.

It did not take long for the brother and sister to turn their steps toward the old parental home where the sister, her heart pounding with joy, presented her brother who had returned from America. The old folks were dismayed as they realized that the stranger to whom they had denied shelter the night before was their own son. But in spite of this the meeting became very precious. The old folks seemed to become many years younger, and both said that never during their long lifetimes had they experienced such a joyful day as when they saw their son from America again.

The news that an "American" had come to the parish spread like wildfire not only in Marbäck but in surrounding areas, and the practical joke he had played on his sister and parents was the subject of conversation for some time. He was the great phenomenon of the parish whom all discussed and all wanted to see. Outside the church on Sundays he was surrounded by inquisitive parishioners. He answered all their questions with such assurance and high airs that the people got the impression he was a great and mighty man. Nor was he adverse to letting the comrades of his youth and the other people of the parish make a hero of him.

He bragged extravagantly about America and made crushing comparisons between "the big country in the West" and the small and insignificant Sweden. During his boastful descriptions of America the old honorable people of Marbäck began to be a little ashamed because they had stayed for all these years in a pitiful little nook like Sweden. And this modest self-consciousness about their country was heightened even more when the American told how he had had to change his name in America so that no one would suspect he was of Swedish descent. The fact that Sweden at that time rated high in culture and had a glorious history he had evidently not discovered. Nor did he know, apparently, that Sweden had given the world a Carl von Linne and America a John Ericsson, and that Gustav Adolf of Sweden had been one of the world's greatest kings. Had he considered all this he would, of course, have been proud of his descent even in America.

Yes, this was really an odd one. He was as remarkable in his own eyes as that new land was great and rich. He was able to judge and criticize everything in all of Sweden in less time than it took the average man in Marbäck to gather his thoughts.

He always appeared in bright clothes, gloves, a high hat, and patent leather shoes. In the pleat of his shirt was a glittering stickpin and on his watch chain dangled a shimmering medallion. In his vest pocket was a big watch that, judging from appearances, was all gold. On his right hand he had two big rings with gleaming diamonds—or perhaps they were cut glass. When he put his hand in his pocket the money rattled, and he liked to pull up a few silver dollars to show how big the money was in America.

There was gossip and conversation about the American. Everyone wondered how rich he was, but no one dared ask him that or anything else about his exploits. At a little coffee party where someone did question him about his work in America the answer was brief and cryptic: "I have a business." "Does he have a business?" murmured a little old lady with a question mark over her whole face. This irritated the American so that his answer was short and sharp: "Missus should know that businessmen in America do not take insults from anyone. Insulting a businessman has cost many their lives, which Missus should know." The conversation was immediately changed to the weather and other safe subjects so that the coffee party would not be spoiled by explosives. The stranger's occupation remained a secret until another occasion when he happened to say that he was a specialist in liquors, from which the farmers gradually drew the conclusion that he probably owned a tavern. This later proved to be right.

After a few weeks in his home area the American went to Stockholm because he wanted to see with his own eyes "if Stockholm really is a city or only a little village where the king lives," as he expressed it. He was to come back later.

They waited in vain for his return. At last there came a letter from New York saying that he had had to return to America unexpectedly because of his business. Condescendingly he greeted all the Marbäck folk and wished his relatives "good luck."

Thus this uninvited character disappeared from the parish and from the country, but his memory lived on among the people like the memory of a bad dream.

When speaking of strangers we must also mention a group of

less welcome transients who came to the parish at times, namely the gypsies. These people roamed about the countryside and seemed to have their home everywhere and nowhere. They stayed mainly near the highways, preparing their food by the roadside and sleeping in their poorly covered wagons. Two or three horse-drawn wagons of men, women, and children usually constituted the fellowship. No one knew where they came from or where they intended to go: they came when they wanted to, stayed as long as they wished, and moved on when they found that to be good. In the meantime they begged and traded according to their taste.

They had a very bad reputation. It was well known that they could fool the farmers in horse trading, but it was also alleged that they stole beautiful children, and one could never find out what they did with them. For that reason small children were kept close to mother and father when "the nasty group" was nearby. It was also said that their women could tell fortunes and that they engaged in foul tricks. The old folks really believed that a gypsy woman had a good relationship with the evil one and had received from him much dangerous power over human and beast. Nevertheless, some youthful daredevils would occasionally put themselves in closer touch with the gypsies. The most daring were those concerned about getting married, for they would take refuge with the strangers and let a gypsy woman tell their fortune rather than grope their way through the labyrinth of love and remain uncertain about their prospects for marriage. No matter how serious the warning not to deal with the evil business, it did not help.

Remarkably enough, the fortuneteller could answer nearly all the burning questions of young hearts. The answers were, of course, not very exact or enlightening, but at least they were something. Then the inquirers simply had to wait and see if the oracles came true. The gracious Lord spared the inquisitive ones from open, immediate punishment, and they hoped that the small voice of the soul had not been damaged by their visit to the gypsy, particularly since they had been thoughtful enough to recite the "Our Father" quietly while she was telling their fortune.

The gypsy had her little hocus-pocus ritual as she told a fortune. Usually she sought prophecies in the bottom of a coffee cup after she had made some mysterious swings with it to strengthen the faith of her customers. For her prophesies she asked twenty-five öre, or more if she thought the person could pay.

When the gypsy band had bled the pocketbooks of the parish in many ways, they moved to another area to carry on identical operations. Thus they continued their unique nomadic life and seemed to be satisfied.

Chapter Four

Childhood Days

Seen from a broad perspective, all human experience is much the same. "To be born and live and die away at last" is the life story of all generations.

But seen from another viewpoint, no two people's life stories are identical, just as no two people look exactly alike. The outward contours may be similar, but the details shift into numberless variations.

Human life consists of countless little events woven together like the threads in a tapestry. The Master himself arranges the strands for our highest good according to his eternal pattern and lets the bright colors enter playfully among the dark and melancholy as long as our heart beats and our lungs breathe. As yet we see only the wrong side of the fabric with its knots, tufts, and ends. The beautiful pattern on the right side appears only when the work is seen in the light of eternity.

When we look back on past years we remember certain experiences more clearly than others. These are like the numbers on the face of a clock that mark the hours of our lifetime. The events we remember less clearly are like the minute divisions which can be seen only when one is close.

From infancy we have no memories. Not a single event is inscribed on our consciousness from this time when we were helpless little dictators, sometimes giving joy and sometimes being burdens to our parents who patiently and lovingly took care of us.

During infancy the little ones gather strength for the coming labor of life. They sleep sweetly, eat their simple meals, stretch, and grow. Then they sleep again, eat again, stretch again, and continue to grow. Now and then they test their voices and lungs because of pain or hunger.

Small ones in the cradle continually change their habits, every such change being a step toward maturity. To observe children during this unconscious development is not only a joy but an interesting and rewarding study. This is the mother's delight as she carefully tends her child and the father's recreation after the labor of the day. The happy parents willingly and proudly sacrifice society's pleasures because the little one gives them more pure joy in sixty seconds than all their theater tickets gave them during the giddy years of youth.

In this freedom from anxiety we all began our earthly careers. The unremembered days gave us no concern, for we let others deal with the great problems of life and took for granted that the foundations of the earth stood firm. We lived these sorrow-free days of early childhood like the birds in the forest who enjoy life and chirp their song. Life was all sunshine. It was easy to live. Since then it has no doubt become harder.

How fortunate for little ones when they come to this world and are received by gracious hearts and cared for by tender hands. The benevolent God had kind thoughts toward children when he created fathers' and mothers' hearts with a sense of responsibility for the fruit of their lives. The helpless child evokes the noblest feelings in humankind. How a mother sacrifices herself for her child! How a father works to give his son or daughter the best possible wherewithal in life! Such selflessness bears witness to high lineage, a relationship to God, in spite of humankind's fall and many detours.

Long ago in the childhood of each of us, particular events took place that are still indelibly inscribed in memory, either because they made an unusually deep impression at the time or because they were repeatedly spoken of later by older people. In either case we remember such events even into old age while other experiences from the same time have vanished without a trace. Now and then they return in our mind's eye and give us pleasure as we move back into childhood and revive acquaintance with this bright and interesting world.

Kalle, whose childhood and adolescence are in a shadowy way mirrored in this story, was barely five years old when he witnessed a very disturbing event. A well-fed pig had his sty near the barn, and Kalle and he had, in a sense, become good friends, despite the fact that their lifestyles had nothing much in common. For Kalle it had always been a pleasure to frighten the four-footed one and see him run around the yard and field on his short legs. Sometimes when the porker snapped at the grassy bank, crushing cherry pits and acorns with his strong teeth, Kalle would really scare him. At other times when the pig insisted on rooting up the bank or otherwise misbehaving, he disciplined him with stick or stone. Nevertheless, Kalle liked the pig and certainly did not want anything bad to happen to him.

But now the porker had completed his days and was about to be removed from life in the usual way. The great Christmas holiday was approaching when, according to old Swedish custom, one should eat pork headcheese and pigs' feet and also *doppa i grytan*. In order to celebrate Christmas that way many a peaceful Swedish porker had to be sacrificed, however cruel it might seem.

"Tall Soldier," a large dashing man, had undertaken the role of executioner, for he was just as expert in butchering as he was in bearing weapons for the crown.

One clear, snowless, bracing November morning, the yard outside the cottage looked as if something unusual was about to happen, for a butcher bench, several receptacles of various sizes, and a big tub of clean water had been set up there. Inside on the fireplace was a kettle of boiling water. The day was young but Tall Soldier was already on the spot, giving orders right and left like a real general.

The pig in all ignorance walked about the yard groveling in the frozen grass. Because the mother of the house had the pig's confidence it was her job to capture him with cunning. She offered him a scoop of mash, which he ate with relish. Meanwhile the soldier sneaked up behind him and put a snare carefully about his hind leg. But this was in open conflict with Porky's sense of freedom. Immediately there was a fearful squealing and whimpering, struggling and strutting while Tall Soldier's powerful hands pulled Porky backwards, closer and closer to the slaughter bench.

"Such an insolent invasion of freedom," grunted Porky so indignantly that it could be heard at a far distance. "This would be enough to make every honorable pig in the kingdom an ardent revolutionary." At this moment Kalle, standing nearby witnessing the tragedy, would gladly have tried to rescue Porky if only he had dared. But he feared the soldier who, with his powerful grasp, could have thrown him like a ball across the yard. A little one does not have much to say in this cruel world.

Soon Porky's little legs were tied together and he was lifted onto the slaughter bench and held down. He whimpered and squealed so despairingly that it could have cracked one's eardrums, but all these cries of distress did not alter his situation in the least, for after a while Tall Soldier silenced him by forcing a piece of wood between his jaws, the last thing he would ever bite on. He then firmly grasped Porky's snout, drew his big knife, and slit his throat. The condemned one jerked violently but fruitlessly, and little by little the movements grew weaker and weaker. Life ebbed out. Porky was dead.

This was a terrible event for Kalle to witness and it tore him apart inside. What evil had Porky done that he should receive such treatment? Sure, he had often rooted up the grass bank in the yard and had several times opened the gate and gone out into the neighbors' fields, but certainly this mischief was not deserving of death. As Kalle philosophized over the event a bright idea came to him. Like an arrow he ran inside to his mother and in baby talk reported the injustices that Porky had suffered. *"Otatätte fabo Hög, tack isen så dä moa, dä moa,"* he cried, out of breath. "Horrid Mr. Tall, he stuck Porky so he bled, he bled."

Kalle's emotional outburst and burning zeal must have appeared comical to her because the otherwise sympathetic mother burst out laughing and had not a single word of comfort for her disturbed boy. Kalle's philanthropic feelings on that occasion were, of course, misdirected as, for that matter, they have been many times since then. But his disappointment in this serious moment was boundless. That winter morning the entire world seemed askew.

For many years afterwards Kalle was the butt of jokes for his noble sympathies on the day of Porky's death; all of Marbäck seemed to have learned of his outburst. Suddenly he would hear someone mimicking his own piping voice and deep feeling: *"Otatätte fabo Hög, tack isen så dä moa, dä moa."* At last they gave up tormenting him for his sympathies with the butchered pig, but by then they had indelibly fixed the events of that day in his mind and being.

Tall Soldier was a versatile man with a practical bent. He was not only a faithful servant of the crown, the butcher for the whole area, and a good farmer, but also the only dentist in the district. Most of the people in Marbäck at that time rarely needed a dentist.

They lived on simple fare and exercised their teeth on bread as hard as bone, which the teeth seemed to like, because they stayed strong and healthy and seldom caused trouble.

In contrast, teeth now are given new baked bread instead of hardtack, and sweets instead of simple nutritious food, and they really sink into these soft substances. As a result we now have the golden age of dentistry, with America being the Canaan of the dentists. Here people sit in the dentist's chair before they are old enough to go to school, they continue with the dentist year after year in order to preserve their decaying supply of teeth, and when they have become old and gray they still sit at the dentist's—toothless. What drilling and grinding! Porcelain, silver, and gold are cast into people's mouths. Teeth are screwed in and moved almost like furniture at house-cleaning time. They are extracted and replaced, with torment, groaning, and pain.

Tall Soldier did not have a very large practice as a dentist, for there was never a question of repairing a broken tooth. His task was limited to extraction if a tooth became troublesome. This he could do with a firm hand, without consideration for his patients' feelings.

For a long time a merry journeyman tailor had had a toothache. He tried to quiet the pain with snuff, which was thought to be a good remedy, but he found no relief. In the good old days people had been able to "incant away" toothaches and other evils, but because of the rising enlightenment they had lost faith, so "incanting" would no longer work.

"You must go to Tall Soldier and see what he can do for you," commanded his tailor boss. Said and done! On Sunday during High Mass the journeyman directed his steps to Tall Soldier, who lived within the parish about an hour's walk away. Kalle was allowed to accompany him, and for this he was thankful. By then he had been reconciled to Tall Soldier for his cruelty to Porky. When they got there the soldier had not yet arrived home from church, but in a little while they saw him coming, clad in uniform.

"So you have trouble with your teeth," said Tall Soldier laconically, and ordered the journeyman to sit down on a stump in the yard. He made a quick diagnosis of the journeyman's mouth, and then went in after the tooth forceps, which he decisively adjusted to the sick tooth. He made a quick jerk. The tooth came out and the toothache was cured.

The whole operation took place without hocus pocus while the sun shone and a few flies sang to the patient. There was no antiseptic washing—only a dipper of cold water to rinse the mouth. Blood poisoning and other difficulties were not feared, nor did they occur. The journeyman joyfully paid the usual fee of twenty-five öre, and he and Kalle whistled their way home again.

The following episode is an example of how a toothache was cured by unusual means. Kalle's grandfather on his mother's side was a powerful and dauntless warrior who, by the end of his career, had won promotions from private to color-sergeant. Once when he and his men were out on field maneuvers he developed a toothache that gave him no peace night or day and made him so irritable that it was not wise to test his patience.

Among his subordinates in the field was one man who dared to undertake an original experiment in order to cure the old sergeant's ailment. Philosophically he told his commanding officer that he possessed an excellent cure for toothache though it was a little difficult to apply it by the tooth.

"Medicine or witchcraft, who cares, just so I get rid of the pain," roared the sergeant. "Be so good as to sit down then," said the soldier good-naturedly.

The sergeant sat down on a stone and the soldier pretended to take medicine out of his pocket, but in a flash closed his fist and boxed the sergeant's ear so hard that he almost tumbled end-over-end. The old sergeant, who never wanted to hear of any foolishness among old people, became angry over the insult, and a mighty warrior oath was on his tongue.

"Did it help, Mr. Sergeant?" asked the soldier, with a broad grin. Indeed, the toothache had disappeared! When the sergeant realized it he burst into a hearty laugh, reached out his hand, and thanked the soldier for such a powerful and original treatment. Finally he said firmly, "Such a man deserves promotion in the service."

In this case what really cured the toothache? Was it the cuff on the ear, the resulting mental disturbance in the patient, or a combination of the two? The question may be an interesting problem for the reader to consider for a time. However, the sergeant was cured, and that was the point of the matter.

Chapter Five

Mischief and Mishaps

People sometimes say that boys and puppies should be whipped, because if they haven't done something wrong yet they intend to. This is obviously false, because first, it is wrong to place boys and puppies in the same category, and second, it is wrong to contend that either puppies or small boys entertain evil motives and designs. Little ones, whether they walk on two or four legs, think very little; they only live, and life plays in them and with them.

People also say that virtue is rewarded, which presupposes that one has freely chosen the good when one could have chosen the opposite. But small children cannot consciously choose good or evil, so if they sometimes stray from virtue it is not with evil intent. Their wrongdoing springs from the impulses of the moment, which they follow without reflection or reservation. They act first and think afterwards, which is, of course, true of many older and more experienced people also.

Young children do not know of any "misdeeds," but learn what they are when they are exhorted and warned about them. For this reason punishment for misbehavior comes as a complete surprise to the children, who see themselves as being what they should be, but then get a scolding and slap on the fingers or elsewhere. First then, children grasp the fact that they have not been good children.

For the most part the mischief and misdeeds of small children are only accidents. They have has not yet learned to control their lively limbs. Children stumble and spill the milk, brush by the flower-pot and knock it down, break the windowpane, trample the garden, and tear their clothes. None of these things happens out of wickedness or the desire to destroy; rather, they are the result of chance. When similar things happen to adults they are readily excused, not called mischief. Why then give children's actions uglier names than the corresponding deeds of adults? Children are not helped by such injustice; nor does it do credit to those who perpetrate it.

It is the duty of adults to teach children what is right and good, to urge them to be virtuous, and to discipline them wisely if needed, but it is grossly unjust to punish them harshly and unwisely, to spank them in anger, or to call them names that are abusive to the child and unworthy of the disciplinarian. Only after the child is older and displays clear signs of disobedience and rebellion should punishment be serious, but even then the disciplinarian must be fair.

Interesting volumes could be written about small mishaps during the tender years. The reader surely remembers several such incidents from childhood which, even after decades, bring a smile amidst duty and struggle.

One beautiful summer day when Kalle's father and mother were away, Kalle and his three-year-old sister were at home, along with another little girl about the same age from the nearest farm who had been promised that she could spend the day with them. The three children had fun running, jumping, and playing. One innocent prank followed another and their recreation was full of sunshine.

In the afternoon the little girl from the farm began to feel a housewifely impulse so she started to bake cute little cakes of sand and water which then dried in the sun. Meanwhile, Kalle played warrior, and among other weapons he used a little hatchet which he swung around boldly in authentic warrior fashion. Like a Charles XII he attacked the hated Russians unmercifully. In his lively imagination he saw them fall like grass before the scythe. Drunk with victory he cut such deep wounds in the grassy slope that sparks flew when the hatchet hit some hidden stone.

While the war to defend his native land flamed in all its horror in Kalle's fantasy, the girl sat calmly putting her cakes in order. She had just finished her baking and was wiping the "dough" from her hands on the grass carpet when Kalle made one of his warrior cuts as if to slash the skull of the Czar himself. But instead of hitting the grass he hit the hand of the little baker and cut the tops of three of her fingers just above the knuckles. The little girl shrieked violently and burst into tears. Blood flowed from the three gaping wounds. Kalle's warrior heart immediately softened and he began to cry with the one who was hurt. When his little sister saw and heard the others crying she also joined in. Here were three bleeding fingers and three pairs of weeping eyes but no mother at hand to bind the wounds or comfort the distressed. This pretend war brought wounds, blood, and tears just as real war does.

Kalle, however, knew his duty in this critical moment and tried to be a doctor as best he could. He found a clean handkerchief in his mother's drawer and wrapped it carefully about the little girl's wounds, whereupon she hurried home for further treatment by her mother.

Kalle and his sister were now alone to ponder the sad events, but as is typical of children, they quickly forgot them and continued in lighthearted play. What happened when Mother came home and Kalle had to account for the events of the day he has not related, so we cannot read about it here. In a short time the little baker's hand healed, but as long as she lived she bore scars on her three fingers as a reminder of the day when she baked sand cakes and Kalle went to war with the Russians.

Because Christmas is the festival of festivals in Sweden, it is eagerly anticipated in palace and cabin and its mood is absolutely unique. Young and old make secret plans to surprise friends and kin with Christmas gifts as far as means allow. The people of Marbäck seldom had enough money for big and luxurious gifts, but there was always something practical for the children no matter what happened with the older folk. The children of that day valued their practical gifts just as much as little ones today value the trinkets brought by Santa Claus.

On winter evenings Kalle's mother sat by the light of the fireplace and knitted mittens. One year before Christmas when Kalle wanted to know who the lucky recipient of the mittens would be, his mother was reserved and averted his questions repeatedly. He knew that the mittens would not be big enough for a grown person; who then were they intended for? Obstinately he continued with his questions. In order to avoid them, Mother found a way to fool her boy by saying that they were a Christmas present for the girl at the farm. This explanation satisfied curious Kalle. Eventually the mittens were completed, washed, and deposited in Mother's drawer.

Finally the long-awaited Christmas holiday arrived. On Christmas Eve Kalle's mother had all she could do before the celebration would begin. In the afternoon Kalle, who was always busy and self-willed, took the new mittens and, without asking his mother's advice, delivered them to the farm as a Christmas present to the girl whose fingers he had almost chopped off. He was pleased and happy that he was doing a good deed.

In the evening when the presents were to be given in Kalle's home, his mother could not find the mittens anywhere. They had disappeared without a trace. She questioned Kalle, and to her great surprise he confessed that he had already given them to the girl at the farm, which he thought was entirely fitting and proper. Now, however, on Christmas Eve itself, Kalle received a well-earned scolding for meddling, for he had given away his own Christmas present before he had received it himself. To be sure he had only followed his impulses, acting honorably and in good faith, but even so he had acted wrongly.

Now, as in many other instances, it became the mother's task to correct Kalle's mistake. How she managed on this occasion is not told, but she succeeded in retrieving the new mittens by Christmas Day. Kalle had them as a Christmas gift even though he did not receive them on Christmas Eve.

Another year, another Christmas, solemn and festive, in Kalle's home. As usual, his parents were thinking of the children and had arranged presents for them. For Kalle they had ordered a new pair of wooden shoes made by "Grandpa" from Bäck who had begun to make shoes in old age. If at the earlier Christmas the hands had received mittens, on this one the feet would have their wooden shoes. As the apostle remarks, when one member rejoices, all rejoice, and in keeping with that, Kalle's whole body was warm whether he got mittens or wooden shoes. The new shoes he received were broad and had upturned toes; they were substantial and splendid, and clean as new-fallen snow.

The second day after Christmas Kalle was determined to go out sliding on the ice in his new wooden shoes, and he was promised that he could go in the afternoon. That would really be fun!

Near the cottage was a stream that froze smooth during the winter. At the edge of the ice was a gray yard fence, and directly in the path was a stile for those who wanted to step over it. As we know, boys do not habitually use stairs, but leave them for stiff old patriarchs. Fresh as the kernel of a nut, happy as a bird, agile as a squirrel, and stimulated by the crisp winter air, Kalle rushed ahead, put both hands on the fence, and leaped over like a cat. With a sound like a shot he landed his full weight in his wooden shoes on the other side. The ice cracked and the water trickled up through the fissures which, however, soon froze shut again in the cold. But his right wooden shoe was worse off. It was split open—and he had not had time for a single slide.

What a terrible disappointment! And how embarrassing to have to tell Father what had happened! Who could be sure that there would not be a spanking in store? But the Christmas spirit made the father milder than usual toward his boy. He took the matter philosophically and exhorted him to be more careful in his play. Now if Kalle had only been allowed to order "Grandpa" in Bäck to make a new wooden shoe things would have been all right and the accident would soon have been forgotten. But he was not allowed to. Instead, the father took an old rusty iron band out of an odds and ends drawer and nailed the cracked shoe together. Kalle had to be satisfied to wear the shoe as if nothing had happened.

Kalle grew up in the "golden age of wooden shoes," for nearly everyone in the area wore them six days a week, if not seven. Only the gentry and the curate were exceptions. One must honestly admit, however, that this now-abandoned footgear was not so foolish. Most importantly, it was much cheaper than leather shoes, since the raw material was just outside the cottage; all one needed to do was bore a hole in a birch block, hollow out with proper tools a space for the foot, and shape the outside of the block. Also, wooden shoes kept the feet warm and dry in all kinds of weather, and in that respect no modern rubber shoes can compare. But of course they were not very suitable for people who wanted to tiptoe or to sneak up and assault someone. Those who have evil intentions use slippers rather than wooden shoes.

Why not introduce wooden shoes again, not just as curiosities but as practical footgear? It would help lower the price of shoes if some prominent women and men would organize a wooden shoe society and wear them on certain days of the week. The sign of membership would be nothing more than the wearing of the shoes, but it would not hurt if one wore a miniature shoe on the lapel or wrist, too. Some entrepreneur ought to start manufacturing wooden shoes and by intensive advertising create a market for them. Certainly the American people would be interested. Just think what a clatter there would be on State Street in Chicago or Fifth Avenue in New York! And no one would need to fear having their toes trampled in a crowded elevated train.

But back to our story.

Once more it was cold and snowy winter, and twilight had come after the short day. Kalle and his two younger sisters were alone in the cottage because their father was at work elsewhere in the parish and their mother was out in the barn milking and feeding the animals. Kalle and the older girl sat on the hearthstone, warming their backs at the fire and watching the shadows and the reflections of the flames on the wall. They were not exactly afraid of the dark but they would have liked it better if Mother had been there. The pine wood crackled as it burned, throwing sparks around the children far out onto the floor. They paid no attention to the playful sparks, for it was good to be warm and good to sit at the fireplace.

As he sat there, Kalle's back became unusually warm, so he turned a bit. He became still warmer. His skin smarted, so he reached his hand behind his back. At once he realized that his clothes were on fire. He stood up and began to shake them, which made the flames spread more freely. For a moment he stood there frightened and perplexed, but then like lightning it occurred to him that he should roll in the snow outside the cottage. He rushed out and threw himself backwards into a drift, turning to the right and to the left, and he heard the flames and sparks hiss as they were extinguished in the cold snow.

In that moment of danger, whence came the impulse to the eight-year-old to throw himself into the snow? Thinking of the children, the Master said, "Their angels always behold the face of my Father." Perhaps this explains how help came on this day.

The fire could have been disastrous, but the results were comparatively insignificant. Kalle's coat, vest, shirt, and skin had burn marks, but nothing more. The coat was the worst, but as it was not old it could not be thrown away, and since Father was an expert in repairing clothes, he soon inserted in the center of the back a square patch the size of a little window pane which looked like the ticket shutter in Aneby railroad station. Then Kalle, despite his protests, had to wear the coat as if nothing unusual had happened to it.

There were plenty of mended coattails and sleeves in school that awakened no notice, but Kalle was the only one with a square patch in the middle of his back, and for this he became the object of pranks and jokes. Nor did explanations help in the least. Just as schoolyard play was in full swing some rogue would knock on Kalle's back as if he stood at the ticket window in Aneby and shout, "Third-class ticket to Stockholm, please." As Kalle would turn, another comrade would take advantage of him and knock, requesting a first-class ticket to Haparanda. Then the travelers would take flight before Kalle could double up his fist and give them a ticket in the ear. So Kalle had to endure much pestering because he had once sat too close to the fire and because his family was not wealthy enough to give his coat to the rag-and-bone man.

Sometimes both young and old have to suffer innocently in this world, and vexations like these are not worth getting riled up over or losing one's head for. It is better to take them calmly and render them harmless with a good-natured smile.

Chapter Six

Errands and Chastisement

A boy's first work usually consists of performing little services for his parents or his sisters and brothers, and in this way he begins his training for the struggles and toil of life that lie ahead. Hardly has the little one learned to walk on a level floor before he begins to do these jobs for Mama. "Please pick up the ball of wool for me," she says to her little tyke, and he obeys immediately with a broad smile on his round face. Or she may say, "Dear Pelle, can you find the mischievous spool of thread which ran and hid under the table?" Pelle happily retrieves the spool and returns it to her. Then she pats him on the head and says, "Thank you so much. You will soon be a big strong man like your papa."

These first little services lead to other responsibilities which grow as the child develops in years and ability. This is wholesome and good.

Wealthy parents who keep servants rob their children of much useful training for life; this is one of the curses of wealth. Children who grow up with modern comforts in large cities often experience the same loss even if their parents are not wealthy; this is one of the curses of modern urban society. All young people should become accustomed to good useful employment, without which they tend to become lazy and awkward weaklings who have difficulty taking care of themselves. Those who have received better training in the race of life easily pass them on the track.

But children, like older people, are not always inspired by the spirit of willingness and service. They can often be cross and obstinate. Though they may bear no ill will toward Mama or Papa, they still do not want to obey and cannot be induced to carry out even a very easy assignment willingly and cheerfully. What is the reason for this strange situation? The intractable will, which sits there crosswise, heavy and unmoved, like an automobile that the driver cannot start.

From time immemorial people have tried to bend the wills of children by force and have succeeded in extorting apparent obedience. A box on the ear, a pull of the hair, or a stroke from the switch or cane have coerced children to obey. If a boy has chosen to say, "I do not want to," the answer has been, "You have no will," and with clenched fist the adult has tried to drive that lie into the boy's brain. But the child always has a will, even a strong will. How can one shape it? This is a good question for educators and leaders, and if it could be answered satisfactorily many other problems would also be solved. If scientists could give us a dependable formula for bending the will, thousands of employers, politicians, and evangelists would quickly make use of it.

Children, however, are children, on holidays and weekdays, at home and away, outside and inside, whether playing, sitting in school, or running errands for mother. They are easily distracted, they become occupied by the impressions of the moment, and they have difficulty concentrating on a specific task. They have good eyes and ears and the potential for a good memory, but they still forget easily.

If a child is sent on an errand and is asked to hurry, the child may promise to do so and be very sincere about it but neglect to keep the promise. For example, a boy goes on an errand for his father. He runs along the way until he notices a bird's nest in a tree. This captures his attention, so he climbs up to investigate what the nest is like and whether there are any eggs in it. Down again from the tree branches, he notices beautiful butterflies sailing freely and begins to chase them through the meadow. During the chase he discovers little wild strawberries which stimulate his appetite, so he picks and eats them. In this way the hours pass. Eventually he turns his steps toward home without having done the errand on which he was sent.

Exactly the same thing happens to little girls. Stina goes on an errand for Mother. On the way she meets little Lisen who has received a new doll for her birthday. A confidential conversation unfolds between them about the doll and her dress, and they sit down by the wayside to continue their deliberations about other things that interest young girls. The hours hasten by. Not for a moment does Stina remember her mother's orders because her attention has been completely captivated by something else. This happens now and then to the best of children, and parents and guardians should carefully take this into consideration.

One summer on a glorious Sunday morning Father sent Kalle across the parish on an important mission. Gently he said, "Hurry now so that you'll be home in time for church." Kalle trotted along and came to the designated place without any unnecessary delays. But then the friendly lady of the house invited him to coffee and cookies, and since at that time he was very vulnerable to such invitations, he agreed to wait. It was quite a while before the beautiful coffee tray was ready with its rusks, *pepparkakor,** and coffee pot, and Kalle really enjoyed the dainty morsels. Finally, with a deep bow, he thanked her for the excellent treat and said goodbye. He knew he had already been delayed so he took a shortcut along the lake and hurried, but at the shore new temptations met him. In the clear still water he saw little lively fish darting to and fro and little black crayfish trying to hide under the stones. He rolled up his pant legs—he was already barefoot—and waded into the water, lifting the stones and noting how the crayfish nimbly scrambled backwards to other hiding places.

It was such fun this Sunday morning by the lake with the little fish and crayfish! In this idyllic setting how could Kalle be expected to think of his father's prosaic exhortation to hurry home? But eventually even in this fascinating environment he became thoughtful and the reality of disobedience confronted him. He ran home as fast as his legs could carry him.

When he arrived, Father had already gone to church in rather bad humor because the boy had not returned, and Mother was also agitated at this new evidence of Kalle's disobedience. His excuses and explanations could not satisfy her. "Obedience is better than sacrifice," was her laconic reply to the boy's efforts to justify himself. "Put your legs back on and run to the church," she commanded

---

* gingersnaps

in a tone that could not be misunderstood.

Kalle sensed he was in trouble and ran up and down the hills the whole quarter mile to the church, arriving in time to hear only the last part of the sermon and the announcements. At the conclusion of the worship hour he made himself obvious to his father so that he would see with his own eyes that Kalle had been there. Worship seemed to have calmed the father's disturbed mind so that he had neither a harsh word nor a hard look for his disobedient son as they went home from church in fellowship with other parishioners. Kalle was naturally glad that this sensitive matter was not discussed but was allowed to be forgotten.

Like most men of that day, Kalle's father had the ugly habit of using snuff. The craving for this stimulant was evidently quite compelling for those who used it, so there always had to be some on hand at home. Father kept his supply in brown bottles with cut-off necks. The snuff went from the bottles to the snuffbox to the lips.

For a long time there had been no order from the store, so the bottles were empty and the last grain in the snuffbox had been used. In the face of this critical situation Kalle was sent to the store at the old parish poorhouse in order to buy the indispensable stimulant. The storekeeper, Målberg, an old gouty man, and his sick, wrinkled wife of the same age lived in an attic room of the poorhouse and sold coffee beans, candy, writing materials for the school children, snuff for the old men in the parish, and other necessities. On this occasion, Kalle had strict orders to shop with Målberg and then hurry home. He jogged along on the narrow, stony path through the pine forest and then on the highway to Målberg's store.

When he arrived he found that the storekeeper was out of snuff; he hardly had a pinch for his own nose. However, he had sent his son, also named Kalle, to buy some in Aneby and he was expected home in a couple of hours. "If you're not in a hurry, you can wait," said the old man. "Yes, it's no doubt best that you stay," piped the wrinkled old woman from the edge of the bed.

So Kalle decided to wait. Meanwhile he could play with the corporal's boys who lived nearby along the highway.

It took all day for Målberg's Kalle to return, for he too was just a boy, and on the way he had had to pass the waterfall at Stalpet and the station at Aneby where switching locomotives and freight cars were all in motion and all fascinating. Late in the afternoon he came home carrying his purchases.

Meanwhile, during his play with the corporal's boys, Kalle had forgotten to eat. Now hunger began to pinch his stomach, so when he finally had the snuff weighed up in a brown paper cone he hurried home. There the mood had been gloomy all day because Father had lacked the necessary inspiration for his work. In vain he had looked out over the road for Kalle. "He is going to get a spanking," he said repeatedly, for Kalle had blundered so many times before when he had been sent on errands that it was absolutely clear that this time too it was only carelessness that kept him so long.

Kalle had hardly gotten his foot across the threshold before the thunder began to roll. As usual he tried to explain, but his father would not listen, so Kalle simply grit his teeth and let the storm rage. The judgment had fallen without inquiry and now the punishment followed. First a cuff on the ear so that it sang in Kalle's cranium and he almost fell over. Then a newly lacquered red ruler which made him dance to a lively tempo. He cried for compassion and forgiveness as the stick whistled through the air and delivered blow after blow.

Crack. The brand new measuring rod broke. One of the stumps whined through the air and hit the weight on the wall clock so that it gave a lovely tinkle. This must have seemed like an omen to the angry one because immediately he became calm and the punishment ceased. He crossed the floor, took a pinch of snuff, and quiet as a wall began his work at the tailor's bench.

Then Mother took the "culprit" in hand. Kalle told her the reason for his long absence and was relieved that at least she was willing to listen to his honest confession, although he continued to feel that he had been treated unjustly. The mother set out some food, and the boy soon forgot how warm he was around the ear and where the yardstick had hit hardest. The broken stick disappeared in a few days and a new one quietly took its place at the tailor's bench.

From this story the reader might get the impression that Kalle's father was a cruel and brutal man. It would be wrong to let such a misleading idea take root, however, for his whole disposition was tender-hearted and loving, though he was easily upset and on such occasions did things that in calmer moods he bitterly regretted. Whenever a violent impulse takes the reins in a human being the person must prepare for adventure and collapse, and then sound reason may again be restored. The event we have related shows how dangerous it is to let violence dominate when children are being chastised. If punishment is to be beneficial it must first of all be just.

During his school days Kalle used to buy writing materials from Målberg, and if now and then he received a penny to spend he took it to Målberg's to trade it for *polkagrisar.** Since all the children did the same, the little store in the poorhouse was very crowded every day after school.

One day when the store was filled with schoolchildren, old Målberg lay tired on the bed, and his whining, wrinkled wife limped around to wait on the customers. Kalle was one of them. He bought a slate pencil for two pennies, but in her hurry, the woman forgot to take the money he had ready in his hand. Her mind worked slowly just as her whole body felt the burden of old age. After a while the crowd clattered down the stairs. Kalle followed them and the two pennies followed Kalle. This was entirely unpremeditated, for he had really intended to give the old woman the money.

Should he go back and pay for the slate pencil or should he keep silent and not be so particular? This was the troublesome question for him when he came down onto the road. The tempter whispered, "Keep the two pennies because it was the old woman's fault." The tempter's words sounded good to him and he felt a childlike satisfaction over a successful business transaction.

When he came home he told his mother quite frankly what had happened and what a good business deal he had made. In his childlike innocence he expected a bit of praise because he had saved the home two pennies, which was no small sum according to his understanding of money values. But his mother's face became serious and anxious. Her mild eyes looked piercingly at the boy. "What have you done, my child?" she asked, and with a firm voice that could not be misunderstood, she ordered Kalle to go back to Målberg's immediately and pay for the pencil. Kalle objected and tried to prove his innocence, but it did not change his mother's decision. "Go immediately," she commanded. "You have acted disgracefully, my boy, and you bring shame upon our name before both God and man; go and pay your debts."

Kalle became silent under his strong-willed mother's command; it was as if his slow thought machinery had stopped. Later when

---

* peppermint candy

48

he came to and could think a little he was already on his way to the store in the poorhouse. On the lonely path in the pine forest Kalle felt almost afraid of the dark, although it was still daylight.

Kalle was by nature shy, and he felt ashamed as he walked along the path. To present himself at Målberg's and pay for the pencil seemed to him terribly difficult. He wanted to escape the mandate to meet the Målberg woman and confess to her that he had done something wrong, but he did not dare defy his mother's orders. Whichever way he turned there were severe problems.

As he walked and pondered the matter, he received some unexpected help, which was still not the best. The tempter who had lured him not to pay for the pencil in the first place now joined company with him and showed him a way out of his dilemma. Kalle again did not recognize the quiet voice and was unaware that a new danger lurked in his way. The tempter whispered, "You have done nothing wrong. It was Old Lady Målberg's job to see that she was paid. You had the two pennies ready in your hand when she walked away from you without receiving her money."

Kalle liked these whispers. They came like a caressing spring breeze on a cold and dismal winter day. Now the tempter proposed that Kalle bury the pennies in the sand pit, then go home and pretend that he had been to Målberg's and paid for the pencil. Kalle thought this was a wonderful idea because then at some later time he could dig up the coins and use them to buy candy.

The sand pit, where Kalle had often played on his way home from school, was on the very edge of the forest near the main road. Here he sat down and mechanically began to dig. But uncertainty still bothered him. He wanted to follow the tempter's advice because it would help him out of his difficulties, but he also knew that disobedience did not bring lasting happiness.

Then the tempter became more insistent and moved the hesitant boy to action. "Why should you stand ashamed before the old Målberg lady when you have done nothing wrong? It is her fault entirely. Bury the coins and go home. No one needs to know anything about this, but even if someone finds out it will be better to get a whipping at home than to be disgraced over in the poorhouse." So urged the tempter. Finally Kalle consented. He carefully bedded down the copper coins in the sand at the foot of the pine, being careful to note the exact location. Then he pulled himself together and walked toward home, undaunted.

In nature all was pleasant and the sun was still high in the heavens, but in Kalle's heart there was twilight that threatened to become night. As he walked home he felt strong urgings to turn around and expedite his errand according to his mother's will. But the tempter used his spurs. Conscience must be silenced if it cannot be calmed, so Kalle increased his speed and whistled a tune to lift his spirits.

"What did she say?" asked Mother when Kalle came home. "She said 'thank you,' " Kalle answered without looking up, and he began to play with the cat out in the yard, glad to be free from further conversation on this delicate subject.

This event has important lessons that we would do well to reflect upon. Here was a boy who because of circumstances was beguiled not to pay for what he bought. Here was a well-meaning mother who looked upon the boy's deed with pain and wanted to teach him the importance of being honest.

But the well-meaning mother did not consider the fact that dangers could lie in wait even on the way she ordered the boy to go. If she had been aware of that and had acted otherwise, the danger could have been averted. Suppose the mother had spoken confidentially with her boy about the dangers of not being completely honest so that he had seen the matter as seriously as she saw it. And suppose that she had then said, "Now, my boy, I will go with you to Mrs. Målberg and we will tell her what happened. You will ask her forgiveness and give her the pennies. Then you will see how glad the old woman will be. She will come to like you because you are a good and honorable boy." If the mother had acted in this way, the boy's experiences would have been very different.

Kalle's mother never learned what had happened to the copper coins, which probably spared her some anxiety for the boy's future. And although Kalle tried several times to dig the coins up from the foot of the pine tree to spend them on candy, he never found them. Under the circumstances, this was no doubt best for him.

Chapter Seven

Work and School

Our first steps on the road of knowledge are usually taken under the guidance of Mama, who plants the first wisdom in her child's mind without thinking of anything besides fulfilling her motherly duties. The child instinctively draws from this fountain of knowledge, laying the first foundations for future building. Motherly love and care provide for all the needs of the child. The creator has arranged all things well.

When Kalle was growing up, it was a point of honor for parents to have taught their children to read before they entered school, and it was the mother's responsibility to teach them. Accordingly, Kalle had his first reading lessons from his mother. While she carded wool, spun, and wove, he sat at her feet with a pointer and a book and learned the alphabet and numbers; later she taught him to spell and put words together. From these repeated recitations of the simplest parts of the written language he soon gained proficiency in reading.

If Kalle tired of this work, as he often did, his mother would encourage him by saying that if he read diligently the rooster would lay an egg. Every ABC book of that day contained a picture of a beautiful rooster who had the wonderful ability to lay eggs—not ordinary eggs as the chickens did, but *pepparkakor, polkagrisar,* and lovely caramels. Now and then he could even lay copper coins. This remarkable rooster always knew whether Kalle had been industrious in his reading, but he always laid his "eggs" while Kalle slept. As soon as Kalle opened his eyes in the morning he would look to see if the rooster had laid an egg or not, and if he found a *pepparkakor* or possibly a penny in the ABC book his joy was boundless. Happy childhood when faith comes so easily and there is so little trouble with doubt and unanswered questions!

But the time came when Kalle had to drink a little more deeply from the fountains of knowledge in order to be prepared for the responsibilities of being an ordinary citizen of the community and state, so he was sent to the parish school. Here, in front of the schoolmaster's desk and in the presence of Mother and schoolmates, Kalle had to demonstrate his reading ability and loudly and clearly give his name and age. Then the teacher placed him in the class nearest his age and knowledge. Thus without other ceremony Kalle was registered in the school and had to submit to its discipline just as the rest of his lively schoolmates did.

The school was in the parish house. In the south wing lived the schoolmaster and his friendly wife and two boys. In the north wing was a large square classroom with windows on three sides. Through the window to the north one could see the graveyard with its cross and headstones that spoke quietly and eloquently of human mortality. But also in the cemetery, right in front of the window, was a thriving lilac bush that witnessed to life and hope beyond the tomb. The schoolmaster sat at the desk with his back to this window and kept an alert eye on the pupils so they would not stray from lessons and duties.

The forty students sat on long primitive school benches in rows according to age and achievement, girls and boys separately. At times it pleased the schoolmaster to change the seating arrangement, alternating boys and girls. While this did not please anyone else, it may have helped keep order in the school, and for the teacher this was more important than anything else.

Many pupils had sat on the old worn benches, gaining knowledge useful for time and eternity. With slate pencils, lead pencils, ink, and knives, indelible impressions had been made on the unpainted benches. If the impressions left on the students had been as deep, the teachers would not have worked in vain.

The educational systems of all countries have made enormous progress during the last half century. When Kalle attended school in Marbäck the work was not as comprehensive as it is now, but it was valuable nevertheless. In the schoolroom were maps of

Sweden, the Scandinavian peninsula, the European countries, the biblical countries, and the Eastern and Western Hemispheres, as well as a blackboard with chalk and eraser. Children themselves had to own the necessary books, slate pencils and slate, and later pen and ink.

On the schoolmaster's desk lay a flexible cane keeping watch like a dog at a gate. All tittle and tattle during school hours ceased immediately when the teacher struck one blow on the desk. The cane instilled great respect in the children, and very seldom did anyone need a closer relationship with it, but whether this was because of the good behavior of the children or the compassion of the teacher must remain unknown. Only on very rare occasions during Kalle's time in school would a student's meanness draw the teacher's anger so that he used the cane, and this was never on the flat of the hand. More often the dunce's corner was used for discipline. Time and again the more mischievous boys had to stand in the corner for their own improvement and for the intimidation and warning of others.

Sandberg, the teacher, was a tall, lean man in his best years. He had black smooth-combed hair and muttonchop whiskers. He looked very serious, and in the schoolroom he was sternness personified, so that the students respected him. But his frank blue eyes did not inspire fear. When he was with the spirited children out on the playground he often let a merry smile break across his face, and once in a while he permitted himself a good laugh when he saw how heartily they amused themselves. In the classroom he was the schoolmaster who inspired respect, but outside he was a father and a friend.

In the schoolroom nothing escaped his watchful eyes. However carefully the boys tried to play their pranks the teacher would see them; knowing this, they tried to restrain themselves. Whether he sat at his desk or walked back and forth with his hands behind his back, his eyes were on the children. He knew them well and knew exactly which ones were most likely to play pranks and which ones were prone to be lazy in their work. His eyes followed these automatically.

Because Marbäck Parish was large, not all the children within its boundaries could go to the parish school by the church, and because the people were poor they could not very well have schools at the same time in other places with other teachers, either. In order to solve this problem the parish was divided into three districts, and the same teacher taught approximately fifteen weeks in each one. This meant that the children attended school a comparatively short time each year, but they gathered a good store of knowledge anyway because of the long hours and long homework assignments. The study was intensive.

In the summertime school started at eight in the morning and continued until five in the afternoon, but during the winter the hours were shorter. Usually the children had fifteen-minute recesses during the morning and afternoon and an hour at noon. With few exceptions they carried lunches because it was too far for them to go home to eat.

The daily program included reading, writing, arithmetic, geography, history, and, for the older children, nature studies. In addition to these subjects, much time was allotted to the catechism and biblical history, which gave the education a very clear religious stamp. Because it was felt that education should minister to the religious needs of people, every morning began with devotions and every afternoon closed with singing and prayer.

No one can deny that this religious element in education was very important in the rearing of the younger generation, for in this way the children received knowledge of God, reverence for spiritual things, and a much needed sense of responsibility in relation to God. Their moral concepts were clarified and they became more reliable citizens. Where these religious elements are not sufficiently emphasized in education or where they are bypassed completely, there grows up a generation that causes great anxiety for both state and church, one that says with Pharaoh, "Who is the Lord that I should obey his voice?" (Exodus 5:2).

In older times, memory work was an essential method in education, including religious instruction. Homework assignments were many and lengthy, for biblical history and the Long Catechism had to be ground into the mind. If the children did not succeed in learning them in the evening they had to use the early morning hours, because all the lessons had to be arranged in an orderly fashion on the shelves of memory so that at any moment they could be taken down and presented to the teacher.

During the noon recess the children went full steam ahead in play and innocent pranks. Little ones of that day played much the same as they do now: the boys ran and wrestled, yelled and romped about, giving vent to their oversupply of energy. The play yard was spacious, and on the road no threatening automobiles sped by. The air was always pure, and the sun shone gloriously, seldom hidden by the clouds. There was life and delight in the play yard of the school, and the children were chubby and rosy like peony buds.

Sickness was uncommon among the schoolchildren, who seldom even had colds during the winter. Yet in spite of this general good health the usual epidemics like whooping cough and measles went the rounds in the parish now and then. These did not cause much more concern than children's losing their first teeth, because one knew that they were a normal occurrence. No one died of measles, nor was the doctor consulted about their treatment. One merely used common sense and bided one's time. The school was not closed, but continued as usual.

During his school days Kalle had the "pleasure" of becoming closely acquainted with measles, which he very likely first met in school. It was also in school that he first felt the symptoms of the sickness. He became so tired that only with great effort could he drag himself home in the evening, and when he got there he immediately crawled into bed and slept until the sun was high in the heavens the following day. When he opened his eyes and looked in the mirror his face was so red that he hardly knew himself. His head dropped onto the pillow again and he gladly stayed in bed while the fever raged in his body. But in a few days he was back on his feet and in his usual place at school.

Though the illness itself was unimportant, it still played a nasty trick on Kalle, for during his absence his comrades had progressed from division to fractions and had received the basic lecture on the subject. When the arithmetic hour arrived, Kalle sat completely helpless before incomprehensible terms and impossible problems while his schoolmates counted nonchalantly and wrote numbers noisily on their slates. In his confusion Kalle used his eyes, the providential means of getting help for him who is little and weak. Soon the teacher noticed the pupil's crying and willingly gave him an extra lesson in the strange rules of fractions, which was all he needed. Since then Kalle has managed very well in fractions, even though now and then they have been a bit "fractious."

Because music and song have always been regarded as an ennobling influence, pedagogues have made it a part of the curriculum. Schoolteacher Sandberg, who was also the parish clerk, trained the children to sing patriotic songs and great psalms, forming a choir of the better voices. Membership demanded a fairly good voice and the ability to climb easily in the scales. When Kalle's voice was tested he was rejected; as a singer he was rather unceremoniously thrown onto the scrap heap. Kalle was crushed, for even though he knew that he had much greater skill for climbing in trees and on housetops than in musical scales, it was insufferable to be rejected as worthless material for the choir. He took the teacher's decision so seriously that from that day on for many years he did not open his mouth to sing even in church, and he thought he was a poorer singer than he actually was.

Now and then in a school distressing events can take place that call for tact and wisdom on the part of the teacher. Quarrels can arise, injustices can be committed, and dishonesty and theft can occur. The teacher must handle these situations wisely if the children are to be reared as good citizens and learn the art of honorably tending to their call.

During Kalle's school days a collection was to be made for some good cause. On the day the children were to bring their coins and give them to the teacher, a one-crown silver piece mysteriously disappeared from the pocket of one of the students. The boy soon discovered the loss and tearfully reported it.

The teacher thoroughly searched the whole school, but no one found the lost coin and no one would confess to having taken it. All seemed to be as free from guilt as the angels in heaven. The schoolmaster gave some serious reminders that God sees all and that eventually we will have to account for our actions, and then the matter was dropped for a time. But the teacher remembered the event and watched the behavior of the students. He soon noticed that one of the boys kept himself in caramels more than any other in the school, and since he was not from a wealthy home this awakened suspicion. At the store the teacher learned that the same boy had, on a certain day, changed a crown in silver and bought *polka-grisor* for twenty-five öre.

Because of these findings the teacher arranged a private interrogation of the boy, during which he finally confessed that he had stolen the coin out of the other boy's pocket. Since the theft in a certain sense affected the whole school, the teacher thought that the guilty one should confess publicly and ask for forgiveness from the boy who had been wronged. He saw this as the only way that the matter could be resolved decently.

At the morning prayer the teacher announced that one of the boys in the school had taken the silver crown and that he had confessed his guilt to the teacher and now wished to confess before his schoolmates and ask for pardon. A deathlike silence prevailed as seriousness took possession of the children—almost as if all at once they had been brought before the judgment seat of the Eternal. Then a little white-haired nine-year-old arose and in tears stammered, "I am the one who stole the one-crown." The teacher took the repentant boy by the hand, led him to the boy he had wronged, and said with a trembling voice, "Now ask your schoolmate for forgiveness." While sobbing choked his voice the offender asked for forgiveness and received it. Most of his comrades had tears in their eyes, and even the teacher wiped his eyes with his blue-checked handkerchief.

Then Mr. Sandberg gave a moving speech of exhortation to the whole school, warning against dishonesty and all other sin, and emphasizing this example of how sin brings sorrow and punishment. Then he warned the children against harboring bad thoughts about their failed comrade now that he had openly confessed and asked for forgiveness. There was something extremely touching in these words from the teacher; the children knew that the Almighty himself had spoken to them. At that moment no one in the school could have been tempted to a dishonest deed.

The schoolmates surely remembered this experience a long time, but no one wanted to talk about it. Comradeship continued undisturbed, and the students played and studied as they had before.

Schoolwork was usually arranged so that older and younger children were given lessons on alternate days. This allowed them to help with various tasks at home even during school sessions. And of course they had to work during vacations, sometimes beyond their ability. Both the custom of the day and the economy of the people necessitated that children work. In this way their time for play was cut to a minimum while their ability to work was raised to the highest imaginable degree. There was a rock-firm belief that "one who is idle learns much evil," and people wanted to save the growing generation, at whatever price, from the curse of idleness.

Kalle's father was a master tailor who at times had two or three journeymen and one apprentice. According to custom, a son was to learn his father's trade. In all probability, therefore, Kalle would become a tailor, perhaps a master tailor: so quite early his father began to teach him the basic skills. While very small, Kalle stood by the table and threaded the needle, tied a knot in the thread, fastened ends, pulled out basting threads, and did other such rudimentary things for his father.

From these elementary tasks he went on to learn how to overcast raw edges and how to sew with straight and even stitches, which was not the easiest thing in the world. Hundreds of times Kalle had to rip out his seams and resew them because his father would not tolerate careless work. Kalle did not like the assiduous labor at the tailor's bench, nor did he want to be so meticulous, since he could see no reason for it; but he longed to run the sewing machine and believed that he could do it. Like all other boys, he liked wheels and gears and machinery in general.

The sewing machine in Kalle's home was a Singer, a well-known and very expensive make. It had been one of the first in the parish and at the beginning had been a real curiosity for the farmers, who looked at it with great amazement when they came into the tailor's shop. To sew on a machine in those days was a highly important art in which the master trusted only himself and his oldest journeymen. Kalle had more than once demonstrated that he had greater talents for picking apart and destroying locks and clocks than in putting them together again. Not so strange then that he still had to keep his fingers off the sewing machine.

However, Kalle constantly improved in the trade, and it was said that he had good aptitude. As a ten-year-old he had already learned to sew reasonably good buttonholes, but for a long time yet he could only practice on simpler clothes.

One day Kalle's father said, "Look here, boy, if you sew these moleskin pants satisfactorily you will immediately have twenty-five öre," and with that he threw his boy a cut-out pair of trousers for a lad on the other side of the parish. It was a tempting challenge, for twenty-five öre was big money for Kalle in those days. He took to his task with alacrity. The moleskin was a stout piece of fabric that did not surrender easily to needle and thread, but Kalle's strong fingers and will subdued the obstinate cloth so that it finally assumed the shape of pants. This was Kalle's first independent job as a tailor's apprentice. The pants were independent too, for when they had been carefully pressed Kalle set them on the floor, and there they stood, stiff and proud like Kaiser Wilhelm himself during his days of greatness. The boy who was to wear those trousers would be able to stand on his own two legs without difficulty.

At once Kalle received his money, the whole twenty-five öre. For the first time in his life he felt like a wealthy man, a real capitalist, and his brain was busy with thoughts of how best to use this large sum. In his head were caramels and *pepparkakor* and other goodies. But his father suspected what he had in mind and prevented the planned gluttony by persuading Kalle to let him borrow the whole amount and keep it for coming needs. Thus he did not have the opportunity to revel in his newly acquired wealth.

It is interesting and cheering to note how the worker's world has improved during the last half century, bringing better living and better working conditions. In the 1870s the craftsmen in Sweden had to struggle unbelievably for their living. In Kalle's home, work commonly began at four o'clock in the morning and ended at nine or ten o'clock at night, with only brief rest periods for meals. As long as there was work to be done, strength must last and the worker must toil; this was the outlook for life in that day. And during the winter when days were short, the tailor had to do most of his work by poor artificial light no matter how his eyes might be strained.

During the so-called "shadow time" just at twilight when the day passes into night, the master tailor and the journeymen carried in wood and water and, in the summer, pulled weeds or cleared stones from the fields. This gave them a wholesome change from the unremitting work at the tailor's bench and was the only recreation the journeymen expected. Playing ball or other games for exercise was unknown, and it would have been considered an unforgivable sin to waste precious time with play when there was so much useful work to be done. In those days anyone in Marbäck Parish who would had proposed an eight-hour day would have been regarded as a candidate for the insane asylum.

It was customary for the craftsmen then to take as little time as possible for meals. To eat slowly and chew well would have been to waste time, so they bolted their food, chewing fast and swallowing quickly. It was part of the efficiency in the trade to take meals on the run; one should be an expert even at dinnertime.

Neither Kalle nor the other apprentices liked this, for Kalle, at least, had a good appetite and needed food to continue growing as well as to sustain previous growth, and it took time for him to be satisfied. But when the "master" and the journeymen left the table the "boy" had to follow, whether he was full or not. At the table the master tailor watched the speed of the journeymen and Kalle, and if anyone lagged he was given a meaningful glance and a laconic command to hurry up. Hardly had they put the last morsel in their mouths before they united, in an almost comical haste, in bowing their heads in a prayer of thanks and returning to their places at the tailor's bench.

While Kalle was growing up it was still the custom for the tailor and shoemaker to go from place to place doing the work the people needed done. A date was made with the tailor and shoemaker far in advance, and preparations were made for their coming. Their stay in a place was longer or shorter depending on how many people were to be dressed up in new clothes or new shoes and how many old clothes or shoes needed repair. Ready-made garments were not available, and since dressmakers had not yet come to Marbäck, the tailor sewed clothes for all members of a household, the women as well as the men. He also sewed caps for the men and boys. The old clothes of adults were cut down for younger people and children. When the fabric was worn bare on one side, the garment was ripped apart, the cloth was turned, and a new garment was sewn for another member of the family, usually one of the boys. At times the cloth was not big enough, so the tailor had to labor a long time to piece it. Once right during the Christmas rush Kalle had to piece together eleven little bits as facing for a coat collar.

For all his work the craftsman received very meager compensation and frequently had to wait a long time for it. The best part of the experience was that as a rule he had good board at the farms. The mother usually wanted to show her ability as the mistress of the household and prepared tasty food for him, for she knew very well that her reputation was at stake.

The tailor trade never appealed to Kalle, but then he did not enjoy any kind of work at that time. Like other boys he preferred to play and have fun and did not like to sit still. "I get so dreadfully tired sitting this way all day," Kalle complained, putting the emphasis on "all day."

"Then go and wash the dishes for Mama while you stretch," answered his father in a dry, cold voice. "Ugh," thought Kalle, "that is a thousand times more boring than sewing." But this was the reward for his complaint, and he had to get on with the dishes before he could begin to sew again. At last he came with a new complaint in order to escape the monotonous tailor's bench, but that was rewarded only with a brief order to go out after an armful of wood for Mama, or some such heavy work. Little by little he learned to keep quiet and work like the others in the trade.

Once in a while for the sake of variety Kalle was sent on an errand out in the parish, and this he liked better. On one occasion during the winter he was sent to the mill to have some rye ground because the flour at home was running low. He put the sack on his sled and started out for the mill two miles away. Uphill was rather strenuous, but out on the main road was the big Långliden slope where he expected a glorious ride down over the slippery ice. He made a long detour in order to enter the main road at the very crest of the hill and thus be able to ride down the whole way.

On top of the hill Kalle pushed the sled with the rye sack ahead of him until he had good speed, then threw himself over the sack and let the sled go. It was glorious! With every second he went faster. But where he lay he began to feel that the uncontrolled speed could be dangerous. He tried to slow down by digging his square-toed wooden shoes into the ice, but in a flash he lost one of them and careened down into the ditch where he, his sack, and the sled tumbled about in the snow.

Fortunately he escaped with only a few scratches on his hands and nose made by the ice and the crust of the snow. The joy quickly ended, and now Kalle had the herculean task of getting the sack back up on the sled. For this, old Peter of Liden was kind enough to come to the rescue. The rest of the way to the mill Kalle drove more carefully, and in this chronicle nothing more can be told of that journey.

Chapter Eight

Melancholy Shadows

On the whole, the home in which Kalle grew up had been a miniature paradise filled with light and sunshine for the eight years since the young couple had united their destinies. During these years three strong, well-formed children had arrived, who by their presence enriched the home with joy and pleasure. The oldest child was a boy and the next two were girls. The fourth, another boy, was born after the clouds had begun to gather and the famine years had begun.

The parents had been able to support themselves and their children without going into debt, but because of the economy this was about all they dared hope for. "When we have clothing and food we must be content," thought the pious couple in true apostolic fashion, and they were happy in spite of their rather stern battle for existence.

The woman was hard-working, brisk, and happy, a good wife and mother. Though she had generally good health, she suffered from epilepsy. How this illness had arisen and how long it had troubled her is not known to the writer, but the children remember her attacks from their earliest years. They came without warning as she sat at the spinning wheel or prepared food at the stove, as she fed the cattle in the barn or worked in the field or meadow or walked on the road. Suddenly she would fall. Her hands would clench spasmodically, her facial expressions would become distorted, and she frothed at the mouth and sometimes bit her tongue. She lost consciousness. The convulsions lasted perhaps fifteen minutes, after which she slowly regained consciousness and realized what had happened. After each such attack she felt tired and needed rest. During the hours that followed she was quiet and listless, but little by little her usual good humor returned. There were always at least a few weeks between the attacks, and during the last half of her life she was completely free of them. She retained good strength of body and soul way into old age.

No doubt the couple felt her illness as a heavy burden, although the children were not aware of this. Parents do not reveal all their griefs and anxieties to their children, nor do children brood over the trials of life or search for subjects of sorrow. However, it was a great miracle that the sick one was never bodily injured when the attacks came so treacherously, and when she had to work at all sorts of tasks because of the economic situation of the family. This home could never afford servants, either male or female.

The man was a good worker and a good head of the family. He was a tall, well-dressed person who walked with long, determined steps and used a walking stick when he was out among people. As a youth he had lost his hair because of illness and therefore wore a wig and a well-cropped full beard. He had one brown eye and one blue eye. One eye looked straight ahead and the other looked a bit to the side, a peculiarity neither Kalle nor the journeymen liked because it increased his ability to see what was going on. He was good-natured, happy, and humorous, a man of great emotion. He was the foremost tailor in the parish at that time and had plenty of work at the farms.

But one Saturday night when he had been out working with his journeymen on a remote farm, he came home over the frozen lake, walking himself warm and then becoming chilled in the winter air. He caught a cold which developed into pneumonia, and though he managed to come out of this dangerous illness without a doctor's help, his strength did not return as expected.

The couple looked ahead and hoped for better times, but months and years passed without any noticeable improvement. If the sick man and his good wife had foreseen this long period of suffering they would no doubt have despaired, but in his wisdom the heavenly Father has so ordered life that we cannot see the future; instead we have to take one moment at a time. In this way our pilgrimage becomes a journey of faith, not of sight.

Several maladies seemed to unite in totally defeating the man who had formerly been strong and powerful. Digestion was ruined, the nerves were broken down, and nearly all the organs of the body were more or less upset. Doctors did not seem to understand his suffering and could do nothing for him.

The illness was very trying. Now and then the sick man felt some improvement, but he soon sank back into even greater suffering. Under these circumstances the journeymen had to be dismissed and customers had to turn elsewhere to get their work done. At times when the illness abated he tried to sew or cut out a pattern, but for the most part it was Kalle's responsibility to sew, though his mother also helped as much as her time permitted. In this way the home had at least a little income, though it was not enough. When the illness worsened so that the father could not even be up to arrange the work for Kalle, the income decreased further. Poverty marched violently into the home on the path that sickness had made. An icy fog that refused to lift lay heavily over the family that had earlier been so happy, and prospects for the future were anything but bright.

When medicines did not seem to help, the doctors ordered a mineral water cure. This was tried, first at Sundhult, near home, then at Medevi. As the father was too weak to go to Medevi alone, the mother had to go also and the children had to be sent away while the parents stayed at the health spa. Helpful neighbors willingly took the smaller children, but Kalle was sent to his grandfather who lived at Tranås, where he also attended school. Thus the home was broken up for the summer, with parents and children separated and thrown into new situations.

All went well for the children during their separation, for they were well cared for, each in their own place, and were free from sorrow as if nothing unusual had happened. But at the spa the situation was quite different. The stay among the guests was certainly a useful change for the patient and his faithful wife, but the separation from the children brought gloom. When no improvement whatsoever could be noted, the sojourn became only a new disappointment in which many bright hopes were buried. At the close of the season the mother and father returned home and gathered their scattered children to the old cottage. Because of his age, Kalle could appreciate the value of home, and was very happy about the privilege of returning, even though his father's illness brought a certain sadness there.

Kalle's parents had been believers for several years. During the great waves of revival in the mid 1870s they had come to the realization that they needed salvation and had surrendered in the Savior's hands and found peace with God. As a result of this there was a change in their lives and home which the children also observed. The tippling that had been so common was immediately discontinued. The Bible came into daily use. They faithfully attended spiritual gatherings both in church and in the cottages when some traveling colporteur came to the parish to "hold prayer," as it was called. Kalle often went along to such meetings where the cottages were packed full of people who read, prayed, and sang spiritual songs with deep feeling. Even today he can still hear the young and the old blending their voices in the song:

Who are these that on the river's edge
Just at the dark brink of the quiet grave
Praise God with palms in hand
Washed in the blood of the Lamb?

This salvation experience no doubt helped the couple sustain their spirits during the difficult times of trial. In the first years of the father's sickness he could usually draw comfort from the Bible, that reliable fountain of power and peace. But the lengthy illness and the resulting economic anxieties eventually affected his spirit so that he became quiet and melancholy. The long darkness around him brought darkness even above. It was as if heaven were barred to him. A mighty host of doubts about God and all holy things stormed forth and surrounded his soul. God's promises, which up to this point had often encouraged him, now seemed to him like extinguished stars in the black night. Indeed, they were sometimes transformed from words of comfort and life into words of judgment. He felt as if God had completely abandoned him to the evil spiritual powers, and he believed himself to be eternally damned.

The parish priest visited him now and then in Christian love as part of his ministerial office. He tried to comfort him, but it gave him no relief. Traveling colporteurs who visited the parish also came to console and help the despairing man, but their well-meaning efforts could not bring light to his doubting soul. All their comforting words and all their quoted biblical promises were rebuffed by the standing objection of the sick man: "This is not valid for me. I am lost."

Doubts haunted him ceaselessly. Sleep evaded him. Like the psalmist, he drenched his couch with tears [Psalm 6:6]. Even Kalle, the deep sleeper, was sometimes awakened at night by his father's melancholy complaint, "I am lost. I am lost." In the darkness it sounded like an echo from the dwelling of the damned. Where he lay, Kalle listened and became deeply sad; he pulled the quilt over his head and cried himself to sleep.

When the sick man was able to be out of bed he usually sat quietly with his head on his hand. He did not answer if spoken to. At times he walked back and forth with his hands behind his back, now and then uttering a whimpering sound. When he saw how this brought tears to his wife and heard how the children began to cry, he tried to stifle his feelings, but this was like damming up a swelling spring flood. After each such effort still mightier waves of despair broke loose, and he would throw himself on the bed and cry like a punished child until he finally went to sleep. But he was soon awake again with the same doubt in his soul and the same gloom over his mind.

After three years in this condition, relieved by only brief periods of better health and greater hopefulness, it looked as if the sick man would completely succumb. He clearly entertained ideas of suicide. One day he turned to his wife and said, "It is best now that I take my life, because it would be much better for both you and the children." It was like a prayer for her consent. The severely tried wife, who so many hundreds of times had had to force herself to keep up her courage, now had to do her best not to appear broken and downhearted. She answered, "My dear, you must never think about that. God will help us, you can be sure. Look how he helped Job after a long and difficult testing."

He was silent. Then after pacing a bit he put on his cap and went out toward the barn. Mother followed him, fearing the worst, but when he saw that he was being watched, he returned without saying a word.

At times when he was gripped by such attacks of melancholy, Kalle had the task of following him. It was not a happy assignment. "Go home, boy," he would command, but Kalle did not dare leave him. Instead he would follow him at a distance. On one such occasion he turned to his boy, patted him on the head, and said, weeping, "It's a poor father you have, little Kalle. It would be better for you if I were gone." Still, in spite of all, Kalle liked his father and did not want to lose him. In his childlike way he asked God to help.

This indescribable mental suffering would have been enough to break anyone. It is a miracle that the sick man and his wife could survive this long, dark period of testing, and it can easily be understood that for the children the atmosphere at home was not very good.

The father's illness was now in its fourth year. He had improved, but was still so feeble that he could work only a little while each day. This was, nevertheless, a glorious dawning after the long night of trials, and it was especially wonderful that the terrible doubts had left him for a time so that he could believe and hope again. But as the sun and clouds alternate during April days, so his health varied. He was far from well.

During his father's long illness, Kalle had to work outside as well as inside the house and thus was never able to devote himself to play and pleasure like other boys his age. He was reserved and he walked alone. He had grown old before his time. Nevertheless, the boy still played within him and he had his fun. Every second day he went to school, where among his comrades he forgot the gloom at home. He ran races and pulled "finger lock" with the strongest boys and had other pleasantries with friends.

In school he also traded pens and slate pencils with his comrades. He was, perhaps, as foolish in business as Esau, but the commerce continued just the same. One time he traded a new slate pencil, which he needed in school, for a fishhook. The fishhook was a real treasure in his eyes, the first he had ever owned, and the more it stuck him, there in his pants pocket, the better he liked it. He had never fished, but now that he owned a hook he intended to use it. He took one of Mama's heddle sticks* and a few yards of strong thread for a fishing line and went down to the stream. He found a worm immediately, and for the first time in his life cast out onto the deep.

Beautiful perch swam to and fro in the water. Soon one of them

---

* A heddle stick is a long, narrow wooden rod used to hold up the warp fibers in a loom.

nibbled and was caught on the hook, and Kalle firmly pulled in his first catch. The beautiful fish thrashed so impatiently on the grass bank trying to get back into the water that Kalle almost felt sorry for him. He made his cap into a temporary little fishpond where the perch could play and flounder, but in a little while he took his catch and fishing gear and ran home to show his parents what he had caught.

Mama and Papa complimented him on his successful undertaking, which pleased him greatly. Then his mother whispered, "Listen, we'll cook the perch and prepare a really good meal for Father. Maybe it'll help make him well again." Kalle had other more selfish plans for the perch, but since Mother's suggestion was, of course, better, he agreed without protest. Thus unexpectedly, fresh perch was served to the sick man. No one can say how much this contributed to his recovery, but it certainly did not hurt him, and perhaps it was a refreshing encouragement. Kalle himself was not harmed because he made this little sacrifice for his sick father. Sacrificing oneself for others is a virtue that a person should learn in youth, for selfishness grows strong, too strong, in most people.

Chapter Nine

The Emigrant

Because emigration to America had begun in the 1860s and continued for several years, there were people in almost every parish who had relatives or friends in the young and hopeful country. Between them was a lively correspondence that tended to develop America fever among the Swedish people, especially among the young.

When Kalle had been only a few months old an uncle and aunt had gone to America. After their arrival in "the big country in the west" they had tried to persuade Kalle's parents to emigrate, but this effort to awaken a desire to travel had failed, and when sickness came it removed forever any thought of pulling up roots and going.

However, after nearly ten years in the new world the aunt and uncle sent a proposal. They had concluded that it would be much better for Kalle to come to America in his youth than to remain in Sweden, and as his father was still in poor health they thought it would be a double help if he could begin to earn his living there. They promised to send him a free ticket and to watch out for him until he could take care of himself.

Negotiations were carried on by correspondence. All angles were discussed and weighed. Kalle's parents were convinced that it would be better for him to go, but it was hard for them to reach a decision in the matter. No one asked Kalle's opinion, for his will was not important since he was just a boy, and presumably his parents knew him well enough to know that he would not protest a journey to America if it was seriously considered. Then on a beautiful summer day came his mother's father, the honorable old Sergeant Orre, all the way from Tranås, to speak with the parents about the projected trip. Three young aunts were now going to America, so Kalle could count on good companionship. Besides, Grandfather, as old as he was, was a great admirer of America. Through his persuasion all doubts were cleared away in Kalle's parents, and it was decided then and there that he should be an emigrant.

Kalle was delighted with the decision. Now he could go out into the wide world and see something. He would escape the gloom of the home weighted down by illness and could forever leave the tedious tailor's bench with its needles, scissors, wax, threads, and bits of cloth. Wasn't this glorious! What he might get instead and what the journey would otherwise bring did not worry his eleven-year-old brain in the least. He was going to the splendid America; this was his great fortune, and about this he dreamt night and day.

A couple of months passed before Kalle's ticket arrived. Meanwhile the necessary preparations were made so that the journey could begin without delay. From the prosperous America they had written, "Do not buy new clothes for the journey because they will not be of any value in the new country," and Kalle's furnishings were considerably lessened by these instructions. His old clothes were tidied so they did not look so bad even though they were worn. But he absolutely had to have new shoes because his old boots were so tight they could hardly accommodate more than half his foot. And the wooden shoes? Well, the parents had an intuition that the boy should not go to America in wooden shoes. New boots were ordered from shoemaker Rikt, real blunt-nosed boots according to the fashion of the time, with thick soles and massive cleats or *sinkor,* as they were called. In this footgear Kalle at once felt like a full-grown man and was not ashamed to put his best foot forward at any time or place.

The most important equipment for a journey to America in those days was an ample basket of food, because the Englishmen who owned the ships had the reputation of providing poor fare for the emigrants. Therefore the Swedish emigrants usually provided themselves with hardtack, butter, cheese, sausage, dried beef, and pickled herring. In addition, one usually brought along a little coffee pot and some coffee beans, as well as sugar, rusks, and *peppar-*

kakor according to one's means and opportunity. Kalle's mother did her utmost to provide a good food supply for her son, but the meager resources of the home prevented her from being too lavish even if at the moment she was tempted to be so. However, when he left he had with him more good things to eat than he would have had if he had stayed home. On the journey his provisions were added to those of his aunts, since they had assumed responsibility for him during the trip.

In his joy over going to America, Kalle had not considered how his parents or sisters or brother felt about his departure, but he began to feel the seriousness of the journey a few days before leaving. Father and Mother spoke with him about the meaning of the journey and exhorted him to be a good and obedient boy so they would not need to be ashamed of him. Naturally Kalle gave beautiful promises and meant them seriously. During these conversations with his parents he felt something strange in his breast which made it impossible for him to be really glad.

But the most moving experience was when his sick father asked, with deep emotion, that Kalle forgive him because he had been harsh at times and because he had not been able to give him a better home so that now, so young, he had to go out into the world. Kalle thought this self-reproach of his father was unnecessary, for he himself remembered only too well that numerous times he had been disobedient, deserving more punishment than he had received, and that he had been rather poor encouragement to his parents during their many years of trial.

Tuesday, September 9, 1879, was the day of departure. One of the neighbors had kindly promised to take them to the railroad station at Aneby so that this time they would not need to use their "apostles' horses."* Already the wagon was outside the cottage, but the neighbor did not come in, out of deference to the moment and the feelings of farewell. All morning there had been hustling and bustling. All the possessions of the eleven-year-old except the clothes on his back were contained in a package he could carry under his arm. His parents had also scraped together a few copper and silver coins as travel money.

---

* feet

71

Now again came the tender exhortations, the Bible verses, and tears. The father put his trembling hand on the boy's head and said with emotion, "God bless you, my child." Once more the mother embraced the boy and tried to say something, but her voice failed her. Hot tears rolled down their cheeks. Parents, brother, sisters, and Kalle himself felt the importance and meaning of that moment. Little brother, who had just opened his eyes for the day, began to cry with the rest of them.

Kalle stood there as if in a fog. "Are you not going to say good-bye to your sisters and brother now?" said Mother. "Perhaps you will never see each other again." To bid farewell to sisters and brother with whom he had played and sometimes quarreled was a shattering challenge. Then Mother exhorted them to ask each other for forgiveness, which did not make the moment any easier to live through. Tears and tears, sobbing and loud crying. What a tragedy that the hearts of children and parents must be torn from each other in this way.

The three younger children were to remain at home while Father and Mother went with Kalle to the station. Finally the travelers sat in the wagon, and the farmer struck the horse to get going. Thus the journey began from the old childhood home. The children who stayed behind stood by the window and looked out onto the road. Kalle waved his hand and they waved back. Farewell! For how long? God knows that, and he alone.

It was a beautiful, clear northern fall day. The whole countryside spread its autumn delight as if, in this moment of farewell, it wanted to give the lad the best impressions of his native land's forests, meadows, and valleys. Here Kalle had first seen the light of day. Here he had taken his first steps in the sands of time. Here he had smiled in purest innocence and here he had shed many honest childhood tears. Now he was turning his back to the whole region with all its memories.

All sat quiet in the farmer's wagon as if at a funeral. The solemnity of the moment of parting filled all hearts and thoughts. It was the only subject one could have talked about, but to speak of it was neither useful nor encouraging. At length, during the shaking on the stony road, their thoughts were led away from the oppressive subject so that they could speak about everyday things. Kalle, for his part, thought about America where he would work like a grown man, earn much money, and send some home to his parents so that at least they would not need to suffer want as they sometimes had during his father's illness.

In plenty of time before the train was to leave they stood on the platform at Aneby station, Kalle with a third-class ticket to Gothenburg in his hand. Again there was a monosyllabic and tearful conversation between Kalle and his parents, who were torn apart by the thought of separation. Kalle received their blessings and good wishes and their last words of admonishment. Then the train rolled into the station and the compartments were opened. Passengers got off and others got on. Over there Kalle's traveling companions waved, and Kalle and his parents hurried to greet them. There the parents delivered their oldest son, the eleven-year-old, for them to take care of during the long journey over land and sea. They, in turn, promised to bring the lad to his destination.

The train started. The parents remained at the station and waved tenderly with their white handkerchiefs, which continued to call out their quiet farewell until a curve obscured them from view and made all further waving meaningless.

"It is worst for those at home," said Kalle knowingly, as if to comfort himself in his sense of loss at the separation from his dear parents. His three aunts, Alma, Hulda, and Julia, who were to be his traveling companions, agreed. So he put his tear-drenched handkerchief in his pocket and began to orient himself among his fellow travelers and their baggage. The other passengers in the compartment shook their heads in amazement when they heard of Kalle's journey to America and the illness which was the primary reason for his youthful departure.

When Kalle had been in America a few years and entered the golden age of enthusiasm, he tried to be a poet and wrote the following verses about his departure from home. Like Topelius, he inked a good deal of paper, without in any way becoming like the great author:

Secure in fellowship of friends
And in the hands of the Most High,
He journeyed from fields of home
To distant western lands.
In his best clothes,
With a free ticket in his pocket,
A few small coins,

73

A food supply for two,
He began his voyage.
He became an emigrant
With little joy in the journey,
That is true.

A lad of eleven
With rosy cheeks and light hair,
I carried my baggage in both hands
And set my goal in the distance.
I won't forget the farewell moments,
Trying to hide my tears
When, at the station, I was quickly wrenched
Out of their hands which I had pressed.

Now father and mother have only memories
Of their oldest son.
He himself remembers them and days at home
Because of nature's ancient law.
But as the train rushes forward
And his eyes rest on the passing scenery
All feelings of loss are forgotten
And tears no longer fall upon his cheeks.

In Jönköping, the Jerusalem of all people from the province of Småland, the home of the Bible "readers" and match manufacturers, lived Kalle's distant relatives whom he had hardly heard of, much less met. But now the journey to Gothenburg provided an opportune time to visit them. Their name was Carlson, and they lived at Blacksmith Street 7. He was a glovemaker and she a midwife, and they had a son about Kalle's age. Here for the first time Kalle met the big city with all its luster and glory. He wondered if there could be a more remarkable place even in America. According to his perceptions Jönköping was colossal, but in childhood one becomes wide-eyed before what is comparatively small.

"The fire department is going out this evening. Do you want to come and see?" asked the son.

"Yes," Kalle answered, without really understanding what it was all about.

"Then hurry!"

Both boys scampered out through the city streets and alleys, their flying rush fired by their inquisitiveness. The city boy increased his speed while Kalle followed close on his heels, but the street was barricaded so that people had to stop. The firehose and water jet were hauled out and positioned, with eight men posted to pump water by hand. Other men were placed in a long line to pass buckets hand-to-hand. The fire ladders were arranged. The chief shouted orders exactly as if the fire had been out of control and it had been a question of actually extinguishing it.

The volunteer firemen were trained to serve in case a fire should break out in the city. If this happened they were to leave their work immediately and join in the task of saving the community. Kalle thought the maneuvers of the fire brigade were remarkable, for he had never seen anything like it, nor had he heard it discussed.

The huge crowds on the street impressed him also, as did the big bridges and the boats that sailed on Lake Vättern's clear water and were now at rest in the harbor. At bedtime the eleven-year-old from quiet and peaceful Marbäck could hardly fall asleep because of the deep impressions his young brain had received on that one and only evening he was able to spend in Jönköping.

The following morning at eight o'clock the "America travelers" left the idyllic city on the southern shore of Lake Vättern to continue the trip to Gothenburg. Now they no longer traveled on a local passenger train but on the express train which sped through Falköping and the countryside to the west to Gothenburg, where their journey concluded without any adventures worth mentioning.

Gothenburg, the second largest city in the kingdom of Sweden, was for Kalle a new revelation before which even the glory of Jönköping faded as a flower withers in the sun's rays. Here were more and bigger buildings than in Jönköping. Here were gigantic stores, impressive busts and monuments, splendid parks, and a harbor in which hundreds of large vessels loaded or unloaded their freight and then sailed off to foreign coasts. In this great commercial seaport the strangers now had to find lodging and orient themselves as best they could while they awaited the departure of their steamer.

Countless groups have passed through this port of departure bound for foreign lands, especially for America. Here they have come from their remote, quiet home regions and for the first time have seen big city life and been impressed by the big, wide world.

Here they have gazed out over the blue waves toward distant lands and unknown coasts, and here they have dreamed their dreams of fortune and success.

Kalle and his companions were crowded with thousands of other emigrants on old Sillgatan, or "Herring Street," where they were to arrange for the journey. The tickets were to be inspected and the passengers' accommodations on the ship assigned. Swedish coins were to be exchanged for English or American money at the going rate. A police officer must stamp the emigration certificates that the travelers had with them before permission would be given to board the steamer. The office of the White Star Line positively wanted to separate Kalle and his unmarried aunts, placing them in different quarters on the ship, but since Kalle still traveled half fare and had been entrusted to the care of his aunts, they could not bow to the will of the officer. They insisted on a change and succeeded in getting places for all of them in the family section of the ship. With this arrangement they were satisfied.

The emigrants were looked upon as third-class passengers. In that good old time they had to be satisfied with indescribably wretched accommodations which would not be tolerated now. They were a kind of living freight transported in the cheapest way possible.

They had to bring their own tin plate, tin cup, knife, fork, and spoon because the steamship company did not provide them. They also had to supply a mattress, pillow, and cover if they did not want to lie on boards with a handbag or something similar as a headrest. Out in the marketplace they bought a mattress cover if they had not brought one from home, and from the farmer who was there with a load of hay they purchased straw to stuff it. Perhaps they had brought a pillow, quilt, hand towels, and soap from home, but if not, they had to buy them now, too, or get along without them.

It was mind-boggling for the emigrant to get everything arranged. Then to carry all their possessions on board was not an easy or pleasant experience either. The company took the mattresses out to the steamer in the harbor, but all other belongings had to be brought aboard by individual travelers. Each one had suitcases and bundles in all shapes, as much as could be carried. The emigrants were crowded into a little steam sloop where they and their possessions became tangled up like pea vines, and in that way they were brought out to the ship. A stairway was lowered along the side, on which the emigrants, with baggage, one by one eventually succeeded in climbing up onto the deck. Kalle and his companions, as well as all others in that terrible crowding, nearly lost their patience, but it was even more of a trial for the mother who was alone with several children.

An unbroken stream of Sweden's fresh, young blood slowly moved up the stairs on the side of the steamer, across the deck, and then down to the innards of the ship where they disappeared into the different sections. The young unmarried men glided down to the ship's bow and the young unmarried women to the stern. The families disappeared amidships. Down the crowded stairs streamed mattresses, pillows, quilts, rattling tin plates, food baskets, and people. One wondered where all would find room. A few of the ship's crew showed the emigrants their bunks and after a while succeeded in bringing some order out of the chaos below deck.

Family quarters where Kalle and his aunts found a place consisted of a large square room where several hundred people during the next days would have their bedroom, dining room, and, in case of seasickness, their hospital. Along all four walls were two levels of bunks, upper and lower, where the emigrants lay with their feet toward the center. These bunks were probably forty inches wide and were separated from each other by a board standing on edge. In them the emigrants also had to keep their food baskets and suitcases.

In the center of the room by the stairs stood a couple of long unpainted tables and benches which were carefully attached to the floor. This was to be the dining room. A kind of lamp containing big wax candles spread a feeble light in the room at night; during the day somewhat clearer light came through the portholes. The sanitary conditions in these quarters were always deplorable but were particularly bad at sea when many lay ill. Kalle and his aunts were by no means delighted over the situation, but there was nothing they could do about it because they were simply emigrants who had to be satisfied with the conveniences the steamer *Rollo* provided.

By afternoon everything was clear for departure. The whole deck was now a swarming throng of human beings. All gazed toward shore, craning their necks to find a familiar person on the wharf or at least have a last look at the Swedish people gathered to say farewell to the travelers. Then the rusty steamer sounded its mighty basso voice in long drawn-out tones. The anchor was raised. The pilot mounted the command bridge. The engines were started and the propellers churned the water into a foam. Slowly and solemnly the steamer began to move towards a strange coast.

What persistent waving of handkerchiefs both on the ship and on the shore as many tender ties were stretched apart. Tears moistened many eyes as the travelers looked in parting toward their dear ones. Most who were leaving had already gone through this wrenching at some railroad station in Sweden's countryside, but even these were moved in this final farewell by the thought that this might be the last time they would see the land of their parents, for they had to recognize this possibility even if all of them intended someday to return.

Someone began to sing the beautiful national anthem, *Du gamla, du fria, du fjällhöga Nord,* and everyone on the deck joined in. They stayed there for a long time watching the Swedish coast with its rocks and islets. They remained in quiet contemplation as if at a vesper service, while thoughts of many sped home to dear ones, ahead to the new life that awaited them on a foreign coast, and perhaps upward to the heavenly Father, praying for a safe journey and help to meet their unknown destiny. Unmoved by all this, the *Rollo* steered dutifully on course out to the Kattegat straits and the North Sea, towards England.

Why are these steamers continually leaving with Sweden's young, healthy sons and daughters? Has "Mother Svea" treated them so badly that they could not have stayed at home? Or are her children so depraved that they despise their mother and for that reason go far away to a foreign country? No, neither of these possibilities explains the circumstances. Very few people leave because they harbor ill will toward the country of their birth. The emigrants do not see their departure as turning their back on their country for the purpose of never returning. In fact, if they knew that their exodus would result in an altered attitude toward the country where their cradle stood and where their childish feet trod, they would certainly abandon their journey, because love of country burns like a bright flame in their breast.

The emigration from Sweden to America began and has continued mainly as a result of economic factors. The Sweden of a half century ago could not give its working class the enticing advantages that America offered the immigrant, for the United States government had opened large tracts of fertile land for reclamation under very favorable terms, and the American workers in the cities had comparatively good conditions. In contrast, the life of the workers in Sweden was rather harsh in both countryside and city, much more so then than later. These differences in the economic conditions of the workers and in the opportunities to better themselves started the stream of people going to America.

Even though the emigrants leave their fatherland they think about returning sometime, and intend at least to keep up their connection with the land of their birth. However, soon after they move to the new land unanticipated influences intervene, and little by little their thoughts and feelings change. They learn the language of the country, adopt its customs, and are influenced by its thought and culture. They begin to feel at home and believe it will be possible to have a good future in America. Perhaps they experience economic success. By and by they start a home, and as their children grow up they are educated in American schools and become Americanized. These children do not know their parents' old homeland except by reputation. They are Americans, and through them the parents are Americanized faster and more profoundly than they realize.

As the years pass, naturally the former emigrants think many times about visiting the fatherland, and perhaps they continue to dream about being able to go home some time in the future. They still prefer to speak the mother tongue at home, they visit the Swedish church, and they like to read the page on Sweden in the Swedish-American newspaper. When they meet someone who has recently arrived from Sweden and talk together about the country on the other side of the sea they feel as if they have experienced a pleasant fresh breeze on a warm summer day. But in spite of all this they can no longer think of moving back to Sweden, for their roots are already too deep in America to be able to pick up and leave. They have slowly and imperceptibly been grafted into the American ancestral tree. Moving back would be a painful dislocation, and Sweden no longer holds the same attraction as before.

It is not too difficult to break loose from one nation and be grafted into another during peacetime, but if war should break out between the emigrants' fatherland and their adopted land they would have some very painful experiences. Grafting is, after all, an unnatural condition, and even if one is ever-so-well united with the new tree, something of the old still remains in the blood. This condition is inalterable.

But these thoughts were not in the minds of the emigrants as they left Gothenburg.

The steamer had brought its precious cargo out to sea, and each hour it drew nearer the coast of England. The English businessmen sent their ships directly to a Swedish port to get the emigrants, brought them across the North Sea to their own little island kingdom, and finally shipped them on other steamers across the Atlantic to America. The English therefore served as ferrymen for the mighty stream of emigrants not only from Sweden but from other countries, thereby earning large sums of money.

At first good weather prevailed. The Lord provided glorious sunshine and abundant fresh air. The *Rollo* moved on calmly and steadily, and the emigrants stayed on deck and felt well. But the North Sea is a spitfire that seldom keeps a good mood for many days at a time. It likes to rage and foam and strike fear into seafarers, and the autumn winds like to rile it into the wildest fury. On the second day out of Gothenburg the winds began to play in the rigging. The waves grew and the *Rollo* rolled and pitched and lurched in the agitated elements. All the emigrants had to stay below deck in their crowded bunks.

As the psalmist puts it, "All their wisdom became as nothing" when the steamer was tossed about on the water. Inside the *Rollo* seasickness was as violent as the winds and waves outside. The women moaned, the children cried in competition, and otherwise bold men lay apathetic in their bunks. Some ruffian swore a sharp oath over the wretchedness, but that was all he could manage. A whimpering feminine voice was heard saying the "Our Father" in an undertone while someone else recited "I poor, sinful man," etc. Here was suffering and terror for all, and no one in this rocking misery had strength to think of etiquette or good manners. Of course there was no thought of a doctor either. A couple of seamen went about carelessly throwing sawdust on the meals that had been thrown up, and later, at a more fitting time, they cleared away what could be cleared and then hosed the floor clean.

After half a day of this, the raging weather eased somewhat and the sea became less turbulent, which was an immediate solace to the ill. But for some time the galley felt the effects of the storm. Finally both the well and the ill were brought up on deck where they could wash their lungs with the fresh air and their clothes in the sunshine. This was sorely needed after a day's uninterrupted stay in the unsanitary and crowded quarters. On the third day after leaving Gothenburg, the *Rollo* approached Hull on the east coast of England. Now the sea lay like a mirror, and all the travelers felt well in spite of what they had recently been through.

On the ship were emigrants for several steamship lines. They, together with their mattresses and other possessions, were to be sorted in Hull so that the respective companies should get their determined share. As Kalle and his companions belonged to the White Star Line category, they and their belongings were marked with the insignia of that line and ordered into a special group. Then the customs officials of John Bull had to examine their baggage. They did not garner anything for the toll house, but simply put their important chalk marks on it and let them go.

From a commissary on the wharf each emigrant received a big bread roll and, at the long counter, a bowl of soup. Because the time was short and many mouths had to be satisfied, the man in charge rapped the counter meaningfully with his cane and shouted something incomprehensible which meant "Hurry up there." While the emigrants were still chewing on their bread rolls they were driven aboard a train standing by for the journey to Liverpool. They saw nothing more of Hull, so famous on the continent for its shipping and commerce, nor did they see much of England because part of the trip took place after dark.

The White Star emigrant flock from Sweden had to wait three days before the steamer *Britanic* was ready to go, during which time they lived in a simple emigrant hotel in Liverpool. Nothing remarkable happened during their stay there, but, coming from clean and attractive Sweden, they received an anything-but-pleasant impression of the city, for dirt, rags, and poverty stared at them from all sides. Finally the agent of the steamship company came with the command to get ready for departure. A little later he gathered the several hundred emigrants and walked ahead of them in the street; they followed him like sheep following a shepherd. It must have been a motley and interesting crowd to watch as they pressed forward with their suitcases and bundles among carts and horses, but such crowds marched there so often that they probably did not awaken much notice.

Two levels below the steamer's stern deck the emigrants from

Scandinavia and other parts of the world found their quarters. The better places aboard were reserved for England's own sons and daughters who were now also emigrating.

When the emigrants had been brought on board, the gangways were opened amidship for the second-class passengers, who would have a little more style and a little greater comfort. Finally the gangways were opened higher up for first class. Now came the fine people who did not need to soil their soles on the gangplanks of the lower classes. They were, of course, the gentry, who had servants who would carry their suitcases and bow as much as their old pants could stand in order to get tips.

A whole world lies between the "nobility" in first class and the swarming "pack" on the lower stern deck. Our Lord created humankind, but humankind created class distinctions, in which money plays the biggest role. Genius, goodness, and virtue are not offered first class, but anyone, even scoundrels and villains, after acquiring money in one way or another can buy into the upper class and receive its privileges on sea and land. What a perverted system!

Finally the *Britanic* sounded a long, eerie blast of its horn. The gangplanks were withdrawn and the lines were cast off. The propeller began to turn, sending bits of wood and other debris in a merry dance on the turbid waters of the Mersey River. The steamer set a southerly course and slowly moved out onto the Irish Sea where the waves were just diminishing after a storm.

Of course the *Britanic* had to call at Queenstown on the southeast coast of Ireland because many of the Emerald Isle's people were also waiting to go to America to try their luck. The steamer anchored in the harbor while the emigrants were brought on board from two small boats. Meanwhile, around the ship swarmed a multitude of small row boats from which fruit peddlers sold oranges, apples, and bananas. The coins were lowered and the fruit hoisted with great efficiency. An old wrinkled Irish woman, big as she was, was even sport enough to let herself be hoisted to the railing, where she sat in the loop of a rope selling fruit and talking with the emigrants whether they understood her or not. This lively business continued alongside the ship the whole time the *Britanic* was anchored in the harbor. The enterprising Irish in Queenstown must have turned a rather pretty profit.

At long last the signal sounded for departure and the steamer again began to move. There was waving and waving. Many burning Irish tears flowed and hearts ached. People are of one blood even if they speak different languages, have different cultures, and live in different parts of the world. They have the same feelings and they smile and cry the same way, exactly as if they were children in the same family living under the same roof.

Out on the Atlantic the waves soon put on their whitecaps and danced in violent rhythm to the music of the winds. This roughness increased more and more until the third day when the weather became calmer. Meanwhile most of the emigrants were ill and preferred to lie still in their bunks, battling the unpleasant experiences that attend seasickness. In their misery a few again began to pray the "Our Father," while some tried to make themselves well by cussing.

Finally, when the weather was better and the sea was calm, the emigrants emerged onto the deck where they passed the time in whatever amusements suited their tastes. Many gathered around the card table. Others found a common joy in the dance. A few were faithful to the liquor bottle and were soon lying around like swine. Here and there one could see individuals reading, but they were a minority. Many sat in small groups joking and laughing and talking. Here on the stern deck one could see Jews and Turks, Germans and Swedes, yes, representatives from nearly all the nations of the world.

The food service on the *Britanic,* as on the *Rollo,* was nothing to brag about, but it was sufficient to sustain life during the journey and the emigrants had no right to expect more. Breakfast was a big salty wheat roll and black coffee. Dinner was usually stewed meat and potatoes. When evening came, supper consisted of another salt wheat roll and tea. On Sunday the emigrants were given oatmeal for breakfast and English plum pudding for dinner in addition to the usual fare. The hungry stood in line and waited for the food to be ladled from big kettles onto their tin plates. After eating their portion either standing or sitting—if there was a place to sit—they went up on deck to wash their dishes in a tub of warm water set out for that purpose. Then they hid their dishes in their bunks among bedclothes and suitcases until the next meal when they stood in line again to get their rations.

The provisions of genuine Swedish food which they had brought along tasted postively splendid between meals. A bit of coffee out of the Swedish pot and a sugar lump did wonders, and the tasty little rusks and *pepparkakor* were real delicacies. Sometimes a few Swedish friends got together and had a little coffee party on deck. Not only was it Swedish, but out there on the blue billows surrounded by all kinds of people and tongues, it was almost heavenly for the Swedish taste and temperament.

At long last came a sunny morning with mild breezes from the west. The American coast was visible on the horizon. The dark streak became larger and larger until one could see clearly the contours of the land. Now came the command that all mattresses, pillows, and other possessions that were not to be brought into the country should be thrown overboard. With an almost childish glee, old and young dragged their travel items up the stairs. A thousand mattresses, a thousand tin cups, a thousand tin plates, and a thousand other things were now willingly offered to the waves and the deep. From the kitchen were carried large quantities of unused food for the fish to feed on.

Then the medical examinations began. All immigrants had to pass in review before a couple of doctors whose sharp and practiced eyes examined them as they walked by. Those who were suspected of illness were pulled aside for a more thorough examination later. Along with this medical inspection was a compulsory vaccination, without which no one was permitted to go ashore. While all this was going on, the trunks and other goods were being hoisted up on deck and the ship's lines were being made ready for landing.

Chapter Ten

The Narrow Gate

Most immigrants from Europe landed in New York. Though quite a few also came through Boston, Philadelphia, or some other city on the East Coast, New York has always been the main gate through which they streamed into the United States. All the gates are much narrower now than they used to be because Uncle Sam refuses to receive the rabble from the European countries; in fact, he does not even accept all honorable and good people who knock, wishing to enter. The old "Uncle" has also achieved almost unbelievable skill as an immigration inspector so that it is now almost impossible to escape his eagle eye.

At present, before the immigrants can land they have to undergo a very thorough inspection. They are evaluated not only in terms of health and age but in terms of economics, education, and politics. A half century ago things were completely different. The land stood open for all who had average good health, and the only inspection was of the baggage, and that was often perfunctory. But the misuse of this early freedom necessitated more and more stringent immigration laws until we find ourselves in the present situation.

Since 1891 all immigrants via New York have had to land at the government's large immigration station on Ellis Island, where strangers are carefully examined by hired experts. If they are considered fit material to be infused into the American nation, they are sorted according to their destinations and transported to their respective railroads for further travel. If, on the other hand, they are not approved, they are returned to their homelands. On Ellis Island the examination of immigrants is like clockwork, but at the price of freedom. However, the travelers are safe there, and that is the most important.

Formerly the immigrants landed at the memorable Castle Garden, which was in New York City itself on the outer promontory of Manhattan. Castle Garden was a circular building which had once served as a fort called Fort Clinton. Then it was transformed to an auditorium, where, among others, the famous singer Jenny Lind appeared in 1850, captivating her American public with her inspiring song. Later the building was used as an immigration center and now in its place is a fine aquarium.

In this historic building Kalle and his traveling companions set their shoes on American soil for the first time as they entered the "promised land." Here crowds of immigrants had already taken their first steps on American soil, and here day after day other crowds made their entrance. In Castle Garden hundreds of thousands of trunks and suitcases had passed under the scrutiny of the customs examiner, and here some immigrants, even on their first day in America, had tried to smuggle and lie to the servant of the law. What humming of ropes and straps the walls of Castle Garden had witnessed! What Babel's confusion they had heard when immigrants from almost all the kingdoms of the world, all in their own languages, had tried to account for the innocent contents of their trunks and bundles to "Uncle Sam's publicans." Oh, Castle Garden, full of memories!

When Kalle arrived in America the immigrants had all possible freedom in Castle Garden. When the baggage had been through customs and they had confirmed their railroad tickets they could come and go as they wished as long as they were back in time to be taken to the railroad station on the other side of the Hudson River, from which the trains departed for the West.

But this great freedom also held great dangers for the newly arrived and imprudent. Just outside of Castle Garden were con artists who watched the immigrants sharply, intending in one way or another to profit at their expense. Also, all kinds of nearby hotels had clever "runners" who by hook or crook tried to persuade the newcomers to patronize their hotels if for nothing more than to buy a meal before their departure. Not all these "runners" were angels of light, nor were all the hotels dwellings of righteousness.

After the long, exhausting sea journey Kalle and his companions, as well as all the others, longed for a really good meal. When the immigrants were finally finished with the customs officials and had received chalk marks on their baggage, the "runners" had a good opportunity to recruit customers for their hotels. They outdid each other in shouts and gesticulations, offering big meals for cheap prices. They had learned phrases of every imaginable language, which they used as best they could. They were interesting characters, these "runners." Kalle and his companions were enticed by one of them to a hotel a few blocks away, but they soon discovered that it was merely a common tavern that served food along with its liquor, a common practice in America at that time. When they realized what it was they hesitated, inasmuch as they were teetotalers, but the "runner" had dealt with reluctant immigrants before and it was not long before they were inside the door and seated at a table. There they found other comrades from the *Britanic* who had been similarly solicited.

One did not need to order anything because one's presence was considered an order and the food, served on bare tables, was the same for all. Everyone also received a foaming glass of beer, which Kalle and his aunts left untouched. The food, however, was tasty and abundant, and the price was reasonable. With good appetites they consumed their first meal in America even though they were in a tavern and filled with remorse. A crowd of men was at the bar emptying their glasses and smoking their pipes while conversing in a language incomprehensible to Swedish ears. They did not seem to see the immigrants and did not disturb them, so all went well.

However, Kalle and his young aunts had been in a tavern after only a few hours in the new land. They had not expected that this notorious institution would be the first in America to earn a few coins from them, and they were ashamed of having been outwitted. But what could they do about it now? It was over and done. This event shows how innocent immigrants could be led astray and how snares were laid for their feet as soon as they went outside the boundaries of Castle Garden. Time and again immigrants fell into the hands of unscrupulous swindlers, and such occurrences contributed to the government's decision to move the immigrant station to Ellis Island.

In Castle Garden many who had been fellow-travelers from the old country or at least from Liverpool had to bid each other farewell, for they were now to continue to their destinations by different railroads. It was easy enough for most of them to thank each other for good fellowship, wish each other well, and say goodbye, but it was not easy for all, for among the many were some rosy youths who had established a very intimate friendship with each other during the voyage across the sea. In the evening, sitting on the deck in the mild moonlight, they had caressed and promised each other eternal faithfulness, while fellow passengers smiled covertly. But now the hour had come when those whose hearts burned with love must be torn asunder. Destiny had no consideration for the fire so recently kindled, so because of it, their very first day in America became a day of pain and suffering. How long afterward their devotion flamed and flickered is impossible to tell. Perhaps it died as quickly as it had ignited and then, of course, no real harm was done. But that love! It can bind young hearts together in a few moments so that they believe they are absolutely indispensable to each other. And what suffering it seems to cause its victims at times! Has the reader had any such experiences because of love?

In simple railroad coaches with wooden seats and narrow windows Kalle and his companions, along with hundreds of other immigrants, were brought further into the country. The "immigrant coaches," as they were called, have disappeared from our railroads almost without a trace, but when Kalle took his first journeys in America they were commonplace. On this occasion an extra train of such coaches conveyed the immigrants. It did not operate according to a time table but ran as best it could between regularly scheduled trains. Sometimes its speed was frantic, sometimes reasonable; sometimes it stood on a siding waiting for the regular train to pass. While stopped, the immigrants would get out and stretch a bit on the road bed. Stowed between suitcases in soot and dust, they were weary to death of the wooden seats and low back rests.

The long nights were especially tedious and painful. A few could sleep ever-so-heavily, and they loudly disturbed the others. In his desperate fatigue, Kalle threw himself full length in the aisle where he slept like a log until an American boot began to work over his sleepy body. Then he had to take his place again on the wooden seat where he slumped the remainder of the night.

At long last the night ended and the sun wiped the sleep from the travelers' eyes. While the train was stopped on a side track Kalle and many other passengers took the opportunity to wash themselves. With ditch water they scrubbed soot and dust from their hands and faces and then pulled up grass to use as a towel just as real children of nature would have done. Some who did not want to be so primitive used their already sooty handkerchiefs as towels, but they became streaked like zebras. In any case, it was wonderful once more to use water on one's face and know that one had at least tried to satisfy the inborn Swedish sense of cleanliness.

Once or twice during the journey from New York to Chicago the train stopped at a station where the immigrants could buy a cup of coffee, rolls, and other curiosities from the bakery. The hungry rushed en masse to the counter and grabbed what they could so that the clerks could not possibly supervise them or keep track of what each individual took. Some people without a conscience stole away without paying. One of these, who, shame to say, was of Swedish descent, got back on the train and bragged about how he had eaten to the point of bursting without paying a cent. This he thought was well done in America, and presumably it was neither the first nor the last time he practiced deceit. Not all swindlers in America have been reared in America; some have come here as swindlers, lived here as swindlers, and gone to a world where they can cheat no more. One forgets their names and turns away from their evil deeds with loathing.

Finally, at eight o'clock in the evening, October 3, 1879, the immigrant train rolled into LaSalle Street Station in Chicago. Thus in something more than three weeks Kalle and his companions had covered about 5,000 miles from their home to a completely new environment in a strange country. Here the young tree from the North was to be replanted in foreign soil.

At the station the personnel took care of the immigrants who were to travel west or northwest or southwest, guiding them and their baggage to other trains, but those whose destination was Chicago were left to themselves, for the railroad company had now fulfilled its obligation to them. A crowd stood waiting for the arriving immigrants, and at long last people found each other, with visible joy on both sides. But Kalle and his companions remained standing there after all the others had left. No one seemed to be interested in them, which was hardly an encouraging experience.

There were plenty of "runners" who wanted to take the newly arrived strangers to some hotel for the night. However, the perplexed little fellowship showed the address of their destination to a venerable policeman at the station who, with a movement of his head, beckoned a little German driver who was waiting for business nearby with his horse and wagon. With his English and German, a few Swedish phrases, and gestures, the driver persuaded the newcomers that he would bring them without difficulty to the address they had. He put some boards across the wagon box and commanded Kalle and the young ladies to climb up and sit on them. Then he loaded their suitcases and other possessions into the wagon and took his place as the driver.

Satisfied, the German started his horse, which trotted off with its important load to the monotonous sound of hooves and shoes on the cobblestones. It was already late in the evening, and the streets, poorly lighted by kerosene lamps, were almost ghostlike, for at that time downtown Chicago was not as brilliantly illuminated in the evening as it is now. The German drove and lashed his horse, and the gentry on the boards hoped for the best. They went north on Wells Street over the river to Chicago Avenue, where the driver turned left to number 89 which, in the numbering of that day, was between Sedgwick and Townsend streets.

The light coming through the third-floor windows was bright and beautiful. The driver rang the bell, and in a few seconds Kalle's uncle stood down on the street in his shirtsleeves and greeted the strangers from Sweden with a heartfelt welcome. The notice about their coming had somehow been misunderstood, so that the Chicago relatives had been at a different station. He paid the driver for his work and then led the strangers up two flights of stairs to the lighted floor where the queen of the house welcomed them and where three little big-eyed girls whispered and smiled.

A good washing with genuine American soap and plenty of Lake Michigan water soon removed the soot and dust from the long railroad journey. That time Kalle was thorough, you can be sure! Then he combed back his light hair. In the mirror he thought he looked quite presentable, no matter what the others might think. At the richly set table the immigrants were then treated to good-tasting dishes prepared in the genuine Swedish way, and so they enjoyed the best meal they had had since leaving home in old Sweden. It was almost like a real Christmas party.

Chapter Eleven

New Circumstances

The apartment was neat and pleasant, with six average size rooms. Light streamed in through windows on the street side and through a couple smaller ones on the yard side, but the rooms in between lacked direct light and direct ventilation. The rooms were tastefully furnished according to the circumstances of the day among the Swedes in Chicago, with just the right number of pictures on the walls and with rugs on all the floors except in the kitchen, where a scrubbed pine floor bore witness to the housewife's work and sense of cleanliness.

From the ceilings of the best rooms hung two-armed or four-armed kerosene lamp fixtures which could be raised or lowered as desired. In the large room on the street side were several pieces of stuffed furniture and a beautiful little parlor organ, the first Kalle had ever seen, and because it was new to him he admired it more than all the other furnishings, regarding it as one of America's great miracles. The head of the household played spiritual songs and "Björneborgarnas March," which was as far as he had progressed as a musician, and the oldest daughter practiced scales and simple organ music adapted to her age and musical knowledge.

Kalle's cousins, three little happy, lively girls, were as playful as kittens. He now had the opportunity to become acquainted with them for the first time, and naturally, as is typical of children, they tried to engage the newcomer in their play and pranks. But Kalle had been reared in circumstances where play was regarded as almost evil, or at least as a waste of precious time. Besides, he was a few years older than his cousins and was big and shy. He hesitated to become involved in their boisterousness, but their laughter and high spirits and their conversation in English and sometimes in broken Swedish captivated the reserved boy so that he soon threw himself into their play. The girls were victorious over him. For that matter, isn't it the great art of girls to conquer boys even though the boys don't always confess their weakness for the comely sex?

Kalle's uncle and aunt had promised to take care of him and help him become initiated in the new country. Consequently, without any worthiness on his part, this now became his first home in America, his secure refuge for a short time.

The day after his arrival Kalle was outfitted with new clothes from top to toe. In a Swedish clothing store on Chicago Avenue he was provided with a neat, long-wearing suit that cost seven dollars, a white wing collar, a black scarf, and a soft black hat. From Sven Youngquist, a shoemaker on Chicago Avenue who was well known among the Mission Friends in Chicago, some new boots were purchased. These were as pointed as Kalle's Swedish boots were snub-nosed, stiff, and heavy, and they cost all of $2.25. The kind uncle paid for all this, and Kalle thanked him with genuine Swedish bows.

Kalle's aunt ordered him a white shirt from Mrs. Berg on Sedgwick Street, who previously had made shirts, and the benevolent lady sewed it free of charge so that, starched and ironed, it cost only thirty cents, which his aunt paid. Kalle again thanked as politely as possible in good Swedish. Thus in just a few days the newcomer was tidied up according to American fashion so that he looked very presentable, though some could probably still tell that he was only a "greenhorn."

Now Kalle was ready to have his picture taken, so he and his uncle went to a Swedish photographer on Chicago Avenue named L. W. Felt. Felt took real pictures, but at that time photographers had not begun to make big costly enlargements as they do now. On this occasion Kalle was to be photographed on a so-called "tintype" which could be ready in ten minutes. Felt charged twenty-five cents for four tintypes, while Mellander charged five cents more, but then Mellander's studio was closer to downtown. The plates with Kalle's image were hardly dry before one of them was put into an envelope and sent home to his parents in Sweden, clear evidence that he had arrived safe and well and was in good hands.

During his first day in Chicago Kalle stayed in the house except to visit the stores with his uncle and aunt. But on the second day he dared to go for a walk alone back and forth between Sedgwick and Townsend Streets and then way over to the river, where he watched with interest the barges, the laborers, the swing crane, and the muddy water of the river.

As his aunt was to be a kind of mother for Kalle, she soon gave him his first lesson in American work, sweeping the floor, but he was not accustomed to Brussels carpets or American brooms, so he only dragged the broom over the rug.

"No, that will never do," said his aunt. "You must sweep more vigorously, otherwise it won't get clean."

"Well," thought Kalle, "that's possible," and he applied all his old-country muscle power so that the broom bent double and the dust rose in clouds.

But now she stopped him again, took the broom, and showed him how to sweep with quick, sure strokes so as not to raise unnecessary dust. Kalle imitated her example and later received her compliments on a task well done.

Kalle's aunt had almost the same concept of the value and blessings of work as his parents had had. After meals she would ask him to wash dishes, but that task pleased him less, for had he not washed dishes hundreds of times at home in Marbäck? One did not need to come to America to learn to do that. He grumbled inside himself but did not dare to complain out loud. Instead, he did what his aunt told him to, and she gave him such lovely praise for his willingness to help that he finally began to think it was rather pleasant to wash dishes in America!

Then came the first Sunday in Chicago. Uncle and Aunt, who were Mission Friends, attended the old Mission house which was then on North Franklin Street. It was as clear as sunlight that the newcomer would go with them to church; about this they did not ask his opinion, nor was that necessary. C. A. Björk, now long-since departed, was pastor of the church, but was away that Sunday, and editor A. Hallner preached in his place. Hallner had thinning hair, a sparse, reddish full beard and a somewhat husky voice. Neither the sermon nor the service made any noteworthy impression on Kalle, but this is not to say that they were not good. Ahnfelt's songs, so rich in content, were sung, and the service was Swedish through and through, which pleasantly affected the boy. But in the announcements strange phrases crept in again and again. Kalle wondered what it could mean that the Young Men's Society would meet "downstairs i basementet" and that the Sewing Society would meet at "Mrs. Johnson's på Wesson Street, backstairs at the toppen," but most of the people understood what was said, and it was the newcomer's duty to learn what he did not yet know.

The wooden church building had been erected in 1871 immediately after the Chicago fire. In the basement were some small rooms and a living space where a little book business was carried on by Julin and Hedenschoug. The auditorium, which seated perhaps 600 people, had a little balcony across the rear. Across the front was a platform two or three steps high for the pulpit, choir, and organ.

G. Bergbom, who was regarded by the Missions Friends as a musical genius, was the organist and song leader. In the choir one saw Organ-Olson, Skåning-Olson, Norwegian-Olson, John Larson, John Boman, John Gustafson, Albert and Adolph Julin, and others with genuine Swedish names and traditions. The female songbirds were less numerous than the males, but as time passed their numbers increased. The choir sang in parts the mighty Ahnfelt songs as well as the lively and inspiring Sankey ones which had recently come out in Swedish translation.

Among the Mission Friends who were members of this and other Covenant churches one found such appellations as Sewing-Machine-Hanson and Plasterer-Hanson, Grocery-Nelson, Swenson-on-Wells-Street, Johnson-on-Pine-Street and Frederik Johnson, Peterson-on-Superior Street and L. G. Peterson, Lindquist-on-Wells-Street, Eskilson-on-Clybourn Avenue, and John and Martin Larson. One also noted among the Mission Friends Little-Levin, Wetterberg, Svanland, Tidstrand, Palmblad, Engquist, Hendrickson, Björkros, Williams, and Schultz. Among the younger men were C. G. Peterson, August Hanson, Clas August Youngquist, and others whose names are not written in this chronicle.

In accordance with the style of that day nearly all the male Mission Friends had beards, whether they sat in the choir loft or in the congregation, for who wanted to live his best years without this sign of manliness! One wanted at least a moustache, and not a paltry modern one that looked like a little sponge under the tip of the nose, but one that covered the whole lip and could be twisted between the fingers into an artistic turn almost like a corkscrew at the corners of the mouth. Now *that* could really be called a moustache! But most of the men were not satisfied with only that; they wanted muttonchop whiskers or a Vandyke beard or both. Others were even less inclined to apply razor and scissors to the growth the Lord had given them and had very full beards.

In clothing, people of that day were much like today's children, following more or less the goddess of fashion. However, most of the Swedes were poor and were so recently arrived in America that they could not compete with the Americans and the aristocracy in general. Yet they were not completely "separated from the world" in dress. On Sundays, those who had any kind of tidy work, like businessmen and tailors, wore high silk hats. By virtue of their offices the pastor and the mortician also wore them. On the other hand, simpler people were considered properly dressed if they had a good fedora or only a cap. Some wore gloves and used a walking stick but this was less common. White vests and white scarves were extremes.

The women, then as now, were of two kinds in their dress: those who were moderate and those who, at whatever price, followed the fashion or ran some distance ahead of it. Crinoline was still in use though it was losing popularity, and dresses were ankle length and as full as sails. These wide skirts lived on, and when crinoline was no longer used, the long train, which the ladies had to lift at least when they crossed the streets, became stylish. Since narrow waists were considered essential for good looks, the corset was indispensable and the lacing excessive.

Women's hair was done in many artistic fashions, and hairpieces were used if one did not have enough of one's own to look smart. At times the hair was curled, and young women frequently wore lovely pendant locks much as children sometimes do now. Old men and aunts looked upon this as unchristian, but in that day no one dared to propose that hair should be cut short. The only women who used artificial color on their faces were actresses who were to appear on stage.

Sunday after Sunday great crowds of Swedes gathered in the Franklin Street church to hear the Word of life, until at last it became so crowded that the congregation was forced to build a new house of worship. The old church became a synagogue, then it was sold to a black congregation, and finally, after more than half a century, the building was torn down and a garage was constructed on the site.

When Kalle first attended the old Mission church, there was a table in the narthex upon which wew laid copies of the newspaper *Missions Vännen* which the subscribers could pick up at the morning visit to the church. The paper was then only a monthly and was published by the Lutheran Mission Synod. Making the church a distribution center for the paper was acceptable in that day.

In the narthex every Sunday one also saw Johan Löv, the city missionary of the congregation and the doorkeeper in God's house. He was middle-aged and rather lean, with a light complexion, thin hair, and frank blue eyes. He was a simple and happy soul who always greeted people with a smile and a Bible verse. When Kalle, the shy, newly arrived boy, came up the stairs to the church door, Johan Löv reached out his thin hand, greeted him, and said with a certain intimacy, "I have a greeting to you from our Father in heaven. He greets you saying that he likes you. He says that he loves the whole world and that includes you. Do you hear that, little brother? Father greets you." In this simple happy way he brought greetings every Sunday from "Our Father in heaven," adapting his words as much as possible to the situation of the person. Thus he always had an appropriate Bible verse for the poor and the tired, the questioning one and the one who had no peace. When leaving the church after the worship service one again met him at the door. He would nod engagingly and perhaps ask, "Have you been fed with the bread of life today? Our Father has more bread in the basket. When you get hungry take some." With this he would offer a card inscribed with Bible verses. Löv was at all the smaller meetings of the church also, speaking with people in his prattling way about Israel's consolation as did Simeon long ago. There has never been another Johan Löv, nor have many performed the calling of a city missionary as well as he did during his best days.

Kalle attended this church on Sundays when he first came to Chicago, and in Sunday school, where the superintendent was the well-known Willie Youngquist, he was a rather attentive pupil. In the same church a bit later, Kalle also received his confirmation instruction from Pastor C. A. Björk. About forty boys and girls would gather in the church basement on Saturday afternoons to study the Bible, read lessons in catechism and biblical history, and sing. The pastor was serious and drew great respect from the children. If the room was noisy, it immediately became as quiet as death when he put his hand on the doorknob. He would come in and stand in front and look at the children without saying a word. Those who were guilty of pranks and noise sat with downcast eyes. The pastor would ask some question of the whole class, and then would call on this one or that for an answer, most often naming those who had made the most noise. Being faced in this way with the pastor's searching questions brought a strange sense of responsibility and guilt. With both his person and his instruction Pastor Björk made a deep and enduring impression on the confirmands.

Chicago was a comparatively small town when Kalle arrived, though it had already begun to show an unusual disposition for growth. On the north it hardly came as far as North Avenue, and on the south it was thinly built up when one got to Thirty-third Street. Thirty-ninth was the city limit. To the west the boundaries were equally close to downtown. Originally there had been a cemetery at the south end of Lincoln Park where many of the early inhabitants of the city had been buried, but their remains had recently been moved out to Graceland Cemetery where it was hoped that the dead could rest in peace, far from the clamor and din. But the city grew incessantly and soon enveloped Graceland in its bosom also.

In Chicago the Swedes, like people of other nationalities, had settled in certain neighborhoods where they lived as if in colonies. Some of them lived on the West Side around Twenty-second Street and California Avenue in an area that was high-mindedly called "Stockholm." A larger group lived on the South Side, but the greatest number had colonized to the north. Chicago Avenue was the veritable Main Street of this little Sweden, where Swedes lived in almost every house, Swedish was spoken everywhere on the streets, five Swedish churches had been built, and there were many Swedish stores. Most of the Swedes in the city were young and a few were middle-aged, but there were very few old people. Most had arrived in America within the last five to ten years. None were wealthy by present standards, but here and there were those who had bought their own home on which they made regular payments.

When one walks the streets of Chicago now and compares the city to what it was four or five decades ago one notes unprecedented development—mostly improvement, but in some aspects deterioration. Chicago had, of course, grown up out of a swamp, and in that day was more like a big farmer town than a big city. The downtown had a cultivated appearance, and a few larger buildings had been constructed after the great fire, but only a few blocks from the center itself were many wooden houses crowded together, the result of a lack of building codes. After the fire everyone had wanted to build, and as many as could built however they wished. The streets were only poor roads upon which ashes and other fill were thrown to raise their level. Along them were ditches where water gathered and in the evenings the frogs held concerts, but always with the same program. Except for downtown and a few of the bigger streets that led to the city limits, there was no drainage. It is said that on Wabash Avenue a horse and wagon once bogged down in the loose mud and got stuck. After it came up on solid ground again, a board was put down in the muck with the following warning: "Here there is no bottom. Shortcut to China."

Sometimes there were no sidewalks along the streets, and if they were there at all they were of wood and often unsafe for the pedestrian. Nor were they all of the same height, for people built a sidewalk in front of their own lot without regard for their neighbors', with the result that one frequently had to go up or down a step or two. Yes, sometimes the pedestrians had to climb up and down five or six stairs as they walked along.

In some places, and not in the poorest areas, either, one found not only the woodshed but also the toilet under the sidewalk, an arrangement that was ultimately abolished by the municipal authorities. It was also permissible to have cows, which were led out to pasture on the edges of the city every morning and led home again every evening. Many people kept chickens in their yards, and if one wanted, it was legal to have goats. On one occasion when Kalle came walking innocently up Sedgwick near Hobbie Street, he was surprised by a buck that came out onto the sidewalk from a yard. Whether he did not like Kalle's trousers with the big checkers or whether he had orders to bar the way to all pedestrians he did not say, but he absolutely refused to let Kalle pass, and attacked him unexpectedly with his long horns. Kalle escaped the intended blow only by throwing himself out onto the street. Such interesting episodes can no longer be experienced in Chicago.

At long last the youthful Chicago became ashamed of the deplorable conditions and began to tidy up its exterior, but it took many years to remove the most primitive aspects. With each year the city also grew, so that the more it tidied up the more it had left to do. It was almost impossible for improvements to keep pace with development. The city had no skyscrapers but it had plenty of miserable wooden buildings. The finest hotel was the old Palmer House. The biggest and finest store was Field Leiter and Company, which was later absorbed by Marshall Field and Company.

The city had three different streetcar systems, one in the west, one in the north, and one in the south. They were like the Jews and the Samaritans at the time of Jesus in that they had nothing to do with each other. Their respective cars met downtown where they turned their backs on each other and steered again toward the city limits. The fare was five cents and there were no transfers. Drawn by jogging horses with tinkling bells, the streetcars were all small, with only four wheels. At times one would jump the tracks, and the passengers would step off good-naturedly and help the conductor and motorman lift it back on. These cars were grimly cold in the winter, and in order for the passengers not to freeze their feet, an armful of straw or hay was strewn on the floor. In this way people sat or stood shivering, with chattering teeth. The driver stood outside without any protection against rain, snow, and cold.

After his arrival in Chicago Kalle could have attended school, but he did not want to sit with the little ones and learn how to spell English, so he chose to begin work. He had an opportunity to become a tailor, a trade in which he was already quite at home for his years, but he detested tailoring, and since no parents ruled him here, his own fancy was allowed to determine his immediate future. He began to labor in a factory ten hours a day for $2.50 a week.

When the newcomer received his pay after the first week's work he thought it was a very large sum. With two and a half American dollars in his pocket he was royally rich, and he fancied that it would now be like a dance to swing himself up in America to a rare fortune. In his joy he whistled a melody, but his mother had told him that it was ugly to whistle so the memory of her restrained his outburst of joy. When he came home from the shop his aunt proposed that he send this, his first pay for work, home to his parents as an encouragement, inasmuch as they needed this assistance because of his father's illness. Immediately he agreed. For his young heart it was a unique joy to send his first American pay home to his parents on the other side of the sea.

Life in the factory was not ideal when Kalle was initiated into it. As has been mentioned, he worked ten hours a day even though he was only a boy in his twelfth year; laborers had not even begun to dream of an eight-hour day. Besides, the workshop was primitive in every respect. Among buzzing saws and hissing planing machines, among leather belts and wood shavings and dust, Kalle labored and sweated day after day.

All the laborers were Swedes, honorable men, although some at times took the liberty of swearing sharply in the language of honor and heroism—Swedish. Among other duties, Kalle was the errand boy for the whole labor force. During work hours they sent him for tobacco, beer, milk, or anything else they wanted. At first he had difficulty in the stores because he did not know English, but these experiences forced him to learn the language all the faster.

"Kalle, go and buy five cents' worth of doughnuts," Clas-August commanded, as Kalle carried out the chips from the planing machine.

Kalle gaped, wondering what kind of goods "doughnuts" were. "What shall I buy?" he asked.

"Doughnuts," came the answer, short and clear.

"What are they for?"

Both Clas-August and Organ-Olson laughed and said, "One can never make a greenhorn understand without giving him a lecture or sermon."

Finally they explained what he was to buy, how the objects looked, and where he could find them. Soon Kalle was back with six greasy doughnuts in a paper bag. For his trouble he received one himself, which he devoured and thought tasty.

Now winter came and Boreas breathed frost and cold over Chicago. In the factory big portable stoves of iron and sheet metal were fired by the workers as needed. At times the stoves were red hot with shavings and other flammable materials, yet no one worried about the risk. One cold winter day a worker stuffed a stove full of wood chips, shut the door, and let the flames work and play inside. In a little while a dull "poof" was heard, and the upper part of the stove was lifted off its base exactly as the wind sometimes takes the hat off a pedestrian walking down the street. The flames licked the ceiling. Kalle, who witnessed this event, had the immediate inspiration to report it to the office. Like an arrow he was there. He threw open the door and shouted to the office personnel, "The stove jumped into the ceiling!" The tactless workers began to laugh loudly, and to Kalle's agitated imagination it sounded almost like laughter from hell. They did understand, however, that something must be wrong if "the stove jumped into the ceiling," so they got up and hurried into the factory. By that time the flames were under control and the workers had already put the stove back together. A conflagration had been avoided, but now came stern orders from the office to keep the area around the stove free of wood chips.

This event lived long in the memory of the workers. Almost daily Kalle would hear the echo of his fire signal as some piping voice greeted him, "The stove jumped into the ceiling." One joker even composed a little melody to the words and would hum it when in Kalle's presence. Through these baitings his comrades presumably tried to toughen him for life in America, but Kalle certainly did not enjoy it. At times he even wished he could go back to the tailor's bench in Marbäck, which, in spite of all its vexation, was infinitely better than these insufferable days in the shop.

The factory was a three-story brick building on the north bank of the Chicago River between Clark and LaSalle streets. In it was a primitive elevator on which materials were raised and lowered. Anyone in the factory could use it and operate it as best he could. It was regulated by a loose rope hanging from the top by means of which the leather belt was led into one or the other of two pulley wheels so that the lift went either up or down. It had an embarrassing tendency to fall, and sometimes plunged abruptly to the first floor in spite of all attempts to stop it with the control rope. On one occasion Kalle had a load near the third floor when it started down, and for a few moments he hung by the control rope between heaven and earth. While the adventure did not do any real damage, it does illustrate the dangerous labor conditions in Chicago factories at that time.

In the spring of 1880, Kalle's uncle and his family moved to North Evanston. Kalle was a kind of appendage who had to accompany them, though he was not a child of the house. A big residence with a beautiful garden around it, located about where the Swedish Old People's Home now stands, was rented for the insignificant sum of eight dollars per month.

North Evanston, then a sparsely settled area, was entirely dependent on the Chicago and Northwestern Railroad for its connection with the city. The tracks, which were not elevated as they are now, carried only a few passenger trains per day. As Kalle continued to work in the same factory he had to commute daily, taking a train from the present Central Street station in North Evanston at 6:15

a.m. and getting off at Wells Street, only a few minutes from the factory.

One day a few months after moving to Evanston, Kalle missed his evening train. He could see it rolling out as he arrived at the station but could not run fast enough to catch it. The next train would not leave until nine o'clock and that one did not stop in North Evanston. What was the fair-haired newcomer to do now? Sitting at the station for three whole hours feeling his hunger grow seemed impossible to him, so in order to pass the time he decided to walk the tracks to the Clybourn station and wait for the train there.

When he arrived at Clybourn there was still a good deal of time, so he decided to go on to Ravenswood. Here also he was early, so without a break he continued his interesting journey past Summerdale to Rosehill. This was largely uninhabited territory where there were a few houses only at the stations, and because it was partly swampy, the frogs entertained the lonely wanderer on the tracks with the best songs they could offer. At Rosehill he sat down to await the train. Then for the first time he noticed that he was both hungry and tired after working all day and walking the tracks.

While he was calmly waiting, a young engaged couple came walking, lovingly holding each other around the waist. They asked where he was going. In his broken English he tried to answer them as clearly as possible. Now, however, he learned that the train he was waiting for did not stop at Rosehill or at Rogers Park or at Calvary. This was certainly no encouragement for the tired and hungry traveler, but he tried to appear brave and answered briskly, "Then I will walk all the way home." They pretended that they were sorry for him. When he reflected later, Kalle thought the young man was a strange bird, for he asked Kalle to escort his fiancée home. She lived some distance ahead by the tracks. Kalle could not decide if the man was serious because he could not read his mind, but since he had always tried to be helpful, at times running errands for others without receiving either thanks or praise, he could not refuse the stranger this little service if his fiancée was willing to trust herself with such an unknown and inexperienced cavalier as himself. However, it was then as it usually is with engaged persons, difficult for them to say goodbye, so when Kalle thought he had waited long enough, he resolutely said good night, left them in the power of love, and started for home. The hands on the clock at Rosehill moved toward ten.

When Kalle arrived at Rogers Park, the train rushed by, which he could have been on had he waited for its departure from Chicago instead of embarking on this unnecessary promenade after working all day.

It was almost midnight when he got home. Hour after hour his aunt had anxiously looked out the window for him, fearing that he had been run over by the train or injured in the factory. When he good-naturedly told how he had had to walk more than he had intended, they laughed at him and said, "Such a stupid boy." Then he ate some bread and milk and went to bed. At 6:15 the next morning he stood on the platform in North Evanston ready to go back to the city for a new day's work.

Chapter Twelve

Adolescence

Adolescence, which every boy goes through before becoming a man, is an inescapable breakthrough stage in the program of life. New powers manifest themselves in the youth. Both his voice and his habits change. His self-consciousness emerges in new ways. He becomes conceited and often critical and self-important. To be sure, he is still only a boy, but he wants to become a man immediately so he tries to cut his ship loose from old moorings and set out to sea without having a clear course and without knowing the chart.

During this awkward and perilous time, even more than later, the boy needs a wise father's counsel and a tender mother's patience and love, but he has outgrown her caresses, disdaining them as belonging to the nursery. At this time in Kalle's development his parents were on the other side of the sea; they could not influence him, nor could he lean on them, and perhaps he did not care. His uncle and aunt could not be for him what his parents might have been had they lived in America, but they did their very best to be patient with the boy who had been thrown into their home and whom they had no desire to push out.

Kalle did not amount to much during adolescence, but he excelled at the dinner table and surpassed all his friends in growing. Pants and coat sleeves were always too short, and pants and vest were to each other like debit and credit in a bankruptcy. His feet were always bigger than his boots so that bunions grew in competition on his toes. His hands seemed to be in the way wherever he tried to hide them. In the morning when he arrived at the factory his taunting comrades brought out the ruler to measure his height and determine how much he had grown during the night. When company came home to visit they talked about the weather and how appallingly Kalle grew. Impudent little street waifs shouted "Hello Broomstick" and then ran away as fast as they could. This was a time of trial during which, through no fault of his own, he had to endure suffering and embarrassment from young and old.

In order to escape a bit of this abuse Kalle attempted to sink together and walk crooked like a question mark, but then his aunt would exhort him sternly, "Straighten up, boy." He would straighten up to stand lean and tall, but in a few minutes he would again hear from the saucy street urchins, "Hello Broomstick," or something even more annoying.

He learned easily and was not usually afraid of work, but during adolescence indolence interposed and tried to take him captive. Under this influence he was often truant in his duties, loafing and sometimes excusing himself by saying that he did not like the job. It was a long time before Kalle conquered his laziness and learned to enjoy being busy with work which is such a blessing for man.

During adolescence Kalle was free to be the steward of his own little purse though he was not yet mature enough for the task. His meager income was hardly adequate for his necessities, and with careless management he was bound to encounter problems. He had a taste for fruit, caramels, bakery goods, and other delicacies and spent his coins on them without worrying in the least about future needs. But then winter came with cold and snow. He needed warmer clothing, but had only summer clothes and an empty wallet. The memory of the bakery goods and caramels he had eaten could not keep him warm when the north wind roared around house corners and lashed his body on the way to and from work. In this situation his aunt's serious words were almost as piercing as the north wind itself, but they were wholesome for the boy who, for a moment's mess of pottage, had squandered his small savings. Kalle's uncle and aunt did agree to loan him a few dollars to buy essentials, but with the stipulation that he repay the loan in weekly installments.

As an adolescent Kalle was exceedingly careless about his clothes and his conduct. He would wear his cap on one ear or on his neck or his nose but never squarely on his head where a cap belongs. He swaggered about the streets with his hands in his pockets and played the swell just as some thoughtless preachers do in the pulpit. If a button came off his coat or vest it remained off because it was dispensable, but if a button came off his pants he would usually force a nail or screw through the cloth and fasten his suspenders on that. This method of repair was Kalle's own discovery. If he tore his coat sleeve or any other part of his clothing he mended it with the glue brush, in spite of the fact that from childhood he had been trained as a tailor. He was very inventive in getting by with his rags.

He totally neglected reading, caring for neither books nor newspapers. In leisure hours he most liked to stand on a street corner, whittle a stick, and listen to other adolescents brag, lie, and talk filth. He never had much to say in such company, but he had ears, and learned, therefore, a good deal of mischief. Among other things, he learned to light cigarettes and developed a taste for tobacco, a bad habit which hung on for some years. During this time of his life there was very little lacking for Kalle to become the companion of the prodigal son.

Many strong currents flowed through Kalle's young soul during these years of growing up. The dangerous waves foamed and frothed around the sailor on the sea of time. Still, they were not only unavoidable but useful, because through these experiences the boy was toughened for the coming storms and battles of life. Here he must learn to distinguish between good and evil and voluntarily choose the good. Here the metal out of which character is forged must receive its initial purification.

However, during this time Kalle was very fickle, wanting first one thing and then another, and then not knowing what he wanted. He was indifferent to all and everything, to God and to himself. Now and then he would shake himself up a bit and make a weak effort to get ahead; he would pick up a book and read or perhaps only glance through a few chapters trying to learn something. But soon he would sink again into discouragement and let his ship drift on.

Finally the oppressive chains of carelessness and apathy burst and a new day appeared. All at once he started to comb his hair carefully, trim his nails, take care of his teeth, and shave more often than necessary. He became fussy about his clothes and was annoyed by shoes worn down on one side. He really wanted to buy gloves, too, but his purse could not stand such luxury. It was only his limited treasury that hindered him from becoming a full feathered dude all at once. Yes, in this respect Kalle went through a real conversion in a very short time.

He tried to satisfy his desire for ornaments as impulsively as he had his earlier taste for sweets and delicacies. One evening on his way home from work he stopped on a street corner to listen to a glib huckster selling buttons and rings to passersby. Here was an opportunity to buy himself a "genuine gold ring" dirt cheap— only twenty-five cents of his hard earned money. A "genuine jewel" was set in the ring, and though it was certainly a dirty brown, it must be real anyway, for how could a man stand there and tell lies in public? The huckster called out his wares to the people who came from neighboring factories. He guaranteed that the ring was fourteen carat gold. He did not wish to lie and suggest that it was eighteen carat, he said, but fourteen carat was pure enough gold for any millionaire to wear on his finger. And the gem was a rare kind, worth more than a diamond. He was able to sell his rings and buttons at such bargain prices because he had succeeded in importing them duty-free from Australia, and he would rather sell them directly to the people than to some rich firm that would increase its wealth on the business.

Kalle paid for the ring with jingling silver, and when he put it on his little finger the swindler assured him saying, "Young man, today you have laid the foundation for your future. If you are lucky in making many similar business deals you will not need to work for long in a sooty factory in Chicago."

That sounded hopeful, and Kalle continued on his way feeling that he had risen to a higher plane now that he wore a ring with a genuine jewel.

At home he did not dare to divulge the brilliant business deal he had made so he carried the ring in his pants pocket. But when he went to or from work or sat in the schoolhouse listening to a sermon or was out somewhere with his young friends he always wore the ring on the little finger of his left hand. A few weeks passed. Then the ring lost its original luster and no amount of polishing restored it. It turned and remained blackish green. One sunny morning on his way to work, Kalle indignantly threw the green ring into a still greener pool of water near the railroad station in North Evanston. There it could lie in the quiet peace it deserved.

Whether there was any relationship between the remarkable ring and love is not quite clear, but just at that time Kalle fell in love with a chubby, rosy blond almost twice his age. This was a new and rare experience. Never before had his heart been so attached to anyone of the fair sex, nor had he thought that this was possible, but now he was in a kind of inexplicable intoxication. If people observed this or not, the author cannot decide, but for Kalle these days were very strange. He had never exchanged a word with his goddess; nor did they ever speak about his glowing feelings for her—or about anything else, for that matter. She no doubt lived in total ignorance of his adoration and thus lost the merriment and satisfaction she could have had from the situation. This youthful infatuation lasted only a few weeks and blew over as fast as it had come, but it was a moment in Kalle's development which during later years called forth many smiles. Perhaps this was its most important result after all.

One beautiful clear Sunday morning, May 1, 1881, Kalle went into Chicago on an important errand for his uncle. He felt good about this extra trip because it was his first opportunity to be in the city on a Sunday since he had moved to North Evanston. The only Sunday train at that time left at six-fifteen in the morning. First Kalle was to accomplish his errand up on Sedgwick Street near Chicago Avenue, then he planned to visit the church on North Franklin Street, and then he would take the one o'clock train back home. This was the schedule he intended to follow without deviation.

The person to whom Kalle was to bring his uncle's instruction lived in the basement of a simple wooden house near "Bredberg's Church" on Sedgwick Street. There Kalle met him, along with a few other uncombed men in everyday clothes who were playing cards at a table with a beer jug in front of them. The errand was completed in a minute, but then the men asked their visitor to sit down awhile, which he did, watching their card playing, which for him was a totally new game and new pastime. While they played they took swigs from the beer jug, and when it was empty they sent to the tavern for a refill. It was foaming bock beer they were drinking with such relish, and Kalle had to taste it, said the men. Someone brought a glass from the cupboard and filled it, as if it would have been too shabby to ask a stranger to drink from the jug. He tried to excuse himself, but was embarrassed to confess that he had never in his life drunk a glass of beer. All the men insisted, so at last, with feigned manliness, he emptied the glass and wiped his mouth. The drink was cool and refreshing, but bitter.

Kalle thought all this was strange. Here card playing took the place of the book of homilies on Sunday morning. Here men competed in drinking and swearing. Here was the tavern and drunkenness under the roof of a home on Sunday when honorable people dressed up and went to church. Kalle had never seen this sort of thing before in either Sweden or America, but he was too bashful to say what he felt. After a while they invited him to go with them to see an acquaintance, and he accepted, but as they walked toward the river on Chicago Avenue he began to feel the effects of the beer in his upper story. His legs grew weak and his steps became uncertain. Finally he collected himself, bid a hasty farewell to the men, and guided his steps back to the railroad station. Thus he was free of these enticing rogues in whose company, before evening, he might otherwise have been dead drunk.

Of course Kalle was to have gone to the Mission Church, but he knew clearly that it would have been a scandal for him to attend the worship service inebriated. As he headed toward the railroad station he felt the effects of the beer more and more. The sidewalk on Wells Street was not wide enough, the light posts were in the way, and every once in a while he began to lose his balance. He would gladly have crawled into a stairwell to sleep but he managed to labor on and finally came to the Northwestern station at the corner of Wells and Kinzie streets. There he sat down on a bench and fell asleep.

How long he slept he didn't know, but the station attendant roused him and drove him out of the station. Staggering, Kalle obeyed, but immediately stole back in through another door and got on the train, where he continued to sleep in a corner.

At that time there was a daily "funeral train" from this station to Rosehill and Calvary cemeteries, which were then far outside the city limits. Because the roads were hardly passable, the dead were taken out there by train, accompanied by the mourners as passengers. The train had a dozen coaches packed full of mourners, plus three coaches for other passengers bound for different stations along the way. These three coaches went all the way to Winnetka; the others were uncoupled at Calvary.

In his drowsiness Kalle did not question where he sat down, nor did he notice who got on or off, but remained asleep in his corner. When at long last he awakened he was absolutely alone in the coach. He looked outside and saw tombstones and crosses, but not a living person. Here he was, alone on a sidetrack in the dwellings of the dead because of his intoxication. This was something to reflect upon, and the thought seemed to sober him up at once. He ran outside and looked up the track. In the far distant sky he could see a little wisp of smoke from the locomotive that had probably already brought the other coaches to their destination.

Since there was no other train north all day and no streetcar or other conveyance, Kalle had to use his "apostles' horses" to get to North Evanston. This was rather mild punishment, however, because the day was sheer sunshine and delight. Besides, in this way it was more certain that every trace of the beer's effects would be gone when he got home and had to explain why he had not come on the train. He certainly did not want his aunt and uncle to know that he had been drunk.

Later in the afternoon Kalle arrived, walking leisurely, but very hungry. He explained how the people on Sedgwick Street had tricked him into staying until it was too late for church, how he had gotten into one of the funeral coaches and neglected to change at Calvary, and how in this way he had been left behind and had to walk. This was, of course, true, though not the whole truth. His uncle and aunt were satisfied with this explanation and Kalle never had to tell them of his first experience with being drunk which, fortunately, was also his last. Later he sipped a glass of beer now and then but never did he drink more than one glass at a time, though he had comrades at work who used strong liquor both moderately and immoderately. For a while he took his dinners at a tavern that also served meals, but the strongest drinks he had on such occasions were pop and ginger ale. Never again did he feel the degrading effects of intoxication.

During adolescence and sometimes even later, boys have their own unique way of reasoning, arranging, and planning. They often spend twenty-five cents in order to save five. They gladly walk a long distance out of the way in order to have a short ride. They jump on all kinds of conveyances, risking life and limb. In this respect Kalle was like other boys.

On one occasion he was sent on some errand in the city. It was far to walk, but he made the distance even greater by going down to the railroad and following the tracks in hopes that he could jump a locomotive or freight train and thus steal a ride at least part of the way. When he approached Union Depot from the south on the

Pennsylvania tracks, there was finally an incoming passenger train. He decided to catch it, and began running alongside in order to grab a handrail and get on. But the train was moving faster than he had anticipated. He succeeded in getting a grip on the railing of one of the coaches, but the speed of the train jerked him along. Instead of catching up to the steps as he had hoped, he was thrown mercilessly against the side of the car. He was forced to drop his hold and fell helplessly to the ground.

He fell with a peculiar swinging motion which threw both legs under the railroad coach just after the first wheels had passed. The speed whirled him around on his back so that he fortunately escaped disaster, but the wheels tore his trousers and gave him a light blow on one kneecap.

All this happened in a few seconds. With a pounding heart Kalle rose quickly and took a few long steps away from the tracks. He did not want to converse with some railroad workers who had witnessed the event. He had had enough for this time. Back up on the street he thanked his father's and mother's God for saving him in this marvelous way from being mutilated or even killed.

Chapter Thirteen

Great Changes

For about three years Kalle lived with his uncle and aunt, feeling contented and very much at home in idyllic North Evanston. Now, however, he had to pull up roots and move to the big city, to relatives living on the South Side of Chicago. The shift was the result of an agreement between the relatives in Evanston and the relatives in Chicago and was not his own free choice. He did not doubt their good intentions and no real harm was done by the new arrangement, but this time again he was moved as though he were an object without any will and placed where other people felt he should be, probably where he would be the least bother.

The relocation was an easy matter because he possessed little more than the clothes on his back. During the last evening in his Evanston home he gathered a few things he could call his own, wrapped them in newspaper, and went to bed. The following morning he got up early as usual and ate breakfast. Then he thanked his aunt and uncle for good shelter and good will, said a brief farewell to his cousins, took his package, and went to work.

Never had he missed his parents and his parental home as he did that morning. He felt as if he did not belong anywhere; perhaps no one would have missed him very much if he had disappeared entirely. But this melancholy mood blew away on his way to the station, and later during the day he tended to his job in the factory as if nothing new were in the making.

When evening came he put his package under his arm and

directed his steps to his new home at 2977 South LaSalle Street, where a younger, newly married aunt and uncle lived in a simple four-room flat on the second floor. This was diagonally across the street from the old Mission Tabernacle at 30th and LaSalle. No tears of sorrow were shed when Kalle left Evanston and no tears of joy flowed when he came to his new home; the move was entirely businesslike. And yet when he arrived at the home in Chicago he was as heartily received as he could reasonably expect.

Here too Kalle lived with kind Christian people in as secure an environment as could be found anywhere. But picturesque Evanston with its large houses and big beautiful yards was forever gone. Instead, he now lived near the door of a miserable tavern where loud noise, quarrels, and fights were the order of the evening and ran far into the night. The district was not particularly pleasant, yet quite a few decent Swedish workers as well as other orderly people still lived there.

Kalle continued to work for the same firm, which had now moved its shop to South Clinton Street. The uncle in Evanston was part owner, but when his partner became ill and died, he had to dispose of the business. A talkative American who had big plans but little capital succeeded, with an unbelievably good business arrangement, in taking over the company, and by promising all the workers honorable treatment, steady work, and good pay, he persuaded them to stay in their jobs.

It was not long, however, before one could see that the business was not in sure hands and that the situation of the labor force had deteriorated considerably. Salaries were not paid punctually, but the new owner asked for consideration in a friendly way and assured the workers that things would improve after the first six months because then he expected some large capital to become available. On the basis of this prospect the workers labored faithfully and contented themselves on pay days to receive only half or less of their pay. A few people left to seek other jobs, but most stayed on naively and dutifully in the hope that better times would come. Kalle was one of the foolish ones.

Meanwhile, a fat lawyer came regularly to the office and had long discussions with the owner. An air of mystery enveloped the whole business, and the owner, who walked about stealthily like a cat, did not make the best impression on his employees. Yet suddenly there was a shipment of goods, which pointed to improvement, and the workers hoped that there would be better income for the owner and for themselves. Then one afternoon some half-finished goods were shipped out, and toward evening just as they were about to go home, other workers came to dismantle some of the machines. It was explained that this was only a question of necessary rearrangement and repair. But when the crowd of employees came the following morning the shop was closed and police were guarding the building. The talkative owner was bankrupt.

Now they could see through the whole deception. The new owner had planned from the beginning to cheat them and as many of the creditors as possible. The man was now gone and no one knew where he was. The fat lawyer sat in his office downtown and looked innocent, expressing his sorrow over the outcome for the faithful employees.

When the business closed it owed the workers about $10,000. Kalle, whose salary was a dollar a day, had at least two hundred dollars coming. If there had been fair play and the business had lost money, the laborers would no doubt have remained calm, but here was a well-planned and deliberate betrayal, the act of a miserable scoundrel. No wonder their blood boiled during those days! If the swindler had appeared, he would certainly have needed police protection.

The workers received not a cent of what was coming to them. Though they scrounged a little sum and engaged a lawyer to watch out for their interests, it was too late because everything had been arranged beforehand to the advantage of the owner. Since the laws at that time did not protect the laborer against power and injustice as they do now, such villainy could be perpetrated by rascals without a conscience, and it happened fairly often. The weak one was caught in the squeeze play. Still, the good book says: "Look! The wages you failed to pay the workmen who mowed your fields are crying out against you. The cries of the harvesters have reached the ears of the Lord Almighty" (James 5:4). Truly a higher and ultimate justice is needed because human justice often slumbers.

What Kalle had coming, a real fortune to him, had now suddenly evaporated. While waiting to be paid he had gone into debt for room and board and had become completely threadbare. Now he was also without work. Times were not good. Neither boy nor man, and not competent in any profession, he struggled in these teen years; he did not fit anywhere. In vain he searched for work in many kinds of factories, in the building trades, and on the streets. His friends helped him look, but without success.

A few relatives took pity on him and gathered a little sum to buy a suit and other necessary clothing for the ragged one who was unemployed. Their benevolence temporarily brightened Kalle's situation, though he was not happy about having to accept charity. He was willing to work if only he could find something to do.

At the end of one whole day of job hunting he crossed the river on Eighteenth Street and stopped by the railing to look down into the muddy water. The thought of his fruitless search for work and the memory of his lost money at his former job made him gloomy and bitter. A voice whispered inside of him, "All of existence is a curse; it would be wise to end it all." But instantly he straightened up and said, half aloud, "No, never!" He started for home with a quickened step and tried to whistle a tune to refresh his spirit.

After about three months of unsuccessful attempts to find employment, Kalle finally got a job with the Melville Clark firm on South Canal Street near 16th. This cheered him immensely. He began to see a brighter future and no longer believed that providence had condemned him to beg his bread. He plunged into his work, determined to pay his debts as soon as possible.

A few months later he not only had paid all his bills but had sent a little sum to his parents in Sweden and could put a coin in the collection when he attended the Sunday worship services in the old Mission Tabernacle. He bought better clothes and felt as if he was on the same level as other respectable people. Now his great temptation was to live too luxuriously and clothe himself too well, but even this was a passing phase.

A person develops slowly, growing continually from one stage to another and learning from both the bright and the bitter. When, in more mature years, one looks back on the way one has walked and the experiences one has had, the individual sees clearly that all of life has been an education.

The child has a staunch belief in parents and their faith; the child never questions whether they or his teachers have the right view of life. But eventually the child develops a need to understand and examine. Questions about God and the human soul crowd forward and demand answers. The boy and girl, or perhaps more accurately the young man and young woman, must make a personal decision about their relationship to God in whom they have believed since childhood only because their parents have, rather than because they themselves have learned to know him as God.

Kalle, like so many other adolescents, discarded his childhood faith, and though he did not throw himself into dissipation or licentious living, he was drawn farther and farther out into the world by the less dangerous amusements and by his worldly minded comrades. His conscience warned him of the hazards of the way of the transgressor. The powers of good and evil battled for dominion over "the city of man's soul." Yet he attended church regularly. If the pastor's message was searching and hit home, he felt crushed and miserable. If the message was tender and gentle, his feelings were warmed and he was ready to throw himself at the foot of the cross of the Compassionate One. It seemed to him that he stood at the very gate to the happy world of grace but did not dare knock and request entrance.

One day while he stood at his work, the words came to him with wonderful power: "The just shall live by faith" (Romans 1:17). He took courage and thanked God. The fog scattered. All afternoon there was a song in his soul, but he was too bashful to mention the experience to anyone at work or at home. He wanted to confess, but did not dare, and in a few days the tender impression was gone and his inner world was again dark.

In the late winter of 1885 under the ministry of Pastor F. M. Johnson, a spiritual revival took place in the Mission Tabernacle on the South Side of Chicago. During this wave of renewal Kalle made a decision about the relationship of his soul to the Savior. He had just had his seventeenth birthday. With this religious awakening, ambition and desire to read were also awakened; it was as if his sleeping mental powers had been aroused all at once. In more than one respect he became a new creation.

In the fall of 1889, by a definite leading, Kalle's thoughts were transported to his parental home in the high North, and he developed an irresistible desire to visit. He became certain that this was the right time to make the journey, so he decided to celebrate the next Christmas in the country of his forebears.

He was then almost twenty-two years old. He had survived the years of hard struggle in America and now had enough income to dare to embark on the journey. Two traveling companions joined him: Kalle Gustafson from his home parish and Anders Anderson from Värmland, both good friends from Chicago.

Preparations for the trip were easy, and when the train left Chicago all sorts of well-wishers, including some from Småland and Värmland, were present to wave goodbye and send greetings to all of Sweden. Farewell, farewell!

The three young men sat up during the boring ride to New York because sleeping-car comfort was a luxury none of them had considered for even a moment. They arrived at their destination happy, though tired, dusty, and sooty.

At about four o'clock in the morning of December 6, the steamer *Etruria* of the Cunard line sounded its long drawn-out signals for departure. Most of the passengers wanted to see the ship pull out and were therefore on deck, shivering in the icy morning air.

On the voyage across the Atlantic, past England, and over the North Sea, nothing happened than was unusual or worth relating. Thousands of people have had similar experiences traveling third class on the same kind of journey. Perhaps the reader is one of these.

Three days before Christmas the companions arrived in Gothenberg. The Swedish coast lay clear and cold in beautiful new-fallen snow. The countryside as well as the commercial and seafaring city bore witness to the approach of the great festival. After his ten-year absence, it seemed to Kalle that Sweden had an unimagined glory to offer its homecoming sons. How different it felt to come home than to go away! How conditions had changed in ten years and how insight had broadened!

Neither Kalle nor his companions had told their families about their plans to celebrate Christmas under the roof of their old homes. They had intended to surprise them completely. But courage failed them in Gothenberg, for they felt it would be cruel to arrive without previous warning, so they informed their families by telegram that they were already on Swedish soil and that they intended to *doppa i grytan* and eat *julgröt* and *lutfisk* at home.

The author's pen will not lend its service to a description of the moment when Kalle, on Christmas Eve after a ten-year absence, was reunited with his dear parents and his brother and sisters.

While he had been gone, his parents had attained some new and deeper furrows in their faces and were now crowned by a sprinkling of gray. But Father was cured of his illness. Mother was no longer subject to epilepsy. The sisters were now young ladies and the brother who had been in the cradle was now a tall boy about the same age as Kalle had been when he left Sweden. Kalle himself was a tall young man dressed in American clothes, with a passable moustache and glasses.

The beautiful Christmas festivities in old Sweden now became a thousand times more beautiful because Kalle and his parents, his brother, and his sisters could, after ten years, celebrate together for the first time. It was also the last time.

At *Julotta* Kalle sat in the old church of his childhood, an attentive listener. The mood was solemn and beautiful, but hardly to the degree that Kalle had expected. Memories of previous Christmas matins in Marbäck had made him anticipate a greater festive mood than he now felt. The candles twinkled beautifully and the sexton snuffed them when necessary exactly as in former days. The old familiar psalms were sung slowly, accompanied from the organ loft by Frederick Sundberg, the parish clerk and schoolteacher. But the teacher's brother, Rector Axel Sundberg, had been promoted to a larger pastorate, and the service was conducted by Rector Löfgren, whom Kalle did not know.

No, the impression was not exactly what Kalle had expected, but in all probability it was because of changes which had taken place within himself. He had spent ten of his most formative years in a strange country, had lived in a big city, and had been incorporated into a freer church structure than the State Church of Sweden had at that time. The twenty-two-year-old youth from America was entirely different from the eleven-year-old boy who had emigrated. Now he saw with other eyes and heard with other ears. The intervening years had changed him, which was both natural and necessary.

During the worship service Kalle's thoughts sped to the big leading country in the west, to Chicago and the Mission Church on the North Side that was his church home at that time. There he had been present during many *Julottas* and heard the tall pastor, C. A. Björk, the preacher by God's grace, deliver the Word to large crowds. There he had listened to the great choir that, under N. R. Göranson's firm leadership, sang the good news harmoniously and well. There he had attended the large Sunday school's impressive Christmas festivals and enjoyed its rich programs led by the sure hand of the well-known superintendent, A. V. Julin. At that time everything was just as Swedish in that church as it was in Sweden.

Soon, however, Kalle came back from his mental journey and was present body and soul in the old church in Marbäck. He understood now better than ever that he had been quite thoroughly Americanized as a result of his stay in the new land and that America had a mighty attraction for him. He was at home on the other side of the sea.

In the church Kalle saw many old familiar pilgrims who had become gray and wrinkled during his absence. He also saw a younger as well as a middle-aged generation, and many old schoolmates whom he hardly recognized. The former boys now looked very manly, having grown beards of some kind, and were becoming citizens in the community. The former schoolgirls did not trip about as playfully as before but had another appearance and other manners.

At the front of the church sat Petter Anders of Eket, and on the other side of the aisle, the women's side, sat his better half with a cotton shawl on her head, well tied under her chin. There sat Carl Johan of Biarp, Carl Johan of Berg, Gustaf of Smedstorp, Kalle Rikt, Johan of Kvarnen, and even Peter of Carlstorp. There also were the Notåsa people, the Lilla Högaskog people, the Limna people and the miller of Stalpet. And there sat Kalle's traveling companion Kalle Gustafson from Chicago and his old father, Gustaf of the millhouse. The juryman and the church warden were there and a fine array of gentry from Fagerhullt, Vrangsjö, Herrestad, and Öringe. The gentry, as well as the common people, need to hear the message of grace from above.

On the slope outside the church at the close of the worship service the people encircled the "Americans" who had come home. In the light, new-fallen snow and the fresh morning air there were greetings and conversation; old friendships were renewed and new acquaintances were made. The curious parishioners would perhaps have lingered till noon if necessary to ask all their questions about America and about friends and acquaintances over there. In their thick high-top shoes and substantial boots they did not feel the cold on the hill as Kalle did in his American laced shoes with comparatively thin soles. Johan of Kvarnen's little boy, who was also interested, remarked with surprise, "Look he has only ski boots on."

After the "Americans" had, by prearrangement, conversed a little with each other in English about how pleasant it was to come home for Christmas and the listeners had marveled over the fact that such strange sounds could have a rational meaning, they said goodbye and started towards their own homes to eat a breakfast of *lutfisk,* headcheese, and other good Christmas food. Then Kalle Gustafson turned as if he had forgotten something and shouted to his companion from America, "Merry Christmas!" But the other took to his Swedish and answered politely, "Tack, Tack! God Jul!" For both of them this holiday celebration became a happy and good Christmas.

Långliden slope

Volume Two

Preface to Volume Two

In 1926 I published *Son of the People,* which received a warm commendation in the press. It was a simple account of my childhood and adolescence, closing with my visit to Sweden after ten years in America.

The following chapters (Volume Two) are a continuation of the story. The fact that I speak here in first person rather than in third as in the earlier volume should not be seen as a desire to let the ego intrude, for there are entirely different reasons for this.

It is not my purpose here to write an autobiography, but only some autobiographical sketches, some portraits that reveal the Lord's guidance in my life, how I was called into the ministry, and how this calling developed through the years.

Much could be told about what has happened during the swiftly passing years that would be useful and pleasant for the reader, but only a few fragments can be presented.

Today it is exactly fifty years since I landed on the American coast for the first time. Thoughts of this bring forth heartfelt thanks to he who has led my steps and whose promises are my joy and comfort.

C. V. Bowman
Chicago, Illinois
October 3, 1929

Chapter Fourteen

Christmas Festivities in the Northland

At Christmastime in 1889 after a ten-year sojourn in America, I had the joy of visiting my fatherland in the North, my childhood home. Old and young were tuned to festivity, and celebration was conducted in such great seriousness that not even the most prosaic person could escape its influence or remain untouched by its religious meaning.

Christmas has a unique ability to awaken noble emotions and move people to beautiful acts of loving service both to close friends and to hapless strangers. At Christmas we open wide our arms and hearts to our fellow travelers through time. Never do we feel as close to each other as we do then, nor will we be difficult and contentious then. No, at that season we all want to be kin.

The Christmas season gathers and unites those who during the rest of the year have to be separated. Sons and daughters, even those in foreign lands for whom a visit home is difficult and costly, try to come home at Christmas to take their places at the old family hearth, and if they cannot do so they still send their hearty Christmas greetings to the folks at home and in other ways show their feelings for and interest in the old home and those who still live on the old place.

The preparations for Christmas in the home of my forebears were, as they presumably were in all of Sweden, extensive and thorough. In rural areas people began butchering and baking long before Christmas and continued working day after day until everything in the house and yard had been decorated and refurbished. If the resources of the house permitted, the shoemaker and tailor improved and renewed the wardrobe. People also gave their bodies the most thorough bath of the year in the washtub before the actual celebration began. When Christmas Eve arrived people were at least outwardly prepared to participate wholeheartedly in the rich and varied program of the Christmas celebration.

The festival began on Christmas Eve with *doppa i grytan,* a taste of excellence for everyone, including the hungry children. Don't we all remember the festive moment at the saucepan! Later came the real Christmas Eve dinner of rice pudding, *lutfisk,* veal loaf, potato sausage, *limpa,* juniper ade, and other delicacies. Then came the distribution of presents and the happy dance of children around the Christmas tree which was generously decorated with apples, *pepparkakor,* wrapped candy, and bright paper decorations.

But the climax of the Christmas celebration was *Julotta** in the old parish church. People of all ages from near and far gathered in groups as they approached, quietly and solemnly going to the house of the Lord where the service would begin at five o'clock Christmas morning. Many came on foot, but the well-to-do farmers and the gentry from the estates came riding in sleighs under warm lap robes to the jingle of sleigh bells and the rhythmic hoofbeats of horses on the frozen road.

Inside the church hundreds of lights twinkled in chandeliers and windows. Impressively the immortal hymn sounded forth, *Vår hälsa shöna morgonstund.*** The congregation listened with interest and patience to the sermon about the Savior who had come to earth, even though they were shivering in the unheated church. The festive mood was high and it can be truthfully said to the credit of the parishioners that no honorable person in Marbäck would let any trifle be a barrier to attending *Julotta.*

Because Christmas, as a celebration of the Savior's birth, is completely religious, songs of praise and spiritual contemplation are eminently fitting as expressions of the Christmas mood. Yet it seems as if there is a universal need in people to celebrate holidays by eating and drinking. This in itself is not evil. When Israel was delivered from Egypt, the Passover feast was instituted as a commemoration.

---

* Christmas service before daybreak.
** "All Hail to Thee, O Blessed Morn"

And when the Lord Jesus was ready to bid farewell to his disciples, he instituted the Holy Sacrament by participating with his disciples in the Passover meal. In our day also, eating and drinking are part of family, social, and church gatherings.

As a rule, the Swedish people enjoy having festive meals and perhaps tend to overdo it. In the wealthy person's home and the poor person's cottage such meals occur frequently, especially at Christmas. When I went home in 1889 I shared in more festivities and Christmas parties with family and friends than I was able to enjoy. Just as Job's sons and daughters feasted in each other's houses in former days so we did in Marbäck Parish during this occasion. The Christmas holiday of 1889 became the unsurpassed party period in my life.

No one in Marbäck could be persuaded to undertake any work during the Christmas holidays; only the most essential tasks received attention. Nor was it worthwhile to put on working clothes between the numerous following holidays, for along with Christmas there was always *Anan Dag Jul* and the third day as well. Then came the usual Sunday and then New Year's Day with its day after. Then Epiphany was at the door. Only on the twentieth day of Knut could Christmas be ushered out.* These weeks, however, were the great festive periods of the year which young and old looked forward to and in which they rejoiced.

Christmas was beautiful there at home. Nature itself seemed to be heavenly minded—so peaceful and quiet. The thick snow blanket had made the whole area round and smooth, and the newly fallen snow was like clothing, a Christmas gift from the Creator. The tall trees of the forest stood knee-deep in it, while only the tips of the shrubbery peeked up through it hopefully. Fences were hidden except for their gray poles. Here and there were red cottages with white trim and a white snow roof through which the chimney rose, pouring out a pillar of smoke from the fire in the hearth. At times rosy-faced youth rushed by on supple skis over the hard crust.

The memory of Christmastide 1889 is indelible for me, not just because of the great festivities and the glorious winter scenes, but even more because of the unforgettable visit with my parents in the home of my childhood. The ten years had changed our appearances so that we were unrecognizable to each other. The four children,

---

* *Anan Dag Jul* is the day after Christmas. Christmas festivities lasted twenty days until January 13.

particularly, had to become reacquainted, for we had outgrown the childhood play that had been our natural element when we separated and now had youthful interests. When I had left, the black cloud of sickness had hung over our home. Now that cloud was gone and the sun of health was shining again. True, there was now a sprinkling of gray in Father's and Mother's hair and the plow of time had begun to furrow their faces, but no real change had taken place in them; their hearts were exactly as they had been.

The province in Sweden and the city in America were, of course, very different at all times of the year, but now this came to me in an overwhelming way. Everywhere the contrasts met me as I thought about this Christmastide in the Northland and Christmas as it had been celebrated in Chicago during the preceding ten years.

At Christmastime in Chicago one threw aside working clothes for a day at the most, then pitched oneself back into the rush and noise and restless struggle for existence. In the American city with its belching smokestacks, its humming and bustling factories, and its hurrying masses of people, one could hardly, even at Christmas, attune one's thoughts to festivity. In contrast, the Christmas mood and celebration in Sweden was really gripping, with a completely different spirit reigning. And yet it was, to be sure, the same subject being celebrated on both sides of the Atlantic.

Neither Christmas nor other church festivals are celebrated fully and fittingly by the American Protestant denominations, which have been so strongly influenced by Reformed church thought that they have done little or nothing to stimulate their celebration. The Lutheran church, which has always given more attention to church holidays, has had a wholesome influence in America by awakening more interest in them, but there is still much to be desired in this area of church life.

Our Swedish people in America have always tried to emphasize Christmas by gathering in churches to sing the immortal old Swedish Christmas hymns and listen to the message of the Savior's coming. *Julotta* has attracted them as no other festival service has been able to do, and Americans notice these gatherings and are surprised by them.

In 1888 the American Congregational pastor F. E. Emrick visited the North Side Mission Church in Chicago for *Julotta*. His interest in the Swedes and in the Mission Friends in America was warm and he was then learning to speak Swedish. When he arrived he found the spacious church crowded with people in a reverent but festive mood. Pastor C. A. Björk invited him to the chancel to bring a Christmas greeting to the congregation, which he did, at times in English and at times in broken Swedish, which evoked some smiles. His greeting was approximately as follows:

It is a wonderful and glorious sight to behold these 2,000 people, all sons and daughters of Mother Svea, gathered in the house of the Lord this early morning hour. We consider ourselves fortunate that the Swedish people bring with them to America their religious heritage. That a crowd like this gathers in the house of the Lord at five o'clock Christmas morning to celebrate the Savior's birth is very beautiful. It grips my heart. To my American eyes it looks almost like a miracle. I can hardly persuade my members to gather at eleven o'clock on Sunday morning; to gather them at five o'clock on Christmas morning, I have not even dared to try!

Thus spoke the American pastor at *Julotta* in Chicago. But what would he have said if he had been transported to Marbäck and seen the Christmas celebration that continued for weeks and influenced young and old, man and beast, giving the whole fabric of community life a unique festal tone? This surely would have gripped his heart and left him with an indelible memory!

The main purpose of my returning to Sweden was to see my parents, sisters, and brother whom I had left at eleven years of age in order to seek my fortune in a strange land. At that time the tourist in me had not yet awakened, so I was completely satisfied to spend three interesting winter months in my home area with parents and family. One visit to the town of Eksjö and two or three visits to Tranås, which had recently blossomed from a common station community to a small city, were the only side trips.

During my time in America my parental home had been moved from the Smedhemmet to Klinten, a soldier's home below Eket. The homestead, which has long since been demolished, was ideally located with a view of Lake Råklangen and the beautiful and varied scenes on the other side which inspired the viewer to praise the Creator. I felt more at home here than I could have on any tourist journey. Here was a sanctuary I would soon have to leave to return to the wide world. No wonder I preferred to stay here in my winter quarters.

To see more of Sweden in winter garb would no doubt have been pleasant. I did consider visiting Stockholm and the king but this remained only a thought. At that time I also believed that the Creator had lavished all that was great and beautiful on the American continent and given only insignificant things to other parts of the world, so there would not be much to see in Sweden. Like Americans in general I had developed an immoderate pride in America and everything American. For me the United States was the ideal country, a kingdom of heaven on earth. During my ten-year stay, I had become "100 percent American."

The people of the United States have a strong national feeling expressed in the educational system, the press, and in all of community life. National pride is in the very air. The immigrants are seized by this spirit even though they do not notice it at first. Little by little they go through a national new birth, a re-creation of thought patterns, language, and customs. Only after the change has taken place can they understand what has happened and realize that they are no longer only Swedish but Swedish-American, which is both a gain and a loss.

My high opinion of America and everything American could hardly be surpassed; everything in Sweden paled in comparison. I refused to be moved in the least by Dr. P. Waldenström's biting criticism of everything American, including Swedish-Americans, when he visited the United States in the summer and fall of 1889 and described his impressions in a series of newspaper articles and in a book about his travels. Because the naive enthusiasm of Swedish-Americans about their adopted country and their often unjust comparisons between *little* Sweden and *big* America irritated Waldenström, he was determined to hold up the merits of Sweden and point out all the deficiencies he could discover in America and its people. In this he spared no effort and missed no opportunity. But to change the minds of the Swedish-Americans on this point was a greater order than the learned professor from Gävle realized. With all his arguments, witticisms, and satire, he could not shake our faith in America or our belief that it was greater than Sweden.

Most Swedish-Americans took Waldenström's criticism rather calmly because they liked the man, but some became bitter and could not speak strongly enough against him. We explained the situation this way: Waldenström was by disposition an aristocrat and had never experienced the economic distress that the laborer in Sweden had to struggle with. Therefore, he was not fully competent to judge the situation of the working class in Sweden or America.

It was fortunate, however, that I was a man of few words when I made my first return visit to Sweden. Otherwise I would probably have spoken foolishness and made unjust comparisons between Sweden and America as so many others had done before and would do later. I was spared by my natural shyness from making the obvious mistakes of that kind.

But in spite of this, "America fever" broke out among the young people in Marbäck so that many of them began to think of going with me to the great country in the West. Almost twenty young men and women, among them my two sisters, prepared for emigration to America.

Chapter Fifteen

With the Sun Again

On March 8, 1890, my companions and I set out for America. Winter drifts had melted away, the days had become longer, and the sun had begun to call forth greenery. Soon it would be spring and summer.

Tender emotions were kindled in several homes that Saturday morning because some son or daughter was saying farewell to father and mother, sister and brother. But perhaps emotions surged highest in my own parental home because my sisters and I must all say farewell, leaving our parents and our eleven-year-old brother in the old cottage to endure bereavement as best they could. The emptiness was great and the sense of loss bitter for those who would stay at home. And for those who went away, the longing for home would more than once pinch their hearts.

The wide ocean would now separate parents from children and sisters and brothers from each other, but the distance was not a great gulf that could not be bridged. Hope remained on both sides for a happy reunion, perhaps in a few years.

There comes a time for all young people to leave the nest and prove their own wings. A person cannot depend on parents forever, nor is it harmful to rely on one's own resources quite early in life. A large number of Swedish young people steered their course to America when they left home because America had kindled their imagination as an earthly paradise. And many of them have made their way with honor, some also gaining wealth and prestige in the community and state.

It is a very important moment in young people's lives when they cut the old moorings. They must make new acquaintances and win new friends. They must support themselves. They must choose between good and evil, and in doing so, choose their own future character. Devout parents will, of course, send up warm prayers for their children when they go out into the wide world, and no doubt the young people themselves pray more than they ordinarily do at thoughts of departure into the unknown.

Just as violent storms tear at the world of nature, storms and separation rage in human experience, yes, even in the lives of youth, and this is good preparation for life's fortune and happiness, which we otherwise might take for granted. We all realize that upheaval and sorrow are unavoidable, though we may question why they come and the answer may vary. The philosopher broods over the problem without finding the answer, but the Christian faith finds the right solution because it sheds light on the mystery of life and changes the question mark to an exclamation point. It says trustfully, "In this way my Father in heaven wants to lead me to eternal blessedness in his heavenly kingdom." Supported by the staff of faith, the pilgrim, therefore, treads securely, knowing that this wrenching and sorrow can be a disguised blessing.

For me the approaching journey to America was not a cause for anxiety because I had crossed the sea before and had ten years' experience of what was waiting on the other side. But the mood was quite different for the youth in our travel group who now for the first time were torn from home and with each day entered new ground. Yet young minds seldom admit that they are worried about an unseen future, so all the traveling companions displayed a youthful joy and freedom from anxiety which made the adversities of the journey amusing.

So farewell, you my home in the North! To you I will no doubt long to return from wherever I travel and wherever I pitch my tent on my pilgrimage. Gladly would I again see your fair neighborhoods, walk your old paths, and dream about my childhood. But farewell! Farewell, Father, Mother, and Brother who remain in the modest cottage on the old sod. When you look westward over Råklangen, let your thoughts speed over the wide surface of the ocean to us out there in the land of the West. In the same way on wings of thought we will fly to meet you. Our hearts are united with bonds that cannot be broken and thoughts that are swifter than lightning. Farewell!

In Gothenburg youthful crowds bent on America gathered from the various provinces of Sweden. The authorities in the office of the Cunard Line prophesied, "It will be crowded on the boats all spring." Even now, at the beginning of March, emigrants swarmed on Sillgatan and at the wharf. All had to have their tickets validated, their certificates of departure stamped, and their Swedish paper money and coins exchanged.

But most depressing were the arrangements for mattresses, pillows, quilts, knives, forks, spoons, and tin plates, all of which had to be procured at the marketplace and carried aboard the steamer. The steamship company did not provide the emigrants with these simple articles of civilization, even though it had made some minor improvements during previous years.

Originally the emigrants had traveled on common freighters that lacked all comforts, but as emigration increased, complaints in the press about the negligence of the steamship companies caught the attention of the legal authorities. Consequently they were required to provide more comforts, but the arrangements on the emigrant steamers were still hopelessly poor in the year of grace 1890. Probably the third-class comforts on an Atlantic steamer nowadays are comparable to the first-class accommodations of forty or fifty years ago.

In Gothenburg there was a society of Christians who carried on a spiritual work among emigrants. They arranged meetings in a simple hall and would seek out the emigrants in the various hotels, invite them to the meeting place, and guide them back to the hotel if they needed this as strangers in the city. This mission had gone on for many years and had proven very useful to the travelers. We were invited to this meeting place on the Sunday and Monday evenings we had to spend in Gothenburg.

Here the saving Gospel was proclaimed in spirit and power. Jesus Christ was portrayed as the one who can fill all the empty places in the soul and be more than father, mother, sister, brother, and friend for those who trust in him. The preacher understood how to remind people of home and loved ones, and spoke about the heavenly home which had more to offer than Sweden and America combined. This glorious land could be won by accepting Jesus Christ as personal Savior. Tenderly and seriously he challenged those who were gathered not to neglect the time of grace but to take the opportunity then while the Lord was calling.

On the whole, the emigrants were sensitive because they had just departed from home and loved ones and because they were thinking of the approaching journey which was as if enveloped by fog. The preacher's challenge made a deep impression and the young people were noticeably affected. Eyes were moist with tears and suppressed sobbing could be heard here and there in the room. Those who were anxious about their sins became subjects for special prayer.

A few of those present found grace to receive salvation and could thank God for the forgiveness of sins before the meeting closed. This turned us to rejoicing, and songs of praise and faith followed one after another. It was so uplifting that we could have sung till midnight, but suddenly the meeting ended because it had to be quiet at a certain hour. To continue would have brought complaints and perhaps even the intervention of the police. Thus the inspiring meeting ended just when the spiritual warmth was greatest, but while the song had to cease being audible, it continued in our hearts while we quietly went down the stairs and on to our respective lodgings.

In this way the Emigrant Mission in Gothenburg left an indelible impression on those who attended the simple meeting place while waiting for the departure of the steamer. Many, no doubt, received an entirely new direction for life and made gains not only for time but above all for eternity.

The following morning life was hurried among the emigrants. The Wilson Line steamer *Domino* was almost completely loaded with cargo and was now ready to take on passengers for the journey to England. There were so many lower-class emigrants that it took several hours to bring them aboard. It was faster, as always, with the upper-class passengers, not only because there were fewer of them but because everything was better prepared for them. It should be self-evident that I traveled with the lowly; with the upper class I would surely have felt lost, like a sparrow among peacocks.

We were herded aboard the ship amidst great crowding, pushing, and squeezing, while agents and door attendants shouted commands over the masses. Little by little the swarming crowds were placed in different depths of the ship and order emerged out of the awful confusion. It was almost exactly the same now as it had been ten years earlier when I had emigrated as a boy. The *Domino* was the same style and size steamer as the *Rollo,* which had brought me to England then. Both were rusty outside and dirty inside, and the interior arrangements were identical. People had to accept things as they found them because the Wilson Line had a complete monopoly on the emigrant traffic from Sweden, and its sole purpose was to make money.

Finally everything was settled. The *Domino* sounded its coarse basso voice announcing its departure from Gothenburg harbor. The anchor was lifted, the propellers began to churn, and slowly the heavily loaded vessel began to move. On deck was a throng of Mother Svea's sons and daughters, anxious to take a farewell look at the city and the shore with its gray cliffs and rock islets. As a favor to them the English musicians tuned their instruments and played *Du gamla, du fria, du fjällhöga Nord,* which at that moment was full of both inspiration and, yes, even pathos, for the vessel now carried them to an entirely different and unknown land.

The air was hazy, and there was a lonesome whine in tackle and lines. But immediately out of the islets the waves, in full action, waited to have fun with the steamer. They began to lift and heave the *Domino* rapidly on strong arms without consideration for the travelers' taste or well-being. Those who now journeyed on the seas for the first time found these initial hours on the *Domino* terrible and ill-omened, and they preached about a wet grave. It did not take long before we all disappeared from deck and fled to our bunks, meek as children who have just been chastised. The vessel lurched in the waves and rolled us in our bunks, along with our suitcases and rattling tin dishes. Of the seasick crowd, those who dared to open their lips and who could speak coherently bemoaned the fact that they had been so ignorant as to enter into such misery. And perhaps a few sick travelers said their "Our Father" or a long-abandoned childhood prayer.

To describe seasickness is superfluous because most of my readers have experienced it firsthand, but it is also obvious that it never follows anyone onto the land and that the memories of it are soon obliterated. Long before the *Domino* reached the coast of England we had beautiful weather and all who had been seasick were well again.

At the port city of Hull, our first stop on the journey, we had to have our baggage inspected at John Bull's* custom house even though our belongings were hardly worth anything. In vain would travelers seek entrance to a foreign land, even if only to pass through, without declaring themselves for inspection before the sentries of the kingdom. Their chalkmarks on trunks and hand luggage open the gates of the country and allow the travelers to continue their journey.

Immediately after the inspection we went to a nearby restaurant to receive, at the expense of the line, a salt-bread roll as big as two fists and a bowl of thin soup. It was exactly the same treat served to the emigrants ten years before—the same menu and the same manner of serving. Simpler and cheaper it could hardly have been.

Then we boarded the train which already stood waiting to take us to Liverpool. As we rushed along to our destination we saw a varied panorama through the window: larger and smaller manufacturing cities, well-cultivated fields, and beautiful landscapes in spring garb. Empty tracts and abandoned farms were nonexistent because the country was densely settled. But for us the scenes before our eyes had only a momentary interest. Our desire was for the young America with its wide borders.

When we arrived at Liverpool the fog lay gray and damp over the city. Ragamuffins and dirty wolfish children played, quarreled, and fought with each other on the streets. We emigrants were transported like cattle to the emigrant hotels near the wharf, there to await the steamer's departure to the land of the future in the West.

We had planned our arrival at Liverpool so as to be able to embark on the *Eturia,* at that time one of the best steamers of the Cunard Line, but the authorities in England had decided to use the *Eturia* for England's own sons and daughters and send the Swedes to America on a poorer vessel. In order to do this they had to use lies and tricks. They told us that there was a strike among the work force so that the *Eturia* could not leave for a day or two. We, of course, took for granted that this was so, but we later learned that the *Eturia* had sailed at the appointed time. We complained repeatedly about the conduct of the line toward us, but the agent only cursed and said that it should make no difference what vessel we took as long as we got to America.

---

* euphemistic personification of Britain, like "Uncle Sam" for the United States

Quite unexpectedly, then, we spent a Sunday in Liverpool. This gave us an opportunity to visit a worship service at Stranger's Rest and listen to sermons from a Swedish and a Danish preacher. We also made small excursions in the city, as much as we strangers dared, while we tried to hide our disappointment and indignation at the rude behavior of the steamship line toward us.

In a few days we boarded the steamer *Cephalonia,* one of the older ships of the line, which was bound for Boston, not New York as we had expected. And instead of a six-day crossing it was now a thirteen-day trip, which also turned out to be stormier than usual. Seasickness raged, and in many a bosom indignation raged also. During these days not a Swede on board had a good word to say for the Cunard Line.

Finally, however, we landed in old Boston and soon forgot the disappointments, seasickness, and all we had thought was crazy on the *Cephalonia* during the two weeks. We opened our trunks and other baggage and invited the customs inspectors to dig as they wished in our poor belongings just as their fellow officials in Hull had done three weeks before. Then happily we lashed our trunks again, arranged for our tickets, and bought coffee, doughnuts, and pie, thankful that finally we could once more plant our feet in "God's Country."

When I went through the landing process on the docks in East Boston I could not have dreamt that about twenty years later I would arrive from the west with my wife and children to assume the pastorate of the Boston Mission Church. Nor could I have imagined that on that very dock where the *Cephalonia* berthed at the beginning of April 1890, I as pastor would go back and forth many times to help arriving immigrants. Nevertheless, the unexpected did happen. We never know what changes will occur on our path of life in twenty years, and it is no doubt best that we don't.

A few hours after landing we took a train to Chicago, where we arrived without any difficulties or adventures. Thus after an absence of four months I was home again. But was I actually home or was I away? When I went to Sweden I said I was going "home" to Marbäck. But when I returned to America I said I was going "home" to Chicago. In both cases I went home, and in both cases I went away.

Home is a dwelling, but it means something more than four walls and some furniture. It is, above all, loved ones, memories, and associations. Inasmuch as we can have these in more than one place in the world, we can look upon several different places, even in widely separated countries, as home, and say at the same time, "home in Sweden" and "home in America."

The people who have emigrated from their homeland and settled in another part of the world experience more than any others a division in their inner being, feeling themselves away and at home at the same moment. Swedish-Americans have their Swedish heart and their American heart. When they are at home in America they are away from home in Sweden, and vice versa.

Our home is our free domain, the resting place where we can be undisturbed by the noise and bustle and conflict of the world. In the home are the near and dear ones, and there love and faith reign. With this in mind, Pastor A. T. Frykman gave this beautiful counsel:

> *Get yourself a little place*
> *Full of love and hope and grace.*

The amusing poet Gösta has poignantly sketched his home in the following verses:

> *My home is small, but jolly and good,*
> *And though my purse is empty,*
> *I'm just as happy with my lot*
> *As the pope with his in Rome.*
> *What little I have, I freely rule*
> *'Cause the rubbish is mine.*
>
> *I have a wife and a son who's good,*
> *With dashing and happy looks.*
> *She is, from morning till late at night,*
> *Not idle for even a minute.*
> *She peels potatoes and washes the pots*
> *And sews by machine.*
> *We set up housekeeping sometime back*
> *On a really memorable day.*
>
> *With two empty hands stood I.*
> *But now I have found me a home—not true?*
> *And that is grand.*

At the stove is a shelf that's high and broad,
With plates and cups and saucers.
Two cupboards are under it: one for wood,
The other intended for food.
And yet it happens more often than not
That empty they stand.

Besides all this, two chairs I own
And finally, a mirror of glass
Where I can look at myself if I wish—
Profile or full in the face.
For this is my home which I freely arrange
'Cause the rubbish is mine.

Chapter Sixteen

Development

We are born with potential for both physical and spiritual development. Our inborn talents, our environment, and our free will all determine what that development will be. Just as the fruit of a tree depends not only on its species but on air, sun, rain, and the care of the gardener, several factors work together to develop and fashion each of us.

Maturity is achieved slowly, over much of a person's life. A few develop faster than the multitude while others seem to stop growing and remain children as long as they live.

We develop without being aware of it while we attend to our daily tasks. Home, school, church, and work or business all leave their imprint on us. When we are old enough to distinguish good from evil it is our duty to choose the good, for when we do we become stronger, better people. But if we choose the evil we fashion ourselves for what is evil. In this respect we ourselves are responsible for what we become. A Sunday-school teacher once asked a boy in his class who had created him. The bright little fellow held his hands a couple of feet apart and answered, "God created me until I was this big, and since then I have had to do it myself." That answer was not so foolish, for when we consciously choose the good or the evil that comes our way we help shape our own life and determine the direction of our growth.

My four-month visit in Sweden had been a pleasant vacation, the first I had had until that time. Now I was back in Chicago working in the factory as I had before my journey. I was, it seemed then, permanently registered on the rolls of industrial life, not because I was so delighted with the factory, but because at that time I saw no other way to earn my bread.

Work, whether in a factory or elsewhere, has its blessings. Even the hardest job is better than idleness, which is a misfortune and a curse. But while work is a blessing, it is not always a pleasure. Just as roses have thorns, work has problems, and no one knows this better than the laborers themselves, who at times have to toil under prisonlike conditions and at times have their pay reduced unconscionably. Often there is a job shortage and the laborers have to pray almost like beggars for an opportunity to earn their living. And when they are no longer able to work as quickly as youth, they are discharged.

Most employers have shown an indefensible indifference to the spiritual and physical welfare of their employees; some have even been inhumane. But there are also beautiful examples of the opposite treatment, and such humanity toward workers has usually been rewarded in many ways. In general one can say that factories nowadays have better conditions, though there is still much room for improvement.

In the long run all work is exhausting, and now that specialization has become so common it has also become monotonous. Workers are now like machines that do the same little task with the same motions day after day, year after year. They never need to think about anything new, for thoughts, as well as hands and feet, move mechanically in this eternal repetition. Thus we shouldn't wonder that workers lose some of the vital interest in their jobs which they ought to feel in order to accomplish their tasks joyfully and well.

During the twelve years I worked in a factory I became acquainted with both the dark and the bright sides of factory life. This period was a worthwhile education which greatly affected my development, although it was not very rewarding aesthetically or intellectually. Well-used free hours helped compensate for this lack, for most of the time I had a book at hand which I read at the dinner recess, on the streetcar to and from work, and in the evenings. Therefore, in the course of a few years I read a great deal; my thought-life was nourished and the monotony of factory life was counterbalanced.

I cared little for the daily newspapers that people nowadays so greedily devour. To wade through a slough of scandals, as some people seem to, is not just useless but injurious. How much more rewarding is a good book for both old and young!

The evening schools I attended over the course of several years were very useful, for they largely remedied my lack of formal education resulting from my having left Sweden so young. To use five evenings a week during the winter for schoolwork demanded sacrifice of much else that could have been interesting and inviting, but one gains nothing without sacrifice and sustained effort. Nor have I ever regretted the self-discipline I had to practice in order to go through the school program.

Ever since I had come to a decision concerning salvation and my relationship to the Savior I had had a warm interest in the church and spiritual work. Now more than ever I became diligent in church attendance. After living on the South Side of Chicago and having my church home in the Mission Tabernacle, I moved to the North Side and made the North Side Mission Church, which had been dedicated in the early winter of 1887, my church home. Among the religiously minded people there I fellowshiped almost exclusively for several years.

In those days this church carried on a particularly powerful work among the Swedish people in that part of Chicago. Great crowds gathered there to hear God's word preached by Pastor C. A. Björk, the respected shepherd and teacher. In the spring of 1888 I was formally registered as a member of the congregation and in many ways began learning to take part in the multifaceted work. For my personal development the membership in this congregation was of indescribable value. Step by step I was led on and prepared for a calling which I then had no notion would be mine.

During the prayer week of 1889 a great revival broke out among the people who attended the Mission church. Prayer meetings were held evening after evening until the beginning of March. The revival came without any human planning and without the help of an invited revival preacher, and it increased in strength like a swelling spring flood. This was a glorious harvest time which followed a faithful sowing of the Word of Life. The meetings were led in a simple unaffected way without any forcing by the pastor of the church; in fact when he had to be absent on several occasions he left the leadership to the chairman or some other brother in the congregation. The awakening spirit was manifest no matter who led the meeting. This was an unforgettable time of visitation when the spirit of God had power over the people.

People came to the meetings tirelessly so that the spacious basement and all the side rooms were filled each evening. But they were not all believers and persons seeking salvation. Almost every night hard, disputatious people also came, some of whom played the role of free-thinkers, theosophists, and espousers of other remarkable ideas. In personal conversations they tried, with subtleties and hair-splitting, to lead the believers into labyrinths in order to exhibit their own superiority, and indeed they sometimes succeeded.

The pastor of the congregation quietly pursued the calling of a faithful watchman. If a dispute arose he went over and became a listener. Then with seeming innocence he took part in the conversation with the result that the astute disputer soon ensnared himself in the yarn of his own subtleties. Because Pastor Björk had a unique ability to capture people in the snares they tried to lay for the feet of others, such persons often went home from the service knowing that they had been rapped on the knuckles. After that they took care not to get involved in a discussion with the pastor.

Some time after I joined the congregation I was elected a Sunday-school teacher, and for a start had a class of lively and unruly nine- or ten-year-old boys. Boys that age do not come to Sunday school to learn anything about God, but rather to meet each other, play with marbles, and trade knives and other things they carry in their pockets. It was not an easy assignment, partly because the classes were not isolated from each other but were located everywhere in the big church, so that the boys could see a dozen different teachers speaking and gesturing before their class at the same time.

Even so, being a Sunday-school teacher gave me an excellent opportunity to train myself as much in the virtue of patience as in the art of capturing attention and holding interest. I hope the class gained as much from my teaching as I did from being a teacher. If they did, the work was not in vain.

In some ways Sunday-school teachers have the same responsibility as the pastor: they must take care regarding themselves and their teaching, the former at least as much as the latter, or they cannot accomplish anything. By careless behavior, many Sunday-school teachers have torn up the good seed they had sown in the fields of children's hearts.

When I began to teach this class of boys, I, like many other youth, had the habit of smoking. Since I did not see this as anything evil, my conscience did not reproach me for it. I continued with this bad habit for a time, but then something happened that opened my eyes. One Sunday morning after I had eaten my breakfast in a restaurant, I lit my habitual cigar, and puffing smoke, made my way to the church to teach my Sunday-school class. As I walked, a little ragged boy came up beside me, holding between his fingers a cigar stump which he had found in the gutter, and said, "Say mister, give me a light." I readily let him "borrow a light," but immediately began questioning, "What kind of example am I setting for the boys who see me smoking?" At the same moment the vision of my Sunday-school class came alive in my mind.

I could not defend smoking, but I could think of many arguments against it. When I reflected on the matter, I put out my cigar for that time. I no doubt lit cigars a few times after that Sunday morning, but it was not long before I decided, in the Lord's name, never to smoke again. About forty years have passed and I have been able to stand by my decision without difficulty. Not that I will get into heaven because I quit smoking, for entrance there depends on other things, but at least it should not be more difficult because I laid aside the cigars, and I have the satisfaction of knowing that the ragamuffins and dirty children on our streets will not learn to smoke because of me.

When I returned from Sweden I was given a different class, this time of older girls. In terms of discipline this group was as easy to handle as the boys had been difficult, but because the students were more mature there was greater demand for lesson preparation. Thus I was forced into a more thorough study of the Bible and related subjects which was, for me personally, beneficial. My work in the Sunday school became very important to me, and that time constitutes a special chapter in my development and preparation for my later calling.

In the summer of 1891 the teachers decided to visit all the homes in the neighborhood to seek out the Swedish people and invite them to church and the children to Sunday school. The teachers were paired, one older and one younger, and then assigned certain blocks to visit—if possible, every home on the block. This interesting and useful project was completed on Sunday afternoons during the course of a month.

My comrade in this work was the genial August Julin, who later settled in Sweden. We had many interesting experiences during these house visitations. We met all kinds of people: Swedes, Norwegians, Irish, Germans, French, Jews, Christians, nominal Christians, doubters, and blasphemers. We met people who were sober and people who were staggering drunk, people in everyday clothes and people in Sunday dress. To all we tried to bring a greeting from the Lord and his Church, inviting young and old to the house of God, but we paid greatest attention to our own country folk, who were by far the most numerous in the area.

The Mission congregation also had a strong Young Men's Society which had originated back in 1868 and now had about eighty members. Since most of them had been born and reared in Sweden and most had been converted during the times of revival and were still actuated by great spiritual warmth, the whole society was characterized by Swedishness and religious seriousness.

This society met on Tuesday evenings and used only Swedish. We had Bible study and Bible discussions almost exclusively, though we did change off with prayer, testimonies, and song. A little later we arranged so-called social meetings once a month when a simple program was presented consisting of song, music, and a declamation or speech by some member, but a few ascetically inclined brothers were displeased with these meetings and thought they did not have a sufficiently spiritual character.

An example of this narrow view of what was appropriate at the meetings occurred when editor D. Marcelius, who was a member of the society, on one occasion recited Malmstrom's beautiful poem, *"Vi suckar det så tungt uti skogen?"* ("Why does it sigh so deeply in the forest?") Some of the brethren became uneasy. They looked upon the reading of this poem as a sign of worldliness and protested against it. We did not for a moment doubt their honest motives and we were all willing to respect their good intentions, but most members probably doubted their sound judgment on this question.

Inasmuch as most of the members preferred spiritual edification, most of the meetings had this character. However, a few younger brothers born and reared in America felt that the Young Men's Society had another mission besides. They were good faithful members, but because they were a bit dissatisfied with the one-sided character of the meetings they eventually organized, hired their own hall, and arranged meetings for discussion, declamation, speeches, and literary practices in general. At first interest was quite high, but in the long run it proved difficult to sustain the program. In time the inspiration subsided and the meetings ceased.

This little schism among the young men in the church at the beginning of the 1890s is an example of how different training and viewpoints on rather unimportant questions can lead to divisions. Varying opinions and vehement debates on the questions of politics and church life are, more than we sometimes realize, rooted in a difference in education and disposition of the quarreling parties.

Nothing can be more useful for youth than to make themselves acquainted with the Word of God. The Bible discussions in the Young Men's Society were usually very rewarding, though we were, of course, unable to penetrate very deeply into biblical truth. Our limited insight and confused apprehensions were always revealed when Pastor Björk was present and made his remarks after our discussions. Then he turned what we had said upside down, or perhaps it would be better to say that he corrected what we had turned upside down. But his remarks were so fatherly and genial that they sank into good soil. We all appreciated his visits to our meetings.

If Pastor Björk was not at home, Henry Palmblad usually came to our meetings. His contributions to our Bible discussions were a bit mysterious and very possibly left in our young minds a sediment of pessimism. He continually emphasized the importance of walking in the fear of God during our alien pilgrimage on this earth and the necessity of watching for the evil of depraved hearts. He urged sincerely that as young men we should learn to know both "poverty of spirit" and "the riches of grace." His talks always revolved around these thoughts.

Whenever we met Henry Palmblad he struck a minor chord, but in spite of that we liked him pretty well. One day as I came home from work I met him on the street. After the usual greetings he asked, "Well, my dear young brother, how are you getting along with faith these days?" I answered with youthful frankness, "Well, it is no doubt good." Then the old man with the gray beard and eagle nose gave me an admonitory look and said seriously, "Pray to your merciful God that it may not go too well for you." With this he left me, and I went on my way reflecting on what he had said. Perhaps my happy answer to his searching question had awakened fear in him. Perhaps he thought I was in danger of spiritual pride and wanted to awaken me to serious self-examination.

I do not remember if his words on that occasion moved me to any particular self-examination or not, but the warning did no harm. Perhaps it is sometimes necessary to loosen the strings on the instrument of spiritual inspiration, particularly when it has become fashionable to give an enthusiastic but superficial confession thoughtlessly. So it seems that our departed brother had a special purpose, to relax the strings of the instrument and transpose the song from the major to the minor key.

At one of our Young Men's meetings in the fall of 1889, Palmblad's remarks dealt with the enticing power of sin, and he related how he had seen a little bird on the lawn, seemingly enthralled by some power so that he could not stop hopping, as if against his will, in a certain direction. Then he saw a snake in the grass, whose enchanting eyes had captured the little bird. A man took his cane and delivered a blow to the snake's back, and at once the bird flew away, free from the snake's spell. When I came home I wrote a few verses which I include here as an echo from our Young Men's meetings four decades ago.

My own dear brother, sister, friend,
Redeemed from the Egypt of sin,
You have, as of old in Sodom, a Lot
Who was warned by the Lord, yes, seriously warned
To escape and redeem his soul.

Have you left the world with its lure of sin
To seek the heavenly city?
Do not look back, that you shall not taste
The misery and pain that the unfaithful heart
Will receive in fire eternal!

O dearly bought soul, in the Word we see
That the devil has sworn us death.
He wants to destroy us so we'll not inherit
The glory eternal which the Lord of heaven
Has promised to give the faithful.

Turn your eyes to the goal and haste ahead,
Let sin not enchant your mind.
You pine and yearn for the crown which awaits

And finally you land—though you came through fire.
You've won the struggle at last.

For a while C. R. Carlson, an alert man from Värmland, was
the chairman of the Young Men's Society, but he decided to get married and thus lost not only his position but his membership. The
constitution was clear and inflexible on this point, but he was willing to give up both for his Amanda and for the sake of being a real
man. So the society had to sacrifice even this respected member on
the altar of matrimony, thanking him for a faithful watch and for
good fellowship on the interesting path of bachelorhood.

In the election of a new chairman I was chosen without merit
or worthiness. I accepted this trust and challenge and responsibility with true fearfulness, exactly as I think old Palmblad himself
would have done, determined that I would serve to the best of my
ability. Of course I created no great sensation as chairman and the
society performed no miracles during my leadership, but we sought
to do the Lord's work faithfully. On Sundays we gave out tracts and
invited our fellow Swedes to church to hear the Word of God. We
visited the sick and the poor and helped those who were in economic difficulties. And we continued to hold our meetings as we
had done before.

The eighty members of the Young Men's Society have since scattered in all directions. During these forty years many have finished
their pilgrimage on earth while others are now graying and respected
members of church and state wherever they live. Here, I think especially of such men as Emil Forsberg, John Carlberg, Hjalmer Lind,
J. A. Johnson, Oscar Holmgren, Emil Youngstrom, F. A. Lindholm,
Carl Bergstrom, John Melangton, John Hultman, and G. Dahlquist.
Four members later became ministers, namely G. Wideberg, D. Marcelius, P. A. Strom, and myself.

Until this time the Young Men's Society and the Young Wom-
en's Society had met separately, a traditional arrangement in the
church, for evidently there was a certain fear of joint young people's meetings. Perhaps people thought that such meetings would
lead to romancing among the young people as well as other dangers.
In any case, up until then there had been no Young People's meetings nor had anyone encouraged such a thing.

But youth like motion and activity and have common interests
that their elders cannot share. A young man and a young woman

do not willingly sit alone in their rooms in the evening, but want to go out and be with their friends the same age. Thus on Saturday evenings when I walked with other young men along the shore up to Lincoln Park and saw large crowds of Swedish young people spending a few hours of the evening the same way I did, it occurred to me that it would be useful to hold young people's meetings in the church on Saturday evenings, to which they could be invited. I called this to the attention of the Young Men's Society and we decided to ask the church for permission to hold such meetings there.

The good brothers on the church board wanted to support all good work and did not wish to oppose this undertaking if it could serve the cause, but as it was something new in the work of the church some had reservations; still, we received permission to try it.

From the very beginning these meetings had good attendance, and eventually the spacious lower room in the church was nearly full every Saturday evening. A good string orchestra helped to freshen the song, testimonies were warm, prayers were earnest, and souls were brought to faith in the Lord. The congregation, therefore, had nothing but joy from them, and after a few years the Young Men's Society and Young Women's Society gave up their own gatherings and concentrated their efforts on the Young People's meetings.

In the fall of 1891 I was given another position of trust in the congregation when I was elected to be a deacon, even though I was young and inexperienced. In this office I perhaps did not accomplish very much, but working with the older brothers in the congregation became very important for me. More than before, I learned to know the inner life of the congregation and gained insight into its problems. The deacon meetings were not always encouraging, however, because almost every agenda included questions of discipline, involving at times reconciliation between Christian brothers, at times restoration of those who had fallen in manifest sins, at times help for some who were in spiritual enervation and indolence. Each case became the subject of discussion and prayer. Now and then we had moments of joy when our efforts to heal the hurts, mend the broken, and lift the fallen were crowned with success, but we did not always accomplish what we set out to do.

As a deacon I was automatically a member of the board of the congregation, the *bestyrelsen* or "management committee" as it was usually called. There was good reason for this name because the board managed nearly all of the church affairs. The congregation did not have monthly meetings as is common in Mission churches, but had an annual meeting at which reports were received and officers were elected. The management of church business was left to the board, and if special questions of importance arose, an extra business meeting was called.

By and large the members of the board were good and wise men who took care of their responsibilities with honor and usually had a unity of spirit which gave a feeling of stability to the whole work. During the years I was privileged to serve on the board, opinions were sharply divided only once, and if that question had been brought before a church meeting, it would certainly have divided the congregation. This was the situation. The late missionary F. Franson, who had previously resided in Chicago for a time and participated in so-called "prophetic conferences" among both the Americans and the Swedes, had now returned from a stay in Sweden and other European countries. He had been sincerely gripped by a distressed call for help from missionary Hudson Taylor requesting from among Christians in all parts of the world a thousand new missionaries for China. Now Franson decided to awaken interest in this cause among our Swedish people in America also.

He sought to arrange so-called missionary and Bible courses to be held for a few weeks each in different cities of the country. He began with several such courses in the eastern states and then announced in newspapers that he intended to hold a course in the Mission church on the North Side of Chicago, but since he had neglected to first ask Pastor Björk or the congregation for permission to use the church, the announcement caused dismay. Franson's neglect or arbitrariness, whichever it was, did not sit well with the members of the board, much less with Pastor Björk.

The question of whether Franson should be allowed to hold the intended course in the church was now on the agenda of the board meeting. Most of the brethren, with Pastor Björk as leader, felt that the church should not be opened to him. Their contention was that it had never before been opened under such conditions and should not be so at this time. But others felt that Franson's improper action should be overlooked inasmuch as he was inspired by a good cause. I aligned myself with this group, perhaps a natural decision since I was the youngest and understood perhaps least of all the importance of the question and the wide ramifications of the board's decision.

The result of the discussion was a decision to inform Missionary Franson that on this occasion he could not use the church, but he could hold the planned missionary and Bible course in the Mission Tabernacle on the South Side where Pastor August Pohl was the pastor and teacher.

Though the North Side Mission Church was closed at this time to Missionary Franson partly because of his neglect to consult with authorities in the congregation, two other reasons were more basic. One was that Missionary Franson made common cause with the so-called "Free" people who at that time criticized the Mission Covenant vehemently. Pastor Björk was, of course, the president of the Covenant and the church belonged to it. The other reason was that Franson's plan to send young men and women straight off as missionaries to a culture like China with only a few weeks of a Bible course as preparation was indefensible, the impropriety of which was emphasized seriously and convincingly by Pastor Björk.

Franson's recruiting and sending out missionaries in this urgent and unique way was the result of his firm conviction that the Lord would soon return. So strong was this belief that when he took pledges from individuals or congregations for missionary support he made these promises binding "for three years or until Christ comes." Because he could not conceive of the possibility that Christ could tarry for forty years or more as has now happened, congregations who promised to support a missionary "until Christ comes" assumed a far greater obligation than they realized. Before he was called to cross the border of time, the zealous missionary Franson had recognized the need for a firmer and better order for the support of missionaries and had begun to labor for that cause.

Chapter Seventeen

At the Crossroads

During childhood and adolescence
I never dreamed of achieving a prominent position in life. When I was asked as a boy what I intended to be when I grew up, it is said that I answered decisively, "A thresher or a woodchopper"— evidently the height of my ambition at that time.

One often hears stories of how children reveal through their play some natural talent that foretells their calling in life. However, it is never certain that they will become what the games seem to indicate. Many a man has become a preacher even though he did not play preacher as a child, and boys who climbed up on chairs and tables and preached to an imaginary public have been known never to pursue it. I cannot remember anything in my childhood that indicated I would someday become a minister of the Gospel. I was about twenty-two years old, perhaps a bit more, before I began to be drawn to this vocation.

For many years I did have a lively interest in Christian work, spending my evening hours and Sundays most often in church, but at the same time I dutifully took care of my work in the factory without any thought of giving it up. But the question of whether I should become a preacher was at long last awakened. The cause for this, as far as I can remember, was a conversation I had with the late E. J. Seth, who at that time was in Chicago studying for the ministry, in which he urged me to consider seriously whether it was God's will that I should preach the

Gospel. At about the same time I received a similar suggestion from editor O. Högfeldt, who had recently come to Chicago, and with whom I had become acquainted as a fellow Sunday-school teacher in the North Side church. Now that the question had been raised, I could not escape its seriousness and prayed for grace to understand God's will.

But he who is to engage in the gospel vocation should have natural gifts, an irreproachable Christian character, love for the Lord's glory, and zeal for the salvation of people. When I examined my own life against these requirements I felt that I was lacking in every respect. I valued the well-meant counsel of my good friends but did not dare to depend on this alone. Nor could I depend upon my own inclination; that I understood very well, for old Palmblad's exhortation to be wary of the feelings of the depraved human heart rang in my ears. I stood at the fork in the road and earnestly wanted to choose the right way. But which way was right and pleasing to God?

The question of what is God's will is often very difficult to answer, especially when details of our lives are concerned. How can one be sure that he is called of God to devote his life to the gospel ministry? Does God call by putting this directly into a person's head or does he call through the mediation of the Christian congregation or of individual Christians? Or does he call in both of these ways? If he calls directly, how can one then distinguish this input from the inner voice of one's own will?

I have heard many young men speak with great certainty about how they were guided by the Spirit and called by God to the ministry. But for me the required gifts, the necessary character, and the call of the congregation were all obviously missing. Some have the ability to speak in public, but their living is careless. We can hardly think that God calls men who have not allowed him to sanctify and nurture them to a Christian life through his grace. He whom God calls to serve in the Gospel he certainly equips with proper gifts. There is little doubt that such a person receives an inward prompting, but above all he receives the prompting of the believers and the encouragement of the Christian congregation.

Happy is the gospel preacher whose clear call from God is confirmed by the congregation's support. Even such a one can doubt his call in adversity and moments of temptation, but if he is really called by God, such moments are followed by triumphant certainty and joy in service. His work will also be marked with the seal of authentic progress.

Pastor Seth, who was the first to influence me to become a minister, also inveigled me to preach my first sermon. When he was in school Seth used to preach in the old Mission church in Lockport, Illinois, on Sundays, and one beautiful spring day in 1891 he asked me to accompany him. We met at the railroad station and fellowshiped on the way, discussing everything except the coming meeting in the church, which I assumed he would take care of from beginning to end. We arrived at the church just in time for the meeting to begin, and as he stood up to start the service, he whispered in my ear, "I will call on you to preach." I was dismayed. I wanted to pull his coattails and argue that his bold decision was entirely unreasonable, but he was already at the pulpit announcing the song, "Sabbath Day of Rest and Cheer, Day Divine to Me So Dear." If I had yielded to impulse I would have walked out and left my friend Seth in the lurch, but I did not wish to act discourteously or create a sensation.

There was no alternative but to gather my thoughts around a Bible passage while the service continued. Hebrews 11:24-26 had often spoken to me, and now these verses smiled at me and offered their service in this critical moment. Praying, I made them the text for my first sermon.

I have only a dim recollection of what I tried to present that day, but I do remember that when I had gone on for a while I spoke with burning zeal until I could find nothing more to say. The sermon took perhaps twenty-five minutes, which was short according to the standards of that day, but in spite of that, I fear it had more quantity than quality. However, the good friends in Lockport had the grace to judge my sermon sympathetically without desire to criticize. No doubt this was why I was invited to preach at a mission meeting there a couple months later.

Friend Seth thought he had done well to force me into the pulpit, but it was a daring deed and he should hardly have subjected his congregation to that risk. If it went well it was, of course, because of God's gracious help, but it could have been so disastrous that the worship service would have been destroyed by the beginner's chatter. There are very few who, without sermon preparation, can get along as well in the pulpit as one of Pastor C. H. Spurgeon's students did, according to the following story.

A young man was sent up into the pulpit to preach. As he arose he received a sealed envelope which contained the text he was to use. When he opened it he found these words: "Make a comparison between your own present situation and Zacchaeus's." Without losing his poise he gave the following speech: "My friends, I have been assigned the task of comparing my own present situation and Zacchaeus's. In the first place, we read that Zacchaeus was small of stature, and I confess honestly that I myself have never felt smaller than I do now. In the second place, we read that he came down at once, and I will, with pleasure, follow his example."

My visits and preaching in Lockport prompted me to begin thinking about entering the ministry. I considered discussing this with Pastor Björk because he knew me better than most people; I had been in his confirmation class, I had been a guest in his home many times, and I had participated in many ways in the work of his church. Finally I shared my perplexities with him. We had a good intimate discussion in which he emphasized the importance of having pure motives to enter this vocation. He wanted to know what position I took on the whole question, if I myself had initiated the idea, or if it had of itself crowded in upon me. He pointed out great demands that the Word of God and even people make of a gospel preacher. He questioned whether my voice would be strong enough so that I could make myself heard as a preacher. Besides this he pointed out that I was already involved in church work and suggested that I should continue in this until I was absolutely certain that I ought to take another step. Finally he added, "If this is of God, then it will not be frustrated."

After this valuable discussion with my pastor I felt calmer because I was certain that the Lord would lead me to full clarity on this important matter. I continued my work and used much of my time in the activity of the church, as I had done previously. During the following winter we were not very busy in the factory so I received permission to work only in the afternoons. In the mornings I attended classes and lectures at Moody Bible Institute without registering as a student. This was while Dr. R. A. Torry was president.

In the fall of 1892 I decided to begin studies for the ministry. It would have been convenient to apply for admission to the Swedish department of Chicago Theological Seminary where Professor Fridolf Risberg was the teacher, because the school was in Chicago and offered many advantages to students. But since the Mission Covenant had opened a school in Minneapolis the previous year (which later moved to Chicago), I felt duty-bound to go there even though it would cost a bit more and I would have to leave Chicago and my large circle of friends. I believe that in this decision I acted more wisely than I knew. Pastor Björk wrote my recommendation to the school, sending it directly to Professor Nyvall, who was the president. What hopes and fears Pastor Björk expressed about me I have never learned, but eventually I received a letter from the president containing a brief and hearty welcome to begin my studies in the Mission Covenant School in Minneapolis.

It soon became known in the congregation that I intended to leave for seminary. City missionary Palmblad found out also because he and the pastor of the church were like David and Jonathan. Even Pastor Björk had once upon a time looked upon seminaries as superfluous, but he had changed his mind, whereas Palmblad was still of the old opinion. To be sure, he could tolerate the "preacher factories" but he did not favor them or regard their product highly. Once when we met after he had learned of my plans, he looked at me seriously, almost with pity in his eyes, and characteristically asked, "But what is it I hear about you, my young brother? Surely you do not intend to take the factory route into the holy preaching office!" I do not recall if I had any answer to his question, but I do remember his look and how thoughtfully he stroked his full gray beard. He added, "You should have continued to read your Bible and songbook and simply work hard in the school of the Spirit."

Between Christmas and New Years 1892 I left the factory where I had labored for eight years and where I had had many instructive, if not always happy, experiences. I was promised that I could come back if I so desired, which was pleasant and comforting, for if I should fail in my studies or on my new path I could then return to the work that I now concluded.

At that time I was invited one afternoon to a social gathering with the Adolf Lydell family. Pastor Björk and other friends were also present. During our conversations he told the friends that I had heard the Lord's voice calling and had answered with Isaiah, "Here am I, send me." He pointed out how important this step was for him who takes it and how eternally meaningful it could become for many souls. Then he said with great earnestness and feeling, "Let us now pray to God for Victor, that he may be spared from bringing sorrow to the Church of God as so many gospel preachers have done because of the devil's seduction.''

In these words of the revered pastor there was great wisdom and spiritual insight. He did not request prayer that I would have great victories in my ministry, but that I would be spared from bringing sorrow to God's congregation. More than once he had seen the endless damage done to God's Church and the gospel ministry when pastors had fallen in sin or when preachers had indulged in carnal criticism in a proud spirit instead of declaring the crucified and risen Savior. It was therefore especially fitting to pray that I would not bring sorrow to the Church of God.

How often during the past years have I remembered the pastor's words, and on each such occasion this prayer has arisen in my heart, ''Protect me, God, so that I many not become a subject of sorrow for the congregation.''

The enemy of the soul always aims his fiery arrows at preachers, seeking to fell them first and foremost because he knows that if a preacher falls it is more beneficial for his cause than if an ordinary Christian falls. And the devil has thousands of strategies for attack. He seduces us to coarse sins. He entices us with the world and seeks to lead us away from what is spiritual. He fascinates us with lofty spirituality and a high-strung fanaticism. One person he seeks to capture in the snares of pride, another in the bonds of depression. For this reason the singer says impressively:

Fear that Satan lays the snare,
When you least expect it there.

Chapter Eighteen

A Winter in Minneapolis

Ideally, those who devote themselves to studies should begin when they are young and continue without interruption until they have reached their goal. But not everyone who is hungry for knowledge has the privilege of doing this, for economic and other circumstances sometimes hinder. My education was interrupted when I left for America at eleven years of age. Then the factory became the practical school I attended for more than twelve years without becoming a supervisor or graduating to any position higher than common laborer. But now I left the workshop and tools to devote myself to school and books.

The Mission Covenant School in Minneapolis was founded by Pastor E. August Skogsbergh for newly arrived Swedes who wanted to learn English and get a basic cultural education in order to make their way in America. In 1891, when it was transferred to the Covenant, it also opened a three-year seminary for the training of ministers, and Professor David Nyvall, who had already been Pastor Skogsbergh's colleague at the school, became its rector.

The seminary was now in its second year, and though it was still very limited, it filled a need among the Mission Friends in America. In that day few of our members laid claim to profound learning, and a preacher did not need to be very much beyond the common people in this respect. All the seminarians had been born and reared in Sweden except for two who were Norwegians. Generally, the students were quite mature in years, and a few had been preaching for a time before they came to school. On the whole they were rather coarse raw material upon which the school needed to make a deep and lasting impression.

In the second-year class of the school the following students were enrolled: Alfred Ahnfeldt and O. G. Olson, both of whom have now died, M. Thornberg, O. W. Bengtson, and K. E. Peterson. We freshmen looked upon these brothers as already powerful oaks in the area of knowledge and respected them almost as our fathers in Christ.

The freshman class of 1892-1893 was larger, numbering about thirty, though some of the members did not continue their studies beyond this one year. A few continued and served as ministers for several years but were then called from the work and struggles to their eternal rest. These included the clever little Charles Ecker, the serious and almost ascetic August Erickson, the amicable Andrew Sjöberg, the genial Jonas Johnson, and the suffering K. E. Peterson, who played the guitar, sang, preached, and won many souls for the Lord before his frail body was finally buried in California's earth.

Some of the other students in this big class who are still in the ministry are Andrew Anderson, M. E. Anderson, John Nelson, Isaac Skoog (whose name was Johnson then), Oscar Dahlberg, A. L. Nystrom, J. P. Lindberg, P. O. Lindman, G. A. Lundquist, Gustav Lindstrom, and O. B. Strandine.

Professor D. Nyvall was a teacher in the seminary and at the same time president of the whole school. He was a fiery young man with a great capacity for work, and he bore the responsibility of teaching and the anxiety of administering the new school without showing signs of weariness. He was in every respect a man of enthusiasm and inspiration and he made a deep impression on his students. To instruct these boys who had recently come from forest and plow and all kinds of other work was no doubt a challenging and trying task. Occasionally his patience seemed to give out, and at such times he did not need his straggling full beard to command the respect of his slow-witted students.

Professor Axel Mellander also taught in the seminary. In his entire disposition he was different from Professor Nyvall, in certain ways his opposite. Where Nyvall rushed ahead, Mellander drove slowly. Nyvall sought to inculcate and develop the great points in a lesson; Mellander was careful with details, numbers and years. Nyvall's purpose was essentially to awaken thought and sharpen insight; Mellander saw his task as storing facts in the memory chambers of his students. Together these teachers were an excellent pair, each fortunately complementing the other. In truth they accomplished much in polishing the raw material the congregations had sent to the school. From these boys finally came more or less gifted preachers, all different, none molded in the same form, zealous leaders in the church of Christ and able men in the state.

In the general school, or business school as it was then called, a large assembly of youth was registered. Professor J. A. Lindblade was the teacher, assisted by Miss Lena Sahlstrom and others as they were needed. The seminary students were free to profit from instruction in this department if, at the same time, they could take care of their classes in the seminary where they really belonged. In that era, however, it did not seem necessary to devote more time to the English language because no one expected that preaching in English would ever be required.

The school's quarters were in the Mission Tabernacle, widely known in the city as "Skogsbergh's Church." When classes were in session, young people abounded in the roomy lower level and every nook was used, making it a beehive of life and movement. Besides the school, the newspaper *Veckobladet,* which was Pastor Skogsbergh's creation, had its office on the lower floor, as well as a small bookstore. The late Pastor K. A. Johnson was chief of both of these.

Sessions were held from morning until evening. On tingly cold winter days neither teachers nor students could keep warm, for the sheet metal stoves, fired by ice-coated wood from the sawmills, were unable to keep the penetrating cold from entering. Both the professors and the students sat in the classrooms during these days wearing overcoats, furs, and, of course, rubbers. Oh, how the north wind blew against the icy window panes in the hall along Eighth Avenue! Of course at some moments blood could rush to one's head as when, for example, in Professor Mellander's class we were asked to account for the dates in the history of Judah and Israel and their contemporary world powers, or perhaps tell what Skorstedt had to say about biblical archeology, which was hard to read. But if the head was warm the feet were that much colder.

It was just as cold in Professor Nyvall's classes when King Boreas made his great incursion through Minneapolis, although Nyvall's teaching was more fiery. The respected man, with unruly hair, thin beard, and nose red from the cold, taught in a fur coat with his cap in one coat pocket and his mittens in the other, and we students sat there stiff and blue so that not even our thoughts wanted to move. Under such conditions how can one give an account of everything D. A. Sunden has to say about Swedish grammar? Of course the professor had it all at his five frozen fingertips and thought that we should have been able to get it into our brains. How we clambered and tripped over the language roots! How we fumbled and stumbled through the exercises with sentences and verbs! At times the answers were so stupid that even Job would have lost his patience; no wonder then if Professor Nyvall lost his! And sometimes they were so foolish that the whole class exploded with laughter and the teacher could not resist joining.

With lessons, repeated lessons, and reviewed lessons came at least average results. Some of the students shone a little brighter than the rest, both in classes and in examinations, but hardly anyone could have been looked upon as brilliant. Yet little by little we received a good foundation of knowledge upon which we could build more.

The students were housed with different families of laborers, who, by opening their homes in this way, had an extra income which they badly needed; during the winter there was very little work in the mill city by the Mississippi. Food and lodging were reasonably priced. The food on the table was simple, as it should be for young people who are preparing for their life vocation. High living and plenty of money have hurt many young men and women, many schoolboys and schoolgirls.

Four of us boys roomed together on Washington Avenue, South near Twelfth Street, with a family named Wideman. The husband was the pastor of a little Swedish Presbyterian Church on Camden Place, if I remember correctly. One of my comrades was Oscar F. Dahlberg and another was Lysen, who studied in the general department of the school. Who the fourth student was I have forgotten. Our room, on the second floor over an empty store, was large and furnished simply. Our heating apparatus was a little sheet-metal stove that was fed with sour wood from the saw mills and had warmth accordingly. The windows were drafty and the floor was ice cold. We could freeze up there when the thermometer registered thirty below zero and the northwest wind blew hard! At times we studied and wrote compositions in our galoshes and overcoats and wanted to put on a cap and mittens as well.

One cold winter night my bedmate, Lysen, and I experienced a chilling episode. He and I were both tall and we weighed a good deal together. The bed was old and frail but nevertheless had been able to give us a defensible resting place for some time. On this night, while my comrade and I were sleeping sweetly under the blanket, the bed gave way under our weight. I do not know how it happened, but I awakened to find myself in an unexplainable position with my head on the floor and feet pointing toward heaven. Lysen lay in exactly the same position but was sleeping as if nothing unusual had happened. Cautiously, I tried to wake him with a nudge, fearing that the bed would fall to pieces if we moved.

Finally we got up, lit the kerosene lamp, found some rope stumps with which we had bound our trunks, and tied the bed together with quick movements. Meanwhile Dahlberg and his bedmate, still under warm blankets, scoffed at us because we were so big and heavy that the bed was unable to support us. After this unexpected little adventure we had a few hours of good rest in the repaired bed. The memory of this episode, like some other school memories, has elicited many sunny smiles when life's stern experience has tried to lower the corners of the mouth and plow deeper furrows on forehead and cheek.

The seminary students were sent out as often as possible to preach in different parts of the city and in the surrounding areas, to which they traveled on Saturday. A few of them who had permanent preaching assignments received better training for their coming vocation than some others, like me, who lacked such opportunities to practice. But now and then I would accompany some fellow student to his preaching station and participate shyly with a testimony and prayer.

On one occasion I did get an invitation to preach on Sunday evening in a hall someplace in the city, I do not know just where. Apparently I impressed the impulsive leader because he appeared exhilarated during my message. He asked me also to return the following Sunday, and when we parted he gave me fifty cents for "car fare." The next Sunday evening I preached again, but my message did not fall into the same good soil in the leader as it had the previous week. After the meeting he told me frankly that I need never come again and that I had to pay the "car fare" myself. I obeyed him and have stayed away to this day.

Why my preaching in that place ended so ingloriously I have

never figured out. Perhaps I said something that was not in harmony with the theological position of the leader, or perhaps my sermon was poor. Both reasons are possible. Preaching is, however, more than standing up to speak for a few moments at a religious meeting in the fashion of giving a testimony. People have a right to ask for something more, and God requires something more. Most importantly, he who preaches should first and foremost have a message to bring to the congregation, and he must bring it as one sent from God. To be able to preach is more than an art and more than a gift. It is grace.

And yet, in addition to the theoretical studies in the seminary the students must also have practical experience in the art of preaching. For this reason preaching exercises are set up, in which one after the other the students preach in the presence of their classmates and teachers. The young preacher has a certain terror of these hours because he knows that the audience listens not only attentively but critically in order to find faults in exegesis, language, presentation, and personality in the pulpit. The listeners are to scrutinize everything and then criticize and give suggestions to the one who has preached. The purpose of all this is good, and much improvement has been accomplished by it, but certainly no young brother has ever been inspired or revealed his real preaching talents on such occasions.

Even during my first term in school I took my turn to preach as an exercise. I chose my text and tried to study it thoughtfully and prayerfully: "Clothe yourselves, all of you, with humility toward one another, for 'God opposes the proud, but gives grace to the humble' " (1 Peter 5:5). I had hardly begun to speak before my schoolmates' pens started to move, and as I continued they seemed to increase in speed so that the paper itself could have caught fire. The teachers also made notes, contributing to my absentmindedness and bewilderment and making my task of preaching about the virtue of humility more difficult. On that occasion the sermon was not long, not rich in content, and not powerful.

As I concluded I anticipated a heavy sea of criticism, but I determined to submit myself humbly in keeping with my sermon. Schoolmates pointed out certain language faults, made fun of some awkward gestures and strange grimaces they had observed, and said that I had spoken too softly and too fast. The teachers agreed in part, but on the other hand, they criticized some of the criticisms. They did point out, however, that I had misunderstood the text, which was aggravating, and that I had not arranged the content of the sermon very well. In spite of all this the criticism was more tolerable than I had expected.

One of the students who in time became a popular preacher looked and dressed in the exercises as if he had just come off the farm. He had written his sermon out and now read it. The criticism hailed over him, but for the content he received a warmer commendation from the teachers than did any other student.

Contrasts were apparent in this class. One of the brethren seemed to preach with all the ministerial airs he could muster, but his sermon was extemporaneous and he spoke to us as if we were all backsliders whom, now in fifteen minutes, he was to pluck like brands out of the fire. But the comments that followed revealed that neither teachers nor students were deeply moved by the fiery brother's revival sermon. The inability to choose a text and tailor a sermon to the character of the audience is a great fault in a preacher, even in a student preacher, though it is easier to overlook in a student.

Criticism in preaching exercises is necessary and in most cases fruitful, for it makes students aware of bad habits and faults that they otherwise might not discover and eliminate. It would be useful if older ministers, too, when the need arises, would criticize each other in a frank and brotherly way, because we also have disturbing habits that stubbornly appear in our preaching and do great mischief without our noticing them. This is illustrated by the following event from my own experience.

During my early days of preaching I spoke rapidly and strained my voice, which resulted in wearying my listeners and wearing me out. In addition, I had the bad habit of never standing still. Like a bear in a cage I paced back and forth from one side of the pulpit to the other, unaware of how disturbing this was to the people. Then at a mission meeting in Marinette, Wisconsin, I met editor Otto Högfeldt, who heard and saw my bad habits. A few weeks later I found in my Bible a piece of paper torn from a notebook on which I read the following words of exhortation: "Mr. Bowman, stand still while you preach, speak slowly, and do not strain your voice, and God will bless you. In brotherliness, O. H." I valued this note highly. In a similar way, preachers could no doubt continually help each other if they used their opportunities and acted tactfully.

Eighteeen ninety-two through 1893 was a good and progressive year for the Mission Covenant school. A large number of young people all wanting to increase their knowledge came in from the country during the late winter when the work was not so urgent, bringing the enrollment to about 300. The finances were in such good shape that the treasurer, the late Charles Wallblom of St. Paul, Minnesota, later used to refer to this as the golden year, for not only could he pay the expenses of the school, but he had a surplus of money to loan to needy students.

Despite the primitive character of the young school and the many discomforts students had to endure, the pupils were generally well satisfied. All were thirsting for knowledge. No one was there only to waste time or exhaust his parents' money. The boys did not try to challenge the teachers or test their orthodoxy or educational methods. We were too old and too old-fashioned to be tempted by the newfangled notions that the later zeal for orthodoxy has spawned.

In those days the teachers enjoyed undivided loyalty both inside and outside the school, which eased their burden of labor. They had not as yet been made objects of suspicion by poison articles in a certain paper.* During the winter, Pastor C. A. Björk and editor O. Högfeldt visited classes and heard the different lectures. They expressed in personal conversation with me their great satisfaction with the instruction, and I felt fortunate to have the opportunity to sit at the feet of these teachers. Yes, I valued this privilege and still do. On the whole these were happy days, and our unity and mutual trust were revealed in our eyes and handclasps as well as in our conversation and writing.

The students' church home was the Mission Tabernacle. We attended other churches seldom and American churches never. When we wanted to share in a high church worship service we visited Rev. Tofften's temple where the ritual was more elaborate than in most other Lutheran churches. And if, rarely, we wanted a completely contrasting experience we went to the Free church where preacher August Davis then presided, swinging the lash at his fellow clergymen and fellow Christians, including Pastor E. August Skogsbergh who, he ironically said, was "trying to save souls in a stove-

* *Missions-Vännen,* the unofficial "opposition" newspaper of the Covenant from 1894 to 1946

pipe hat.'' When he noticed some of the seminary students at his meeting he gave these a lash also, calling them ''seekers after a learning which is spiritually poor.'' To such shouting some of his admirers added their ''Amen'' and ''Praise the Lord.''

I did visit the old Mission house on Bradley Street in St. Paul a few times when Pastor S. W. Sundberg was the shepherd and teacher. I liked his sensitive and inspiring preaching which I felt gave full value for the trip to St. Paul, at that time a rather long excursion because there were no electric streetcars, buses, or automobiles. Pastor Sundberg was always friendly and took a personal interest in me, which was encouraging for a poor and solitary student.

Pastor E. August Skogsbergh, the minister in the Minneapolis Mission Tabernacle, was still at the height of his powers, and the church was the chief gathering place for the Mission Friends of the city as well as for many others. On the north and northeast sides of the city there were already independent Mission churches but they were comparatively small and weak. The stream of people flowed to the Mission Tabernacle, which on Sunday evenings was usually filled with interested listeners. At times it was impossible to find a seat.

Pastor Skogsbergh preached and sang with power and inspiration. Now and then he came late to the meetings, but the choir director, A. L. Skoog, who was always punctual, would announce a song or perhaps two or three if the pastor tarried. Finally the bony little man would enter and briskly climb the stair to the pulpit, or more correctly the little table, while he ran his fingers through his bushy hair and glanced quickly over the assembled crowd. He gave the impression of a general taking the reins. One felt that now something would happen.

And usually something stirring and inspiring did happen. At times it was the sermon itself that was decisive. At times it was the song that became overwhelming. Now and then it was the leadership of the whole meeting that left a certain deposit in our minds that we could not escape and that drew us involuntarily back to the Tabernacle.

Songleader A. L. Skoog was an important fellow worker, perhaps more so than most realized. He masterfully led his large and well-trained choir and unified the congregational singing, which always had motion and speed but was always dignified and impressive. It was never ''Hurrah let's go,'' nor were there any disturbing exercises during the singing. They sang with feeling, not just with speed and volume.

Almost every Sunday evening during the winter, so-called "aftermeetings" were held, to which the anxious and the believers who wanted to help were invited. Occasionally they were held in the auditorium, but the results seemed to be better when they were on the lower floor. Usually the seminary students were present, helping in the meetings while at the same time being helped and inspired to spiritual work and personal conversation with souls.

During this winter the renowned revival preacher Fay B. Mills came to Minneapolis to hold meetings for a few weeks in the large exposition building now used by the M. W. Savage Co., an auditorium that allegedly seated about 7,000. Large crowds streamed there evening after evening to hear the talented speaker, and it was said that no fewer than 1,800 people were converted during this series of meetings. However, the All-Seeing might not have discovered any such number about which there would be joy in heaven. To count conversions is a hazardous undertaking that thoughtful people should not engage in but should leave to the Lord who sees all and knows all. Even so, there were no doubt many who came to faith in our Lord in these meetings.

Later Mills devoted himself to the study of Eastern religious philosophy and was so captivated that he gave up his simple faith in Christ and his task as a revival preacher. With this his influence over the masses seemed to vanish completely. One Sunday morning when I was a minister in Minneapolis I had another opportunity to hear him. This was after he had come to the opinion that our calling is to save the whole world ship and not just the shipwrecked, as he expressed it. He had the same personality and the same eloquence as before, but he had only about fifty listeners. A few years later I heard him again in Boston, where he spoke to only a handful. It is said that Mills finally returned to the faith of his fathers in Christ and to the devotion of his prime, but by then he was already full of years and his ministry had ended. Through experience he had learned that the human spirit cannot live on the straw of philosophy. It needs the manna from heaven, the word of life that has come to give hungry humankind life and health.

Chapter Nineteen

The Young Pastor

The end of April 1893. The last of the winter snow was melting from the shady places and the glorious spring sunrays were beginning to warm the meadows and groves of Minnesota.

At the Mission Covenant School in Minneapolis examinations were over and students could read the evaluation marks on composition and examination papers, the results of the winter's work at the feet of the teachers. He who had received good grades in acknowledgement of his labor was glad, and he who had received no such joy still tried to keep his courage up and was at least happy that schoolwork for the term had ended. In any event, all the students had to be satisfied with the final judgment of their teachers and admit at least to themselves that they had received what they deserved. For them, as for Paul, it was wise to forget what was behind and strain forward to what lay ahead.

The school year closed without festivities. No fine speeches, no feasting, no flowers, no congratulations from friends. And no class graduated because the school was only two years old. The work of the year simply ended, and the students immediately went home or to their respective fields to resume waiting tasks and responsibilities.

All the seminary students had been placed for the summer, partly as interim pastors and partly as schoolteachers in the congregations which in those days held Swedish school during the summer. The calls had come directly to the school, and the president had had the difficult task of assigning people according to the needs of the field and the particular talents and maturity of the student.

In those days when churches called pastors or interim pastors from the school, no one asked whether the candidate could preach in both Swedish and English as is now required, for that need did not exist then. Nor did anyone, either teacher or student, think we would live to see the day when a knowledge of English would be necessary, even if he had the insight to see that it would be desirable. World War I completely changed this situation.

But there were other demands that we seldom even mention now. It was very common, for example, for congregations to seek preachers who could sing and, if possible, play the organ or at least the guitar. There were natural reasons for this. Since most of the Mission churches of that day consisted of young people, the children of the families were usually too young to play an instrument in the church. Also, in many places the work was in its infancy and still lacked an organized congregation.

The students at the school who had musical knowledge and talents were, therefore, especially in demand; their shares were always a little higher on the market than others. When such a brother came to a church, he could gather the talents already in the congregation and organize a little string orchestra to share in the church meetings. This attracted people to the house of the Lord and helped to bring the saving truth home to the listeners. Since musical standards at that time were not very high, people immensely enjoyed the simplest songs and music.

The little Mission church in Escanaba, Michigan, had asked for a student for the summer and had specifically requested that I be sent. For me Escanaba was an unknown place in an unfamiliar part of the country, and I knew no one in the congregation. I was called, presumably, because of a few good words of recommendation by my friend Pastor E. J. Seth, who had preached in Escanaba for a short time and now had the call to Superior, Wisconsin. With joy I accepted the invitation.

Three of my schoolmates also received calls to the northwestern Michigan district, namely August Erickson, who was to be an itinerant minister, John Nelson, who was to be schoolteacher and interim pastor in Iron Mountain, and O. B. Strandine, who was to teach school and preach in Trout Creek, a sawmill place along the Duluth-South Shore railroad, where there was a rather lively congregation.

So we four candidates were to take our first stumbling steps in the career of the ministry. We were about the same age and all well-meaning beginners with whom the Christian people must practice tolerance and patience, in both the home and the church.

August Erickson, John Nelson, and I left Minneapolis on the Soo Line night train heading east. We lurched in the dusty railroad car while the train and the hours crept slowly forward. My comrades were, however, more favored by John Blund the sandman than I was and were able to sleep away part of the time, while I was uncomfortable and a bit jealous, watching hour after hour all night. Erickson and Nelson stepped off the train a couple of stations before I did, but at six o'clock in the morning Escanaba was called and I too got off.

This was a deserted place in the forest with hardly any life evident, but a few birds chirped beautifully their morning psalms to the creator's glory. It was Sunday morning, April 20, 1893.

At the lonely station I soon noticed a solitary figure who turned out to be an old bachelor, a light-complexioned Värmländer named Ingmarson, who had come to meet me and take me to Escanaba five miles away.

In a creaky carriage drawn by bony horses we made our way over the loose sand roads while we talked and became acquainted, the Värmländer and I. We came happily and well to 206 Fanny Street, Escanaba, to the home of J. P. Anderson, usually called Seaman Anderson, where Ingmarson left me after introducing me to the father and mother of the house, to Mrs. Anderson's father, and to the two children. In this home I would live for the summer, though I would have my meals with friends, the Adolf Petersons. I was assured that Mrs. Peterson would not let me go hungry.

When I had washed off the soot and dust from the long railroad journey, put on my Sunday clothes, eaten a tasty breakfast, and thanked God together with my hosts, I no longer felt discomfited and forgot entirely that I was a stranger among strangers in a strange city.

I had expected to preach my inaugural sermon in the morning service or at least make an attempt in that direction, but Pastor M. J. Eggan, who had been minister there previously, was visiting Escanaba, and it was natural that he should preach. I did participate in the evening service, however, with a brief message on the text, "We preach the crucified Christ."

I intended with this text to strike the chord I wanted to hold during my ministry in Escanaba. How I preached I do not remember, but when Pastor Eggan continued he emphasized that we must certainly preach Christ crucified, but should not imagine that we are the only ones doing so. Perhaps I had given him reason to append this criticism, if it was intended as such, but I have never spoken to him about it or tried to find out what he had in mind on that occasion.

The Mission Covenant Church in Escanaba had been in existence only a few years and was by no means large. If I remember correctly, it had thirty-eight members. They had a little church building on South Fanny Street that accommodated about 100 people, and upon which there was a debt of several hundred dollars.

The population of Escanaba was then about 4,000, of whom a considerable number were Swedes or Swedish-speaking Finns. During the summer, ore-shipping provided work for many. In winter many took refuge in the forests to work in the lumber industry. The city had some forty taverns that seemed to have a lively business, especially in the spring when young men came from the forests with their winter's earnings in their pockets. But there were many people who were sober and honorable, and among the Swedes many who were believers. Church work was carried on among our Swedish people by a Lutheran church, a Methodist church, and the Mission church I was now to pastor, which was the newest.

The pastor of a small church must sometimes be responsible for tasks from which the pastor of a larger church is exempt, because a larger church usually has more talent that can be used for people's own benefit and the welfare of the church. Sometimes small congregations also have more difficulties than more advanced and developed ones because the members are too close and differing temperaments cause irritation.

The congregation in Escanaba consisted of people from Värmland, Norrland, and Dalarna, plus a scattering from other Swedish provinces. They were by nature very different, even in their rearing and ways of thinking, so while they were individually all excellent people, this did not keep their relationships with each other from being a bit rough. There were friendships within small groups but not very much beyond this, and certain natures were like fire and water. Over the years, efforts had been made to bring them together for atonement and healing but without permanent success;

old wounds were reopened for the smallest reason.

I had not been in Escanaba many days before people tried to initiate me in the problems of the congregation and point out the position I ought to take. Thus I learned that Old Man Crosspatch had always caused trouble in the church and that I should be careful not to become intimate with him. I was also told that Old Woman Gossip had caused annoyances for the church and the pastor and I should stay clear of her influence. Then there were Adamina Lightfoot, Eva Grater, and Guy Powderhorn who needed to improve considerably in order to stand the test as good church members.

All this was interesting but hardly encouraging for the young and inexperienced pastor. I listened to the statements of the worthy friends but told no one what I thought or what stand I would take. Inasmuch as I did not know the situation sufficiently in spite of this information, I decided to bide my time, keep silent, treat everyone impartially, and preach the Word to the best of my ability. This decision did not result from any special wisdom or virtue on my part; it was simply the natural way for me to act. I hardly need to add that the situation was the subject of my prayers.

People came to hear the Word of God which I preached in fear and trembling, in weakness rather than in strength. The excellent attendance and growing interest encouraged me and the work progressed calmly and quietly, which, under the circumstances, was a miracle in which I was allowed to share.

My call to Escanaba was limited to four months, but when half of this time had elapsed, the congregation tried to persuade me to stay on as their pastor and not be concerned about continuing my studies at the school. The pious and well-meaning friends told me that my sermons were good and that I didn't need to improve them by further study, but this evaluation was far higher than I had expected, and sound reason told me that they had no doubt overrated my abilities.

The congregation decided to write to the president of the school to lay their wishes before him and ask his consent for my staying away from school. His answer was immediate. He pointed out that it was now my calling to be a student and not a pastor in a church, that it was not proper to try to dissuade me from my real task, and that if I consented, my leaving school would inevitably lead to a great loss for me in the future. The fact that the friendly brethren in Escanaba thought I was already a sufficiently good preacher he

177

saw as further reason why I should return to my studies.

The answer did not please the friends, but for me it was conclusive. Still, they overwhelmed me with pleas to stay, and the situation in the church was such that after much deliberation I promised to remain until Christmas. Later this was changed so that I stayed until the following fall, but I was firmly committed to complete my education even if it had been postponed a year.

At the same time I came to Escanaba, the economic depression during Grover Cleveland's administration struck the whole country. The iron industry was hit early and hard; the mines in northwestern Michigan were shut down and the shipping of ore through Escanaba ceased. All other business and industry in the city was also affected.

The unmarried men, who were laid off first, went to other places to seek work. An effort was made to give married men some form of work, at least a couple days a week, but that did not help a great deal. It was a difficult time for many.

Naturally the congregation was also affected by these wolf times. Because some people moved away, membership and, to some extent, church attendance declined. I had been promised a salary of forty dollars a month, which I received at the beginning, but when unemployment became widespread and I saw that it was impossible for the congregation to fulfill this promise, I offered my services for thirty dollars a month, and later for twenty-five. I felt it was my Christian duty to surrender a part of my salary when so many in the church were without work. For me it was a joy to be able to make this sacrifice, and the members of the congregation showed their appreciation in their warm support of the work. God blessed us together in a notable way. The heavy black clouds of the depression hung overhead for a long time, but finally they began to break up and our people again had the opportunity to work for their daily bread.

During my ministry in Escanaba I had many new and interesting experiences. Situations arose for which I was completely unprepared, because, as the saying goes, I had left the master too soon. The freshmen had received no instruction about the pastor's tasks in the congregation or about his official ministerial acts because they were expected back in school in a few months. In many situations I had to rely upon my own reason and resources.

I had not been in Escanaba more than a month before I was

asked to conduct a funeral at Hardwood, a little station settlement in the forest about forty miles away. The family of J. P. Anderson had lost a child in death, and since there was no funeral director or minister there the father had come to the city to buy a little coffin and find a preacher. He asked me to accompany him and help them with the funeral. I had neither service book nor proper ministerial garb, but of course I could not use this as an excuse when it was a matter of helping a grieving family.

In the house of sorrow the father himself dressed the little corpse and arranged it in the coffin while the sobbing mother looked on. A few friends had gathered for the service. I read some Scripture and tried to speak words of comfort to the sorrowing parents. After prayer and a unison song, two men carried the little coffin down the hill to the railroad where two or three handcars stood waiting for the funeral procession. The child was placed on the first one and we all climbed up and stood together on the cars, which were powered by hand. Thus we journeyed a mile or so to the graveyard.

Out there in the woods, in God's great church, the little box was lowered into the ground while the birds sang, accompanied by the sighing of the pines and the glory of the summer sun. Here I read a few appropriate verses from the New Testament, spoke a bit about children and the children's Friend, read the Lord's Prayer, and, after a verse of song in unison, gave the benediction. In spite of its simplicity, this first funeral service in the forests of northern Michigan left an indelible impression on me, and I believe on others as well.

Looking on from a distance in the cemetery were three young men, Swedish-speaking Finns. After the service they came forward and asked me to bury one of their companions from work who had died a few weeks before. As there had been no clergyman in the area when the young man had died, he had been lowered into the grave, but with four boards they had left a shaft through which it would be possible for a pastor to pour three shovelfuls of earth onto the coffin. Since I was the first minister to visit the area since then I was asked to conduct the official interment service.

Now I was ushered into a completely new and strange situation. I had never heard that one who had been dead and buried for weeks should be interred, nor did I know whether such an act was proper, but this was no time for a conference on it. I sensed what feelings the young men had about their friend's burial without a pastor and it seemed to me that it was my duty to respect these feelings even though the meaning of interment was far from clear. I obeyed my sense of what was reasonable, even though I had no service book, since this generally leads to the proper way. Thus with dignity I read the old psalm, "I go toward death where'er I go," and the song, "Time flies away as fast as a dream." Then I spoke for a few moments on the words of the psalmist, "Thou turnest man back to the dust" (Psalm 90:3), read the Lord's Prayer, and threw three shovelfuls of earth onto the coffin through the opening, saying, "Dust thou art, and to dust thou shalt return; Jesus Christ shall raise you on that last day." Then I concluded with a prayer and benediction.

The friends of the deceased were satisfied and perhaps not even aware that the order of service was dictated by the inspiration of the moment. I hope that on this occasion they experienced something of the importance of life and the meaning of living the inner life with Christ in God.

A pastor must always be prepared to perform the services of his office and never be embarrassed if unexpected and unique situations arise. He should act so that he gives the people a good and serious impression. A careless ministerial act is highly culpable and should never occur either at home or in church.

I have never had an urge to become a songleader, I am not qualified to be one, and I have never received a call from a congregation for such a task, but in Escanaba I had to provide leadership. There were a few fairly good singing voices which could easily become a choir if they could only be organized, and inasmuch as no one wanted to take this responsibility I had to do it. Fortunately we had a dependable organist, Miss Lottie Peterson, who furnished the real leadership, though she did not want either the responsibility or the honor of it. We practiced simple songs that we could sing and everyone could understand. Our people, at least, thought we had a fairly good choir.

At that time guitars and other stringed instruments were in good standing in our churches, and we were fortunate to have a little string orchestra, also. Accompanied by the organist, they played and sang simple evangelical songs to the glory of the Lord and our mutual edification.

The Swedes had settled at various sawmills and station communities around Escanaba, but at most of these places there was no spiritual work among them. This became an invitation for me to carry the Gospel message to them. Thus to my parish in Escanaba I added Hardwood, Foster City, Metropolitan, Gladstone, White Fish, and Ford River, visiting them regularly once or twice a month. At the beginning there was some prejudice or even opposition now and then, but as a rule I was well received and became acquainted with thankful compatriots. In most cases the meetings were well attended.

Now after many years when I recall my experiences in this mission work—for it can certainly be called that—I am thankful to God for the opportunities I had and the blessings I received there, which became very important for me personally and for my later vocation in life.

In some of these communities the only place we found to gather in was a crowded home, willingly opened for meetings, but in other locations we were allowed to gather in the schoolhouse. As a rule there were no songbooks; I had to secure them myself and then teach the people to share in the singing, which was the most difficult task. In one little school there was an organ that the rats had chewed to pieces. The next time I came I brought tools and repaired the instrument, which made my shares of stock even higher in the community.

My knowledge of music was very limited, which handicapped me greatly when I held meetings at these mission sites. While very young I had learned to play one song on the organ—number 90 in *Sions Basun,* * "Thou Tender, Gracious Father" by Lina Sandell, a song that always gripped me. I had asked my friend Andrew Sandberg, who could play the organ fairly well, to teach me how to play it and I paid him twenty-five cents in hard cash for the music lesson.

To this day I think it was money well invested, for this song became a saving angel at my meetings. Since it had eight stanzas, I divided it so that it sufficed for the whole service, particularly if I could persuade the people to sing the same stanza several times. Says the proverb, "Better to be without bread than to be indecisive."

I could easily play the melody of hymns, but now I needed to

---

* *the first official Covenant hymnal, published in 1908*

learn to play in four parts. By laboring at the organ in Seaman Anderson's house and at the piano in Adolf Peterson's, I learned to play a new song for each visit to the missions. I could, of course, use the same song at different places until my musical talents were better developed.

The city of Gladstone, on the lakeshore eight miles north of Escanaba, has recently begun to grow and more Swedish people have moved there. At that time, however, it had no Swedish church, though Pastor Eggan had preached there now and then while he was minister in Escanaba. The first time I visited Gladstone was with Pastor August Erickson, the itinerant missionary in the district. A cold rain was falling and clouds hung heavy in the heavens when we stepped off the boat and walked up to the town to look for a Swedish family whose address we had received. But unobliging people had spread the rumor that we were not orthodox preachers, so the wife in the house, who was very zealous about pure doctrine, refused to take us in or assist us in any way.

We informed her that we intended to hold a Swedish worship service that evening in the American Congregational Church and gave her a friendly invitation to come and bring her household. Then we visited the stores and the coal docks where many Swedes worked, announcing our meeting and inviting people to church. We continued in the rain with our suitcases to "Slab Town," a kind of suburb where people lived in poor huts, where we looked for and found a family named Peterson who received us cordially in their low dwelling. At the sheet-metal stove we dried our clothes and shoes and the mother in the house warmed milk for us to drink. Mr. and Mrs. Peterson did not profess to be Christians but they took care of us in a friendly and humane way. Certainly the living God counted that in their favor.

After we were refreshed by the good fire in the stove, Erickson and I went to the meeting. The church was full, mostly with young Swedish men, so we announced another meeting for the following week when Erickson would be alone. Then too the church was filled to the last place.

After that, I preached in Gladstone twice a month, and when the P. J. Lindblad family, who were warmly interested in the Lord's work, moved there, they willingly gave me a place to stay though their house and rooms were small. In time, other believers moved to Gladstone and a few people were won for the Lord, which was encouraging for the few pillars in the little fellowship. Later still, they organized a little Mission church which had nine members, if I remember correctly.

At Christmas 1895, after I had returned to school, I visited Gladstone and conducted *Julotta,* the first such celebration ever held there. The American Congregational Church was crowded with Swedes who had not been in America very long, for whom this service was a beautiful reminder of their home province while at the same time pointing to the Jesus Child of Bethlehem.

Lacking an organist, I had to play, lead the singing, and preach the great and glorious message of Christmas. I remember how difficult it was to play the magnificent hymn, "All Hail to Thee O Blessed Morn," but the people's singing drowned out my wrong notes and my embarrassment as well. In spite of all, it was a glorious Christmas service.

Ford River was a sawmill community about six miles south of Escanaba which I learned about through my Escanaba hostess, who had a sister there. There was no regular spiritual work of any kind in Ford River, but the sawmill company had built a little church that could be used by visiting clergy of different denominations. One beautiful summer day I walked there to reconnoiter and, if possible, arrange for a meeting among the Swedes. I reserved the church for a designated evening and got an American to fill the kerosene lamps, light them, and open the building. Then I wrote notices about the meeting and posted them at the sawmill, in the store, and elsewhere. When I had completed these arrangements I walked back to Escanaba.

When I returned on the appointed day I brought a few singers and guitarists to assist in the meeting. The church was more than filled with Swedes, most of them young mill workers. I preached on the text, "Like cold water to a thirsty soul, so is good news from a far country" (Proverbs 25:25), and when I was finished, a sawmill worker arose, decisively picked up his big hat, and gathered an offering, which he then gave to me.

In the audience was also a young man who was planning to open a tavern and public house in the community. There were already several but he intended to share the spoils. This meeting became the turning point in his life, for he accepted the good news from the distant land and it quenched his thirst for strong drink and his desire for a tavern. He became a sincere and active Christian.

After several years as a member of the congregation in Escanaba he returned to Sweden and settled there.

During my first summer in Escanaba I took part in mission meetings in Trout Creek, Carney, Iron Mountain, and Ishpeming. At that time mission meetings were great festive occasions in our churches; members anticipated them eagerly and visitors came from near and far. Generally there was an awakening spirit so that many were brought from darkness to light, from the power of Satan to God.

At the mission meeting in Iron Mountain I preached woe and doom over the people in a way that many of my listeners long remembered. In one of my sermons I used Isaiah 3:11 as my text and tried to emphasize that the ungodly fare badly in this world even if they have health, friends, money, and power; that they fare badly in death even if they die wealthy and are buried with flowers; and that they fare badly in the final judgment even if they have served as a judge on earth, maneuvered out of a righteous judgment in a human court, or walked so righteously that no judgment was to be feared. At last all the ungodly will be called before the all-knowing judge.

At this mission meeting I had as my companion Rev. J. A. Berg, who later became the pastor of the church there in Iron Mountain and still later transferred to the Augustana Synod. Pastor Berg was a warmhearted and good gospel preacher, but he was disposed to churchly practices and liked a worship service with a high festive mood. He saw the ministerial collar and other garb as almost essential to a proper appearance in the pulpit. I at that time leaned in the opposite direction. In our private discussions I opposed the brother's evaluation, but of course part of my reason for doing so was that I had no ministerial coat and no prospect of securing one in the depression of the Cleveland years. He did look questioningly at my reddish-brown coat and suggested, in fun of course, that I ought to borrow a more dignified one for Sunday, but he was reconciled to the situation and we had a very pleasant time together, my high church brother and I.

During my first winter in Escanaba I was visited by my schoolmate Isaac Skoog, who helped with several services. His unique liveliness of presentation and his singing to guitar accompaniment were refreshing. We also had a meeting in Gladstone. It was bitterly cold on that occasion, and we took the wagon over the frozen lake. The meetings were well attended and Skoog had the opportunity to preach and sing as much as he could. After the last meeting we had to walk back to Escanaba, so Mrs. Lindblad made sure we each borrowed a pair of heavy stockings and warmed us up with a good cup of coffee before we began our eight-mile journey over marsh and ice.

Spruce branches set into the ice gave us direction. Our fresh young blood circulated powerfully during our lively march, but only with great difficulty could we keep warm in the wintry chill of the night. The wind whipped our faces and the wolves howled threateningly from the shore. But at the same time the clearest little stars twinkled in the firmament and the electric lights of Escanaba beckoned us ahead.

Finally we reached our destination completely spent and frozen through, and at one o'clock in the morning, thankful to God, we crawled into bed in my bachelor home at Seaman Anderson's. When we awakened in the morning the sun was already shining. A new day and a new grace had come to the children of men.

The mission preachers of the northwestern Michigan district were a motley gathering with varied gifts, but a most pleasant fraternal group. We saw each other quite often at mission meetings in different places and at other gatherings as well. First and foremost was the patriarchal P. L. Taansberg, who always had funny little episodes to tell from younger days and from his work back in Norway and among the sawmill people north of Sundsvall. He lived in a community called Palestine where industrious Swedes tried to farm in spite of the stumps that remained after logging. The genial and talkative J. Hendrikson was pastor at Ironwood. He never let a question pass in either public or private discussion without participating and showing off his understanding and versatile knowledge. O. P. Anderson, a wide-shouldered man with a bushy full beard, a powerful voice, and a good heart was at work in Florence and Commonwealth. An original and faithful man from Dalarna, P. J. Person, still a bachelor though far from the youngest, was pastor in Marinette and the district chairman. O. Frank had been pastor in Ishpeming for a while but had returned to Sweden, and August Erickson had succeeded him. I have already mentioned that J. A. Berg became the pastor in Iron Mountain, and I myself was in Escanaba.

Now after many years and experiences have leaped away I remember with joy and thankfulness the time when I as a youth sought to do God's work on this field and received support and encouragement from this group of faithful brothers in the ministry. The memories of these days are essentially bright and smiling. But just imagine—four decades have passed since then!

Time flies quickly hour after hour,
Soon your precious years of life will cease,
But on the way the stars of promise twinkle
And you may walk in light of God's good grace.

Chapter Twenty

The First Year in North Park

After the Mission Covenant had taken over the school in Minneapolis, one of its great tasks was to find a suitable permanent location for it. The rooms on the lower floor of the Minneapolis Tabernacle were not very well adapted for classes, nor could they be used for this purpose in the future, so the Covenant Annual Meeting of 1891 appointed a board of directors to choose the best location for the school and to receive pledges of donations.

At that time there was a certain competition between Chicago and the Twin Cities of Minneapolis and St. Paul. Both were strong centers of activity of the Mission Friends and other things Swedish. In both places there were strong wills with local interests at heart but with a common interest in the welfare of Covenant education. The decision makers in Chicago wanted the school moved there. The leading men in the Twin Cities naturally wanted the school located in their midst. On this issue, clearly, wills struggled with each other.

Pastor E. August Skogsbergh and other friends of the school in Minneapolis tried in every way to persuade a few wealthy Americans to donate money and land and thereby, they hoped, make it possible to keep the school there, but they could not awaken sufficient interest or get firm promises of donations. Pastor Skogsbergh was, however, hopeful as usual and tried to convince the school board that they should accept the indefinite promises he had received and let the school continue in Minneapolis. For him this was a glorious city, "the center of the universe" as he used to call it.

But Mission Covenant Headquarters was in Chicago. Most of the members of the denomination's executive board lived there, and these brethren were not as enthusiastic about Minneapolis as Pastor Skogsbergh was. They no doubt felt that Chicago was the center of the universe, even if they did not say it. Rather than working for the future establishment of the school in Minneapolis, they tried to find a place for it in or near Chicago. When different proposals had been weighed and discussed, they accepted a Chicago offer of eight and one-half acres of land, $15,000 for the building of a schoolhouse, and $10,000 for a school fund, providing that the church would promise to keep its seminary there for fifty years. It was therefore decided that the school would be located in Chicago rather than Minneapolis, though a few years later these promises and conditions were changed by mutual agreement.

A school building was constructed on the donated land, and on June 16, 1894, it was dedicated amidst great festivities in connection with the Covenant Annual Meeting in Chicago. Old Main stood completely alone on the wide unsettled landscape. Pastor Nils Frykman gave the dedicatory address for this monument to faith and interest in the Lord's kingdom. In the fall of the same year the Mission Covenant's school opened in that building and its school work in Minneapolis was concluded.

But Pastor Skogsbergh believed that Minneapolis was too important a field for educational work to be summarily closed, so he arranged for a new school to be opened that fall in the lower rooms of the Mission Tabernacle. This continued under different names and changing conditions until it became the present Minnehaha Academy.

During my year and a half in Escanaba, great changes had taken place in the Mission Covenant's educational work. Therefore, in the fall of 1894 when I continued my studies, I departed for Chicago to the newly located North Park College. For me this was like a trip home.

On the first day of registration I was admitted in the new edifice built in the interest of culture and the Gospel. First and foremost, I met my former teachers, Professors D. Nyvall, A. Mellander, and J. A. Lindblade. Then I met several of my old schoolmates and many new ones: A. G. Lundquist, Jonas Johnson, Isaac Skoog, John Nelson, Oscar Dahlberg, Oscar Palmberg, David Brunström, A. T. Frykman, C. J. Andrews, and several others who later became respected men in the state and faithful servants in the Christian Church.

The new building was in a distant border area of Chicago named North Park, which would in time become a community. Then, however, it was an almost entirely unsettled area where the last cabbage heads had hardly been removed before the first "ministers' heads" began to grow. Certain streets had been staked out around the school and some of them had been named, but there had not been time for other improvements. Foster Avenue was then, as now, the main east-west street, but it was unpaved and very poorly maintained, making it a terror for drivers, especially when it rained. In the ditches on both sides of the street there was foul-smelling water for the comfort of frogs. In only a few places were there sidewalks, or boards that frequently lay loose on the ditch banks. Along Foster Avenue were some kerosene lamps placed far apart, giving a dim and sorry light in the darkness of night. This was the best street in North Park; the others were even worse.

During the summer a few of the school's friends had begun to build their homes nearby, thus beginning to develop the new community. Among these were C. A. Björk, Johan Löf, Adolf Lydell, Otto Högfeldt, and John Hagström. Besides these, Claes Youngquist, Peter Youngquist, and Carlson (called *borgmästare* or "mayor") had farmed this area for many years and still lived in their homes. S. G. Cronstedt tried to open his own business just across from the school, but it flowered even less than the community and had to be closed. The schoolteachers rented rooms from the homeowners and together with the aforementioned families constituted the entire population of the community. The students could not be included in the count because they were present only when school was in session.

The school building itself was excellent, but lacked comforts. There was no gas, much less electricity, because these modern utilities had not yet come out from the city. It was lit by kerosene lamps. It did have running water, but the plumbing had to be provided privately, and no other homes in the community had this accommodation. In the "mayor's" yard was a good well and an old pump which served as the waterworks for almost the whole community. There stood professors, editors, students, women, and children pumping water for the needs of their respective homes. On wash days they stood in line at the pump, which squeaked and groaned in its continuing service. At times one heard it at sunrise and again in the evening, when it would blend its laments with the croaking of frogs in the ditch by Foster Avenue.

There was also a pump at the main entrance of Old Main, but because the water there had been condemned by the health authorities it could not be used. If there had been a fire at North Park it would have been impossible to put it out. It is strange that such a situation was permitted to exist.

Isaac Skoog and I roomed together at Lydell's. The lady of the house cooked good coffee and often invited us for the blessed afternoon liquid when we came home from classes. As a small appreciation for this friendliness we often pumped the water for the needs of the house. We pumped and carried it hundreds of times, but she invited us to coffee and delicacies so frequently that in all likelihood we received more payment than our deeds were worth.

Later when the water mains were laid in North Park we were freed from our task as water bearers and the old pump had a well-earned rest. It was a big event when the Chicago waterworks replaced our work at the pump and water began to flow out of the faucets in North Park homes.

Isaac Skoog and I had agreed to celebrate by inviting the household and a few schoolmates to a special feast of coffee and bakery goods. Isaac was without means at the moment, but he had a willing spirit and volunteered to make the purchases if I would provide the cash. Since I had a few coins in my pocket he went to the bakery in Bowmanville and came home with his arms full of biscuits, coffee cake, *pepparkakor,* and pie. The lady of the house, her sister Augusta (later Mrs. Fredrikson), and Anna Larson (later Mrs. A. W. Carlson) took over the coffeemaking and serving, which no doubt gave the party a little more class than it would have had if Isaac and I had presided. We did have fun at our memorable coffee party to celebrate having city water so that we could enjoy baths and other comforts of civilization. The improvement certainly deserved this little festivity.

The whole area continued to depend on kerosene lamps for light in the evenings, however, for it was a long time before gas and electricity found their way to this borderland of Chicago. There was no telephone nearer than the Home of Mercy and the hospital,* but

---

* The hospital Bowman refers to is Swedish Covenant Hospital, and the Home of Mercy is now called Covenant Home. They are four city blocks east of North Park.

we got along without that. North Park was a pleasant community despite the lack of modern conveniences. It was sheltered from the hurry and distraction of the city, and the whole population was one big family. Concord reigned because all were humble and looked with friendly eyes upon each other when they met. The students were treated almost like sons in the homes of the different families. The school was everyone's darling, encouraged and supported in every way.

But the long distance from the center of the city and, above all, the poor transportation were great hindrances to the school's growth. The nearest streetcar was at Lincoln Avenue, a good fifteen-minute walk from campus. From there we had to pay to get downtown. Then if we wanted to go to the South Side or other parts of the city we paid another fare or perhaps two, depending on where we were going. This situation was enough to keep parents from sending their children to North Park even if they saw the value of a school of that kind. For this reason it is not surprising that from the beginning the school had a disheartening small enrollment.

Besides, it should be noted that Mission Friends in Chicago at that time were generally uninterested in the school, with the possible exception of the theological department. On the other hand, in Minneapolis and elsewhere in Minnesota, educational interest had been generated by the school in the Mission Tabernacle. But one could not reasonably expect a large number of students from Minnesota to go to Chicago for a general education that they could get closer to home.

If my memory does not fail me, there were only sixty-four students at North Park the first year, and it was a long time before enrollment exceeded one hundred. It was years before the school had a secure footing in its environment and enjoyed a more general support from our people in Chicago.

Because Old Main was the only building, it had to satisfy all needs. In the east wing of the basement were a kitchen and dining room, in the west wing the steam boiler and coal storage. On the first floor just to the left of the main entrance were Professor Lindblade's classes in which he tried to make businessmen of the boys. In the rooms to the right, Professors Nyvall and Mellander tried to shape into preachers the raw materials that the churches had sent them. The second floor of the building was temporarily arranged as a dormitory by partitioning the large rooms halfway to the ceiling. There the students who had not succeeded in renting rooms with neighborhood families had sleeping quarters and study space and played their boyish tricks on each other. In the east half of the third floor was the school chapel, and in a corner was also the library and museum. Across the way from the chapel was the gymnasium.

Thus in the highest part of the building was the place where we gathered to pray, hear the preaching of God's Word, and sing praise to the glory of the Lord. This was an upper room, just as the apostles had in Jerusalem. But on the same floor was the place where, at assigned hours, the students, under the leadership of A. T. Frykman, had their acrobatic exercises. When these athletes were really keyed up the whole building shook, which later made it necessary to move the gymnastics to a lower level. Where they were held did not concern me in the least because I could never be persuaded to participate even though it might have been good for my health. In regard to gymnastics I behaved like a monk without making a monk's commitment.

The school chapel was the only church in the community. Usually the sermon was given by Professor Nyvall, Mellander, or Björk, though sometimes one of the seminary students preached. I was in the chapel as rarely on Sundays as I was in the gymnasium on weekdays because I was usually away when Sunday came, but both the school "family" and the rest of the community worshiped there quite regularly. The present Mission church in North Park originated from the chapel of the school.

The seminary students were often asked to preach in the churches of Chicago and the surrounding area. Before I came to North Park I had been called to serve the little Mission church in Blue Island during the winter months. The call promised ten dollars a month, free tickets between Chicago and Blue Island, and free meals on Sundays. I was to preach twice each Sunday and on Thursday evenings. The church, recently organized, had rented a little store on Western Avenue and furnished it with chairs, a pulpit, and an old organ. The hall held about fifty people, but it was far from full at the meetings.

At that time Blue Island, like North Park, was hardly more than a countryside, and Western Avenue was worse than Foster. If one walked in the street the clay and mire after a rain almost took the shoes off one's feet.

I accepted the call to this distant place because I wanted to be in active service. I suspected that one could easily become dull and dry dealing with only lessons and school concerns, so I felt the call to Blue Island was from the hand of God and accepted it with thankfulness to him. Of course it is possible that the offer of ten dollars per month also had some influence, because a student had expenses during the school year that had to be paid in a businesslike way.

But to take care of Sunday and Thursday meetings in Blue Island in addition to the lessons at the school was a big job. After my visits there I did not get back to my quarters until one or two in the morning, depending on how fortunate I was in train and streetcar connections. I suffered no damage from this strain, however, for when one is young and full of inspiration for a cause one can endure much.

The winter continued without any remarkable events. In spite of the school's low enrollment and the difficulties of primitive conditions, the work proceeded with youthful inspiration and the hope that better days were coming. The students were of all ages, from fifteen to nearly fifty, though the "theologians" were older than those in other departments. This year there were brethren who had more education than is usually the case in a theological school. Naturally they had more social graces and richer Christian experience than the younger students. In our group there were some who moved with the speed of youthful joy and permitted themselves innocent boyish tricks and practical jokes, and others who leaned toward the serious side of life and were perhaps a bit ascetic. Life mixes and unites different types in a remarkable way.

Some good friends of the school feared that fraternization between the seminary students and other youth of the school would lead to difficulties and diminish the dignity of the ministerial office. They therefore wanted those who were to become ministers isolated in a seminary by themselves. Professor Nyvall, the president of the school, opposed this idea, emphasizing that to isolate the seminary students during their training could easily lead to the formation of a special caste that would stand at a distance from the common people. He wanted to prevent this, because, he said, the Mission Covenant needed ministers who could fellowship with the people to whom they were to preach the way of salvation in order to lead them to the Lord. There was no doubt a great deal of wisdom in the professor's ideas.

But though the seminarians and other students met under the

same roof, at times in the same classes, they did not mix a great deal for there was a certain something which set the seminarians apart as a special group. Perhaps it was their age or the fact that they had different interests on another level. Already during their schooling their life task was more focused.

Our studies kept us busy early and late. If one wanted to do well in the classes one could not lie lazy in bed. Among the schoolmates there were some good students, but also some average ones who were in daily danger of being left behind even though they came through at last—refined by fire, to use a biblical image. One of our comrades, a good and sincere soul but with few talents as a student, continually prayed over his lessons, more than all the rest of us put together. Whether his prayers were heard in any special way is not for me to say, but he did win our deepest respect. Now he has finished his day, a man of seventy years. Peace be upon his memory!

The question of the right use of prayer in different life situations is not easy to answer. But while thought by itself brings a person's hand to the forehead in puzzlement, men and women of prayer fold their hands and find their problems solved in a practical way.

As part of our schoolwork we had to write sermons and sermon outlines, which were then reviewed by the teachers and discussed in class. These homiletic exercises, which revealed the abilities—or perhaps more correctly the failings—of the students to think and express their thoughts in words, were both instructive and interesting. There was rarely commendation, but always criticism.

On one occasion I was assigned to make a sermon outline on the text about Jesus feeding the five thousand in a desert place. I had done my work honestly and now was to give my outline in class. As my title I announced, "A feeding in the desert." Responding quickly as usual, Nyvall said, "Yes, yes, just so, that's good," and with his lovely and unexpected acknowledgement singing in my ears I continued to give the disposition of the contents: main points, subordinate points, and conclusion. When I had finished, the professor sat quietly looking at his Greek Testament. Then he said, "Well, that was like being invited to dinner without getting any food." What a crushing moment! But the professor was right. As I realized later, I had issued an invitation to dinner but had not put anything substantial on the table.

Often during my ministry when I have been preparing sermons, the words of my former teacher have rung in my ears and I have challenged myself: do not neglect to serve spiritual food for souls who come to hear you preach, for an empty table nourishes no one and disappoints listeners who hunger for the Bread of Life.

Chapter Twenty-One

Vacation and Activity

Because vacations provide a useful break from the constant tiring work of the classroom, both teachers and students look forward to Christmas and summer holidays just as the laborer looks forward to Sunday's respite from daily tasks.

Seminary students' longing for a vacation is usually blended with the desire to get out into practical work; they burn to conquer and win for the kingdom of God. More than one has left his studies early in order to devote himself to preaching the Gospel, for most of them are impatient with the long drawn-out preparation in school; the young and zealous brother finds it difficult to understand how it can be God's will to use year after year for education when souls are perishing in their sins for lack of the Gospel. Perhaps it was just such a zealous preacher who composed "The Fisher Song" in which, among other things, he says,

> *Let me out, let me out!*
> *Before the present month is past*
> *I want to fish for souls again.*
> *Should I sit here while many long*
> *To hear about the sinner's friend?*
> *Oh no! I will be on my way*
> *Before the present month is past.*
> *I want to fish for souls again.*

I had promised to return to Escanaba to serve the church at least during the summer vacation of 1895. During my stay in school Pastor O. Ohlson, now in Manchester, New Hampshire, had served there, though during Christmas vacation I had visited Gladstone and Ishpeming and had preached in Escanaba. Since my schoolmate August Erickson was now pastor in Ishpeming, it was particularly tempting to spend a few days of my vacation with him. We diligently discussed all manner of questions out in the broad dominions of theology, on the lots of church politics overgrown with thorns, and on the grounds of changing experiences in the Christian life. We discussed education, school comradeship, friendship, and romance. Erickson and I had always been good friends and enjoyed each other's company, even though in disposition and views we were so different that we disagreed about almost everything. But we could express this without disturbing our mutual respect and brotherly love.

At that time certain political articles about the church were being published which stirred up minds among our Mission people. Erickson took the part of those who criticized the leadership; I took the opposite position. I defended the importance of education for preachers and tried to persuade Erickson to return to North Park and complete his schooling; he contended that this was unnecessary. His success as a minister in Ishpeming no doubt reinforced his view. He felt that time was short and that one ought not use more years than necessary on the school bench. But like a wise, understanding man, he did change his mind on this point and returned to school one winter before he moved to Boston, where, with God's blessing, he accomplished his great life work as a gospel preacher.

Pastor Erickson was a gifted and popular speaker who had the support of both the church members and the general public in Ishpeming. A little episode from his ministry there reveals the great confidence he enjoyed. During a mission meeting there was a quickening spirit, and quite a number who were concerned about their sins asked for intercessory prayer. Among those was a young man for whom two of the visiting ministers prayed. Anxious about his sins, he remained on his knees in deep emotion even after the ministers had ceased, and finally sobbed, "Ask Pastor Erickson to come here and pray for me. Perhaps that will help." Erickson came and prayed for him and it seemed as if his prayer had a releasing power for the young man. However that might be, the man came to faith in Christ, and that was, of course, the greatness of the experience.

After the Christmas vacation in the north I returned to school and to my field in Blue Island, but on Sunday, May 5, I again took up the work in Escanaba. Things were more hopeful now among the church friends and the other people in the city because employment opportunities had improved. Those who had lost their jobs in the depression now returned to work one after another, and all the activity of the church seemed to move toward a brighter future.

From the ministry of this summer I carry the memory of a funeral because the situation was particularly distressing. The Englund family had lost a lovable little girl who had been a ray of sunshine at home and a joy in our Sunday school. For this funeral I composed the following verses which I enter here as an echo from that day.

She rests, your beloved, on strong Savior's breast,
She rests from her illness and suffering.
She dear was to you, and dear was her name,
She is resident still in your hearts.

She now is released from all sorrows and sins,
A pearl in the crown of the Master,
More pure than a star in the heavenly round
To reign with her Savior forever.

Though now in your loss tears burn on your cheek
And empty her place at your fireside,
Your child is enjoying the heavenly spring,
This world is no longer her dwelling.

O, look my dear friends, how she beckons to you:
"Come Mama, come Papa, come children,
Come share in my gladness with Jesus, I pray.
Come here where all sorrow is ended."

So be this your comfort in loneliest hour:
You will see your beloved again
In heaven's dear land, in the grove of the blest.
May grace from the Lord so reward you.

During the summer, attempts were made to organize a Swedish Baptist church. Baptist ministers visited Escanaba now and then, and there was one family and an unmarried woman who sympathized with them. Naturally they tried to persuade members of the Mission church to visit their meetings. They gave out tracts explaining adult baptism and expounding their opinions on it. Some of our members were concerned about the question of baptism, but we tried to avoid agitation and conduct ourselves in a calm Christian way so that divisiveness would not flare up as it sometimes has in similar situations. Our congregation did not suffer any permanent loss even if one or two let themselves be rebaptized.

For me, however, this situation was new, for I had never before come into contact with denominational zeal. As I look back now on this experience, I am thankful to God that I did not become involved in a bitter denominational struggle with its devastating results. A young pastor can easily be damaged for his whole ministry if he is sucked into violent conflicts against brethren in the faith on account of doctrinal differences. What questionable strategies and what lack of brotherliness have not been wrapped in the mantle of denominationalism, thereby destroying the Christian character for the future!

From August 16 through 19 a mission meeting was held that was so rewarding that we extended it over the following Thursday. The preachers were Gustav Lindstrom, Andrew Anderson, and Isaac Skoog. Several were converted by the Lord, and the whole Escanaba congregation was refreshed. We all rejoiced greatly because God's Spirit was working among us.

My summer ministry in Escanaba concluded October 7, but the following Christmas vacation I was there again and stayed through prayer week. We longed and prayed for blessings from on high. At my desk in the Adolf Peterson home I wrote the following verses expressing the feelings that held me captive then and that were shared by many others in the congregation.

Savior, my Savior, I long for all souls
To turn to you from their sinning.
Therefore, O powerful Spirit divine,
Send us a true revival.

Help us reflect on the time growing short,
The days of grace disappearing,
Make us more earnest, our levity chain,
Your peace at last may we find.

Heavenly Dove, make the Savior well-known
And souls to heaven awaken,
Showers of grace from your paradise send,
Faithful we'll be abiding.

On January 12, the day before my twenty-eighth birthday, I preached farewell in Escanaba using as a text Hebrews 3:1-8. The congregation wanted me to return again in the spring to be their permanent pastor, but I was convinced that I should decline their call, though it was by no means easy. Surely this was God's guidance, even though the friends in Escanaba could not see it at the time.

Upon my return to North Park I gave my schoolwork everything I had, for it was important to use the time well during this last term. No noteworthy events took place; the work and the life with comrades was as before.

Shortly after North Park had opened, a tendency appeared from a certain direction to make public in the press alleged faults and neglects of the school and its president. This damaged people's confidence in the school. Before the Annual Meeting in Minneapolis in 1895 it had already begun to appear so glaringly that the conference felt it necessary to accept the following resolution: "It was decided that we who are assembled in meeting deplore and disapprove of the writing which has recently appeared in *Missions Vannen* which is calculated to cast a shadow on our teachers and other brethren and the work as a whole." This was the first time the Mission Covenant adopted a resolution against this newspaper's position, but it was not the last, as we all know.

At the same annual meeting the delegates elected Professor Nyvall secretary of the Covenant instead of Otto Högfeldt,* who was the incumbent in this position of trust. This action and the resolution evidently expressed the same opinion.

As an illustration of the criticism that appeared in the *Missions*

---

* editor of *Missions Vännen*

Vannen, I will cite an event during my stay at North Park. Professor Nyvall, the president of the school, was often called upon to preach on Sundays, sometimes hundreds of miles from Chicago. Thus he could not always return to school for Monday lectures. The editor remarked in his paper that instruction at North Park was neglected. He could also have discovered and informed the public that the professor on such occasions had assigned extra work, but of that he was quite silent.

Of course the students saw the newspaper criticism immediately and were incensed by its injustice. We wrote a rejoinder to tell the public the real situation, and two of the students brought it to the newspaper office with the request that it be published. The editor's office refused. Instead, it sarcastically informed the public that some students had presented a reply, but it had not been accepted because its form needed a review by the teachers.

This handling of our response was of special interest to me because I had had something to do with the writing and style of it. Previously the editors had gladly accepted short articles from my blunt pen, but now when it was a question of correcting the editor's warped account of the school president's work, my style was too poor. Well, my schoolmates and I put the editor's behavior on the shelves of our memory. More than one episode of church politics since then has had extra illumination because of this event.

Someday when the loom is taken down and the weaving of our lives is tested, there will no doubt be ugly knots, ends, and tassels. Happy the one who needs not be ashamed on that day. Yes, God help me to act right in all things and be pleasing to him.

In May 1896 my schoolwork at North Park was over. The commencement exercises were simple but had more of an academic stamp than in any previous year of the school's history. In the theological department the graduates were David Brunström, Oscar F. Dahlberg, J. M. Florell, John Lidén, Joel Ohlén, Oscar Palmberg, C. F. Sandstrom, Isaac Skoog, and I.

Comrades now left North Park College which had become dear to them, some never to enter its doors again. The seminary graduating class has never been reunited all at one time and never will be on earth because some have already left this world of conflict and labor. But fraternal memories linger, and now even after thirty years they cast a bright luster over occasional prosaic and tiring experiences.

When I finished school I was called to serve the Mission Covenant Church in Rockford during the summer months while Pastor F. M. Johnson went to Sweden. I also had a call to the permanent pastorate of the Mission Tabernacle on the South Side of Chicago. I accepted both in fear and trembling because I was young and the fields were large and demanding.

In every way my summer in Rockford was pleasant and instructive. Attendance kept up, and as a rule I found it easy to preach to the people. Prayer meetings were held in several places during the week. Young people's meetings were very well attended and often inspiring.

The congregation had an abundance of spiritual gifts. Several brethren had the ability to preach and on Sundays went out in different directions declaring Christ to our Swedish people. Among these were Andrew Berg and August Johnson, both of whom later became Covenant ministers. Johnson is still a pastor in Belvidere, Illinois. Among the boys in the church was O. W. Carlson, who later studied at North Park and has, for a long time, been an active and good preacher in the Mission Covenant.

There was always special joy and rich edification in listening to prayers and testimonies at the meetings when opportunity was given. Such occasions affirmed the words of the apostle, "the gifts are many, but the spirit is the same." I remember especially a little man from Öland named Johnson, the enthusiastic Frisk, the sensitive city missionary Segerdahl, and several others who always volunteered their varied testimonies at prayer meetings and aftermeetings. To see these glowing faces was a real inspiration for the minister. How well I remember old Segerdahl, who liked to sit in front of the pulpit with his hands clasped over his chest, swaying slightly back and forth while his eyes twinkled at the preacher through his spectacles. When there was something in the sermon that encouraged him he would say out loud, "Thanks and praise!" His sensitive heart often received something for which to thank and praise God.

To have such "assistant preachers" is a great blessing for a minister, making it easier to preach in a very special way. How different it is when some crabby and critical brother writhes in the pew, stares sullenly at the floor, and gives the impression that the "Amen" was the best part of the whole sermon. No doubt there were a few such people even in Rockford, but I hardly remember them after all these decades since I was interim pastor there.

A congregation that is blessed with many members also has, quite naturally, many disciplinary problems, because there are always some weak, stumbling, superficial, thoughtless, and careless persons among the Christians. These behave unworthily toward the Gospel of Christ. We in Rockford also had such difficulties time and time again. The deacons dealt with each case individually and tried to exercise real care of souls, but in spite of this, action in some instances may well have been too hasty. When one is concerned about the reputation of the church before the world it is a temptation to exclude members who fall into sin before they are dealt with according to the New Testament. This is a bad fault.

At the end of September Pastor F. M. Johnson returned from a pleasant trip to Sweden. He was welcomed by his congregation, but above all by his wife and also his children who, though still small and interested mostly in play, received their father with real joy.

My service as interim pastor in Rockford was now concluded, and I departed to assume the work that was waiting for me in the other congregation.

Chapter Twenty-two

Memories from My First Congregation in Chicago

At the beginning of October 1896
I came to the Tabernacle Church in Chicago as shepherd and teacher though I was still young and comparatively inexperienced as leader of a congregation. As a youth in this church I had heard God's Word preached by different witnesses and, twelve years before, had finally been won for the Lord. Never could I have imagined on that memorable afternoon that I would someday become the pastor of this church and use the same pulpit from which I had with deep emotion heard E. August Skogsbergh and F. M. Johnson proclaim the Word of Life, but in this wonderful way the Lord guides our steps and completes his purpose with us.

During my last winter in school Isaac Skoog and I had preached in the Tabernacle because August Pohl had moved from this parish to the congregation on the North Side of the city. During this vacancy J. Gelen, a pastor from Sweden, had also ministered for some time. However, now it was my turn to begin work here.

The old Tabernacle, on the corner of La Salle and 30th streets, was still the meeting place for a large group of Swedes. Sunday-night services required not only the main floor but the balcony as well, and even the Thursday night meetings were well attended. Blacks had begun to move into the area and the Swedes had started moving further south, though many continued to live in this neighborhood. Church members were generally very loyal, attending the meetings and supporting the work with their earthly possessions.

This lively congregation consisted almost exclusively of young and middle-aged people; only a few had gray hairs and furrowed cheeks. The chairman was F. O. Moberg, who faithfully attended all meetings and had a warm heart. S. A. Matson was the dependable and orderly secretary who later served for many years on the executive board of the Mission Covenant. The Sunday-school superintendent was the sensitive and happy A. A. Svenson. On the board were such other men as Soderberg, Malmberg, Siktberg, N. M. Nelson, Akerman, and Clarquist. Fred Erickson and later Axel W. Anderson were the leaders of the Young People's Society.

In the Sunday evening services, which were well attended by unbelievers as well as believers, the quickening spirit was often present. The services were always preceded by a warm prayer meeting and, at an earlier hour, by a good young people's meeting, not to mention "the three o'clock meeting" led by the deacons, which was a free discussion on some text in God's Word. Therefore by the time the main service began many of the believers had been "warmed up" in the previous afternoon meetings and were thus ready to receive rich blessings. Such preparation was very important and supported preaching in an essential and distinctive way.

March 10, 1897, was a great and memorable day for me. I then had an experience for which I have often been glad and thankful to God, but at the same time glad and thankful that I did not have to repeat. I was then united in a long and happy marriage to Julia Nelson, who was well-known at the Tabernacle and in the Bethany congregation where she was an active member. When a minister or, for that matter, anyone else is to be married, arrangements are a rather big problem. Should one invite the whole circle of friends? Will there be room for all of them? If some are eliminated what problems will result? Where shall one draw the line? The simplest procedure would be to invite no one; the marriage could, of course, be just as successful. But for such a meaningful moment one needs to have all one's friends present and consequently have a large wedding.

We invited the whole congregation and many more—in all, about 600 people. C .A. Björk, our Covenant president, read the service, after which he immediately departed for a trip to California, leaving us in the big circle of friends to enjoy the happiness and contentment of the wedding festivities.

We did not take a wedding trip at the time but postponed it

until the end of July when we made a circle tour by land and water. We traveled by boat to Duluth, stopping at several places in Michigan. From Duluth we went to Minneapolis and St. Paul, and from there on the Mississippi River to Dubuque, Iowa. Finally we came back through Rockford to Chicago again. It was a trip full of variety and interest.

When we arrived at Duluth thousands of people were gathered on the dock with waving banners and march music, but the reader must not think that the city had come out because my better half and I were honoring them with our visit. No, hardly. Only one person in the entire crowd was interested in our visit, and that was brother E. J. Seth, pastor of the Mission church, who took us to his pleasant home. The other people were there to welcome Senator Mark Hanna, the big chief of the Republican party, who was coming to campaign for candidate William McKinley.

While I preached Christ in the Mission church, Mark Hanna gave a political address lifting the Republican party to the skies, even to the seventh heaven. The following day the city newspapers carried sensational reports about the speech and about the big crowds that had listened with interest. About our meeting in the Mission church they said nothing, nor did anyone expect them to.

In Minneapolis we stayed with our friends the Palmquists for a couple days and preached in the old church on the north side where Palmquist was the pastor. In this pleasant home we enjoyed warm friendship. Their son Herbert, who is now a respected and well-situated pastor, was then only a little boy who could hardly walk across the floor. Thus time changes us whether we want it to or not.

On the winding waters of the Mississippi, flat-bottomed paddle-wheel boats carrying freight between St. Paul and St. Louis took a limited number of passengers. The trip offered real recreation, providing one did not demand too much luxury and comfort. At each little city the boats docked to take on freight, and the passengers were allowed to go ashore to promenade along the street and inquire what the stores had to sell.

These riverboats had a touch of southern atmosphere about them. As soon as we left the dock in St. Paul, moving slowly down the river with the big stern wheel splashing in the water, a troop of black men with guitars and other stringed instruments came up on deck and began to entertain us with music in authentic black tradition. When they began to pick their strings and in a fast tempo sing "A Hot Time in the Old Town Tonight," we knew that they did not intend to provide Christian edification. Perhaps this song was the core of their repertoire, for they sang it with enthusiasm and glided back to it or some similar street ballad between beautiful black songs like "Old Black Joe."

During each concert the most resourceful man in the company would come with an old ragged hat to receive a collection. His humorous comments and comic grimaces worked like magic, and the coins rolled easily and merrily out of passengers' pockets. Encouraged, the ensemble would continue to play until the collector felt that it was time to move around with the hat again. The harvest was less this time but he entertained the people with his funny stories until the coins came forth. He was indeed a seasoned beggar.

The method of handling freight at the various cities was different than any I had witnessed before, a vestige, I suspect, of southern slavery. About twenty blacks were hired as stevedores to carry sacks of flour and boxes of freight on their shoulders and backs. These loads were so heavy that the strongest men almost buckled under their weight, yet they were expected to trot and run. The captain or his assistant stood at the gangway with a whip in his hand, growling commands. The whip whined through the air. "Get going there, nigger! Hurry up there nigger, you," he hollered, and let the whip brush the naked legs of the running burden-bearers. Thus the loading continued for an hour or more before the steamer cast off again and continued its journey.

Obviously such brutal handling does not evoke willingness in the laborer; the blacks gave ample evidence of this with their truancy whenever the falcon eyes of the driver could not follow them and they were out of range of his whip. I hope that this inhumane treatment of workers on the Mississippi has long since been abolished.

At the appointed time we arrived in Rockford where we were to spend a few days before returning to Chicago and completing the circle of our pleasant journey. When I had been interim pastor there a year earlier I was still a bachelor. Now I was a married man and had, through marriage, become a relative of the pastor: my wife and his were sisters. In the simple old manse by the Rockford Tabernacle we felt completely at home, and from the friends in the city and surrounding area we received genuine hospitality. I preached several times in church for appreciative Rockfordites, and this in itself was very satisfying.

After a month's absence we returned to our home in Chicago and were welcomed by the dear Tabernacle congregation.

Before we went on our wedding trip two events had taken place which are noted in my daybook and also deserve a place in my memory book. On Sunday afternoon, May 9, 1897, two missionary candidates were consecrated in the Tabernacle for work in the northwestern district of Alaska. These were the Eskimo girl Alice Omegitjoak, who had attended school both at North Park and at our hospital and was now returning to her people, and P. H. Anderson, who had also studied for a while at school and was now to become a teacher among the Eskimos.

Alice is now married to Misha Ivanoff, who is in government service, and they have a good home with two fine boys whom they seek to rear for the mission among the Eskimos at the same time as they are unselfishly furthering the gospel work themselves. When I was in Alaska in the fall of 1925 I had the pleasure of meeting these friends of missions and learning about their work of faith and love.

P. H. Anderson did not teach in Alaska very long. He arrived when gold was being discovered around Nome and acquired enough of this bewitching metal to make him independent. He therefore resigned and returned to the States after a time. Neither his own experiences nor those of the Mission Covenant were matters of joy; for the denomination there followed long and bitter conflicts which are best forgotten.

The other event was my own ordination. Though I had finished the schooling for my life vocation, received my license from the Mission Covenant, and was in full action as a pastor, I had not been "dedicated to the priesthood" according to the New Testament. This term is often used but is perhaps less proper than "ordination." After making application and being duly examined and approved by the appointed board, I was ordained at the Annual Covenant Meeting at North Park on June 7, 1897. The sermon was preached by Pastor C. B. Johnson, now deceased, and the ordination was conducted by Covenant president, C. A. Björk.

I have already mentioned the "three o'clock meetings" on Sunday afternoons. A group of Christian men and even women who liked to speak on spiritual subjects gathered for these Bible discussions led by one of the deacons. Not only members of the congregation but people from other parts of the city took part. Sometimes I was present, but usually as a quiet participant. These good meetings brought blessings, but on occasion degenerated and did not lead to edification. Because I was a young minister, most of the brethren who attended were older, and at times one of them would take a potshot at young preachers who did not understand how to care for the spiritual gifts in the congregation. This was really a reproof against me because I did not ask them to help preach on Sunday evenings.

Nevertheless, it was a rather interesting assemblage. Some characters were always there; others came for a time and disappeared. Among the latter was a kind of Melchizedek in that no one knew his derivation. In a quavering voice he gave his emotional testimony, a memorized little sermon about the chrysalis that would soon burst, allowing the Spirit, like a beautiful butterfly in summer, to fly around in the heavenly garden meadows and suck the honey of blessedness in the eternity of eternities. He would unwind similar fine phrases at both the "three o'clock meetings" and the prayer meetings. His wavering voice impressed sensitive natures.

He wanted to become a preacher, this aged brother, and he shared this desire with the deacons, who told him that he should perhaps be recommended to North Park. One Sunday afternoon he detained me for a long time on Wentworth Avenue trying to persuade me to give him a recommendation. He thought that two or three months there would be sufficient, inasmuch as he had rich experience in the schools of life and the Spirit, as he expressed it. Cautiously I tried to dissuade him from his school fancies by pointing out his advanced age and other factors, but he was not easily deterred.

In the course of the conversation I must have looked at his bearded, dirty, and ragged appearance so that he understood I had reservations about his presentability. As if apologetically, he said, "Look, the pastor should understand that I have not had a home for many years. I walked from Moline to Chicago so my shoes are poor, but when I was young, people used to say I looked good. If I go to the school I will tidy myself up." And after a moment he added, "I have two white starched shirts and a pair of newly half-soled shoes in Jamestown, New York!"

Well, that was something, but more is required for entrance into the seminary at North Park. I could not help feeling sorry for him. Shortly thereafter he disappeared as suddenly as he had come. Perhaps he found some other church and with his sermon on the chrysalis, the butterfly, and the heavenly meadows, stirred up emotions in other sensitive Christians. More than thirty years have passed since I made acquaintance with the already aged brother. I hope he has long since found grace to be moved from this vale of tears to the heavenly flower fields. Though he did not qualify to become a preacher, he qualified to be saved.

A young minister in a big American city, perhaps in a small town also, will certainly be visited by all kinds of beggars and be "led by the nose" or "taken" scores of times before he can harden himself against the professionals who knock on his door. He probably wants to do well by all, and he may try to give them a testimony about Christ while he gives them a coin for food or a night's lodging, which in most instances will be used for a drink of booze.

One cold November evening a poorly clad woman came to our home, tearful and short of breath. She told us that her landlord threatened to evict her and put her belongings out on the street if she did not pay her rent within an hour. She took in washing for a living but had been ill for a long time and earned nothing. She gave the address where she lived and in every way acted as if she needed help. I thought of following her to her landlord, but for some reason did not do so but gave her what she requested, intending to visit her and her landlord in the morning. After she had gone, my wife put on her coat and followed her to see where she went. A couple blocks from home she entered a tavern with my four American dollars, honestly earned and given in good faith. The following morning I looked for the address where the woman said she lived and found it to be an empty lot. No doubt this was not the first time she had played this role both for ministers and for others, and in all likelihood it was not the last. That woman was a successful con artist.

At about the same time, a young and neat youth was coming to church now and then. One day he visited our home and told us that he was a photographer from St. Paul, Minnesota, who had come to Chicago to seek work. He said that he had been unsuccessful and had now decided to return home, but needed to borrow money for his ticket. He presented his cause so well that I lent him the money, which he promised to repay at the first opportunity. He asserted his profound thankfulness for this valued help.

After some time he appeared again at our door, saying that he had gone to St. Paul but had failed to get a steady position there. However, he had been offered a job in Chicago and therefore had returned, but could not begin his work for a couple weeks. In order to earn a few coppers and not be idle he wanted to try to sell books by D. L. Moody, and he carried a copy of Moody's *The Way to God* in his pocket. But the bookstore would not trust him because he was unknown to them. For that reason he came to me, asked my pardon for not being able to repay what he had already borrowed, and requested another loan in order to buy Moody books that he could then sell. At that time I thought it was my duty to extend a loan to a person in need without any thought of repayment, so I gave him the two dollars he asked for. He bowed in deep thankfulness.

A day or two later when I was riding a streetcar on Indiana Avenue I happened to see the man walking on the sidewalk smoking a glowing cigar which he had, perhaps, bought with my coins instead of buying *The Way to God.*

A week or so later he turned up again, saying that he had his promised position and would even be allowed to live with his boss. Therefore things looked bright. But a new difficulty had arisen about which he wanted to ask me for a little help. During recent nights he had been forced to take very cheap lodging where he had become full of lice, and since he could not, of course, go to his new home in that condition, he needed to borrow a dollar to buy a new suit of underwear. It would not be long before he would begin to pay his debts.

But I had already swallowed enough of his lies so I steeled myself against all his prayers for help. I told him frankly that the infestation that troubled him was in the heart itself and this required more than two suits of underwear to remedy. He seemed deeply distressed that I had such a poor opinion of him, and said he would prove himself right and convince me that he was an honorable man. More than three decades have passed since then, but I have not as yet seen or heard anything about the man's pretended honesty. He was, and perhaps remained, a scoundrel.

It is unbelievable how many strangers have begged money from me since I became a minister. They have come to my home. They have waited for me at the church door. They have spoken to me on the street. Some have been men, some women. Most have been middle-aged or older, but a few have been young. All have told stories of adversity, sickness, unemployment, or theft. As I look back on the whole motley crowd, I cannot remember one who later proved to be honest and repaid the loan. Rather, they proved to be deceivers, professional beggars, and parasites. Sound reason tells us that if a person happens to be insolvent, he has, as a rule, a friend or a few friends who can assist him so that he does not need to beg for help from total strangers.

A few years ago after a visit with one of these characters I wrote the following little rhyme:

> *Fall winds are raising their voices,*
> *Singing their ballads in minor.*
> *Lazybones asks for a five,*
> *Tearfully telling his saga.*
> *He moans of the Father's chastening,*
> *Lies without shame, the scoundrel!*
> *Winds singing ballads in minor*
> *Tell of panhandlers and con men.*

But a pastor in a big city is also visited by other kinds of beggars who volunteer to give concerts, exhibitions, or lectures in the church and share the income with the congregation. Others want a collection for this or that cause, and some appear to be satisfied simply to present their cause. All of these strangers have made this kind of begging their life's work.

One of these came to me several times asking for the privilege of presenting to the congregation his children's home mission somewhere in Persia. Finally I brought his request to the board and he was allowed to speak after my sermon on Thursday evening. He talked in broken English with obvious intent to pull heartstrings, which he eminently succeeded in doing. He did not ask for money but for intercessory prayer for the neglected children in his country, but before he finished he announced that if anyone wanted to make a donation he would receive it as people left the church. He stood by the door and the people crowded around him to give their dollars. If it had been a well-known mission perhaps the dollars would not have come out of their pockets and purses so easily. Oh, how emotions can bewitch people! About fifteen years later I met a man in Boston who begged for a children's home in Persia, and if I am not mistaken it was the same person who had appeared in the Tabernacle in Chicago. Did a percentage of his money go to Persia? Who knows? The man was well dressed and presumably living at the expense of gullible people. This business of his year after year seemed to have prospered.

Time after time we were visited by well-known and respected traveling ministers who, as a rule, were welcome to share their spiritual gifts with us. I remember particularly a little episode that took place in connection with a visit one Sunday evening by J. Ledén, who later settled in Sweden. When his postcard came telling us of his intended visit I was away on a mission meeting, so my wife gave it to the chairman of the congregation, F. O. Moberg. He thought it was the respected C. J. Ledin who was coming, and therefore announced the visit as forcefully as possible.

Sunday came, and for the morning service Ledén preached in the Bethany church. Several Tabernacle members who lived near Bethany had the habit of sometimes attending there rather than taking a streetcar to the Tabernacle. Among these was Axel W. Anderson, who thus heard a sermon that morning by Ledén on Jacob the patriarch. But inasmuch as Ledén was not very gifted, it was not a very inspiring sermon. The pastor in the church saved the situation by making some striking comments. After the service and on the way home Anderson, in his characteristic way, lamented that such meagerly gifted people were allowed to enter the ministry.

Then came Sunday evening. Anderson, like a good Tabernacle member, made his way to the evening service and learned from his friends that C. J. Ledin was to preach, which naturally pleased him. But imagine his disappointment when I introduced J. Ledén, who came to the pulpit, read his text about the patriarch Jacob, and gave the same sermon he had given that morning, except that he introduced it with the thoughts that Pastor F. M. Johnson had presented in closing the service. So Anderson and two others heard the same sermon which they thought rather shabby twice on the same Sunday. The preacher was not likely aware that some people in the audience had heard him in the morning, nor did he know what Axel Anderson felt and thought as he listened in the Tabernacle on that occasion.

Like other pastors, I often had opportunities to serve not only my church members but others through ministerial acts. About most of these people there is nothing of particular interest to relate, but three of the fifty-three funerals at which I served had to do with unusual deaths and therefore left a deep impression both on me and on sorrowing friends. On one occasion I served at a double funeral for two sisters who worked in a hotel and perished in a fire. They were so badly burned that permission to review the remains was refused. It was a beautiful spring day in May when we encircled the two coffins in Oakwood Cemetery and pondered the present tragedies, the uncertainties of life, and the beautiful and eternal hope of the resurrection.

On two occasions I conducted funerals for suicides: for a man who had hanged himself and for a woman who had taken poison. To serve in such situations does not bring gladness and one would rather avoid such an assignment, but since this would not be useful one goes with a heavy heart to do what the office requires. The man and his relatives were completely unknown to me, but I was acquainted with the woman, and there was something of pure compassion with her.

She had attended the revivals in the North Side Mission Church which continued into prayer week and beyond, coming to the meetings evening after evening. She was deeply affected by the Spirit of God, but though Christians had serious discussions with her and many made her the subject of intercessory prayer, she did not clearly surrender herself to the Lord. She had an attractive personality, and it became known that she kept company with a distinguished man whose economic circumstances enabled him to provide a good home for her. But he was a doubter, and perhaps it was this acquaintance that hindered her from coming to faith in the Lord. They were married and remained away from the church.

About six years later when I became the pastor in the Mission Tabernacle on the South Side, the couple, who by then lived farther south in the city, came to church now and then. When I visited their home both husband and wife were amiable to me, but in conversation about spiritual things they had the same viewpoints as before. He was still a doubter, she wanted to believe but could not do so. She was melancholy and anxious, and not long after my visit her husband called to break the sad news that she had ended her own life by taking poison. It goes without saying that the funeral was more than usually depressing, but I will believe that God, in spite of all, has saved her soul and will not hold her responsible for a deed committed by her befogged mind. I am certain that God did what he could for her salvation, but in my message I had to speak more warning to the living than comfort because of the departed one. God help us all to believe in Christ and experience in life and death his gracious presence.

Many great changes have taken place in the Tabernacle since I became pastor. In 1897 the spacious building on 30th Avenue was the church home for many Swedes. Now it is owned by a black congregation. Many members of the old church are scattered; some belong to other churches, and some have died. Others have stayed together and meet in the newer and more beautiful Tabernacle on 62nd Street. As for myself, I was then a hopeful young man still in my twenties who stood at the beginning of his journey as a Gospel preacher. Now I must soon pray with the disciples on their way to Emmaus, "Lord, abide with us for it is toward evening, and the day is far spent."

But it is not only the congregation and I who have changed. The city itself has changed, as have conditions over the whole world. When I was pastor in the Tabernacle most of my members lived in houses heated by movable stoves. In better homes gas, rather than electricity, was used for lights, but most had to be satisfied with kerosene lamps, and no one cooked with gas. No church member had a telephone at home. When the first automobile coughed its way forward on the aristocratic Michigan Avenue, the daily newspapers described it as something marvelous, and all the horses were frightened by the wonderful carriage. In that day most people rode the streetcar, but a few of us had begun to use the bicycle for the sake of change and contentment, even though some pious people questioned the propriety of a minister's riding on two wheels which ran one behind the other. Yes, much has changed since I became the preacher in the Tabernacle congregation in Chicago. But the Lord is still the same.

Chapter Twenty-Three

A New Field of Labor

In July of 1900 I received a call to become the pastor of the Mission church on the northeast side of Minneapolis, the present Salem congregation. As I had never preached there and was almost unknown to the people I think some good friends must have recommended me; I can hardly believe that I had won this call by myself. But perhaps it would be more accurate to say that the call came because of God's guidance. God certainly leads his people if he is allowed to, and does it in more than one way.

I thought that the nearly four years I had served the congregation in Chicago was long enough, especially since I was young and perhaps not as comprehensive in my preaching as a more experienced and urbane minister might be. After prayer and thorough, serious consideration I saw this as the right moment to change my field of labor. Yet a person becomes attached to a congregation in sharing spiritual gifts with them and feels a wrenching when he is to leave. In this situation the young people in the congregation made a special effort to persuade me to stay by preparing and signing a resolution. Assuredly I did not want to challenge their will, but I was convinced that I ought to leave. Thus on Sunday, October 14, I preached my farewell sermon in the dear Tabernacle church using the text in Acts 20:32.

We arrived in Minneapolis October 18, 1900. For a few days while our parsonage was being prepared we were guests in the beautiful home of our friends the Aaron Carlsons. The house, which the owner later donated to the Northwest Mission Society, has now been converted to a home for the aged. The parsonage was on Washington Street near 17th Avenue, only a few blocks from the church.

The wooden church building was not particularly imposing inside or out, and though it had served its purpose in the earlier phase of the congregation, it no longer accommodated the people attending. Before my arrival something had been said about building a new church in the near future. Now all saw the necessity of taking action and no longer being satisfied with talk. After deliberation, the board recommended that the congregation move on the building project with dispatch, and the congregation agreed to do so. It was also decided that if anyone had reservations about the building he should avoid speaking about it so that the project should not be hindered, and I think this policy was adhered to very carefully.

This unity in the congregation augured well for the building enterprise. In contrast, if a proposition to build is railroaded through, as sometimes happens, both the project itself and the congregation's inner peace are disturbed. We escaped such an unhappy situation because the members put their shoulders under the burden and helped, with smiles and singing. This is the way a genuine Christian spirit makes itself known.

It is also noteworthy that the congregation decided not to burden their pastor with collecting money for the building project. In most situations the minister would have to assume leadership in this area, but they had seen examples of what difficulties the teacher of the congregation can have if he devotes his time to fundraising. It goes without saying that I did not dislike this decision. Many duties, not the least of which are money matters, tend to distract a preacher from his real spiritual interests, and this is always a curse.

We decided to build a good church, well suited to its purpose but free from unnecessary and costly luxury. If possible we would dedicate it without debt. We also agreed not to beg money from outsiders but to try to bear the burden ourselves. All this was meant honestly, but we ourselves hardly understood how heavy the burdens would become. The congregation then had 155 members, but with two or three exceptions they were all workers of rather limited income. Only Aaron Carlson, John Olson, and August Anderson had their own businesses. We sought to believe in God and work for the good cause as best we could.

It was a pleasure to see the willingness with which all the members helped. Both the preacher and the secretary worked at times on the building as did all men in the congregation; even outsiders thought it was good fun to enter the group and work. When it was nearing completion, about twenty men used to come from their jobs to help in the church for an hour or two before the evening lowered its dark veil over us and the project. Sometimes the women came to serve coffee and good things to eat. Before we went home we would sing a verse of song and thank God. I have never had more pleasant working companions, and others felt the same way.

We had sold the old church for $1,700, if I remember correctly, and the subscriptions had been paid with unexpected haste. But now that the building was almost finished we realized that several thousand dollars more were needed if we were to dedicate the church without debt. Should we try to get pledges for the necessary amount? That was almost unthinkable, but even so we dared to try. A few members felt that we should not burden people now with a new subscription list, but the majority favored the idea and the required sum was pledged to be paid within a year.

To the dedication, which took place October 1, 1901, we invited the president of the Mission Covenant, C. A. Björk. It was a great and glorious celebration. The new church seated about three times as many as the old church, yet it was filled to capacity with interested worshipers. The congregation, deeply thankful to the Lord for his wonderful help, decided to take a special thank-offering at the dedication festivities to go to Covenant missionary work. Pastor Björk was pleasantly surprised by this gesture because usually the offerings on such occasions went to the building fund. He publicly expressed his joy about this interest in missions and prayed for God's blessing on the congregation and upon the holy missionary cause.

We viewed the fact that we did so well in the building enterprise as a special blessing of God, but the unity of the congregation and the leadership of the building committee had much to do with it. In the committee the late August Anderson, who was chair of the church, John Olson, and Aaron Carlson were very active. Olson's calm and wise dealing with people and Aaron Carlson's indomitable will and ability to see progress clearly even when it was difficult, contributed immeasurably to the success of the project. Working with the brethren was a joy. Never did we have a bitter experience within the committee for they worked like a well-oiled machine.

Now that we had a new and roomy building we decided to invite the Mission Covenant to hold its Annual Meeting in our church during the summer of 1903. The invitation was accepted. I had, of course, been present at several Annual Meetings, but now as pastor of the congregation I had to be the host, a new and pleasant experience despite all the work connected with such a gathering. The delegation was very large, as is always the case when the meetings are held in Minneapolis, but we succeeded fairly well in feeding and securing lodging for the people, even for those who had neglected to tell us they were coming. There were, perhaps, more such then than now.

This Annual Meeting was in many ways a very important one, for it transacted difficult business that had lasting and bitter results. The gold discovery in Alaska a year or so previously had led to complications with the former schoolteacher P. H. Anderson, who had been sent to Alaska as a Covenant missionary. Anderson had acquired a profitable gold claim and had donated some money from this to the Mission Covenant. But then came gossip that the gold he had found really belonged to the mission. One did not know what to believe. An agreement was reached with Anderson and he was given a "release" signed by the president and the secretary of the Covenant. In this way the dispute was thought to have been settled satisfactorily. But before long new rumors arose and certain people wanted to nullify the "release" on the grounds that it was not legally binding. There had already been an injurious newspaper battle which had inflamed people's minds against Anderson, and the results were felt in the charged atmosphere of the meeting. A resolution to nullify the release that had been given Anderson in good faith came before the assembly. It was approved by a large majority, though there were powerful voices against it. This decision opened the possibility for a lawsuit, and a former missionary, N. O. Hultberg, assumed the responsibility of presenting the Covenant's claim in court. With this fateful step the Covenant moved into seemingly endless legal proceedings against Anderson. Not until 1920 was this tangle concluded in a peaceful settlement between Anderson and the Mission Covenant, and by then both parties were completely exhausted by the complicated court case.

Activity in the Minneapolis congregation continued calmly and quietly. No miracles were performed that we could parade in the newspapers. We held annual mission meetings that brought great spiritual blessings. (The conferences so common now with their prepared programs and announced speakers had not yet become the fashion.) The spirit of prayer prevailed, and now and then souls came to faith in the Lord, though we did not have a revival in the usual sense of that word. The membership grew year by year but not as much, perhaps, as might have been desirable. In the summer we always had Swedish day school taught by Alma Johnson and our school students Th. Norberg, Renius Johnson, and C. O. Nelson.

Among the great events during my ministry in Minneapolis I count the visit by the well known and respected Swedish teacher Dr. P. Waldenström. Many people had heard him in Sweden and, since arriving in America, had read his letters and edifying articles in different newspapers. Thus it was obvious that he would draw large crowds wherever he appeared. During his travels in this country in 1902-1903 he visited Minneapolis and preached in our church to a packed house, as well as at a united meeting in the old exposition building which is said to accommodate 7,000 people. This building was so crowded that many could not get in, and I, delayed because of a ministerial service, was one of these. According to Waldenström, this was the largest audience he had ever spoken to.

Minneapolis had many varieties of religious thought, denominations, missions, conservative Christians, spiritual mystics, and fanatics, and almost all of them were represented among our Swedish people. Every now and then someone came forth with what he said was an indispensable light and attracted followers for a time. I especially remember one person who appeared in our neighborhood holding meetings in homes and gathering some Mission Friends, Methodists, and Baptists around himself. He condemned denominations, churches, and ministers. He emphasized sanctification and baptism by the Holy Spirit. When more and more people wanted to hear him he hired a hall on Central Avenue at 25th Street, and it was said to be crowded to capacity for a time.

At a minister's meeting I spoke on strange spiritual movements of our day, and my comments were then published in *Veckobladet.* * What I had said therefore became known by the new prophet, and one Sunday evening, according to someone from our church who

---

* literally, "The Weekly Sheet"

was there, he used my article as a text for his message. He held *Veckobladet* in his hand, read something from my lecture, and said, "So says Bowman." Then he read some Bible passage that was supposed to contradict my words and added, "Thus says the Lord." Then he asked, "Who is right, God or Bowman?" and the people shouted, "God is right." Then he read farther in my article and some other Bible passage which was presumed to contradict my words. Again he asked the people, "Who is right, God or Bowman?" And the people cried, "Bowman lies."

After examining my lecture in this way with the audible approval of the audience, he pretended that the Spirit had fallen upon him. He lay prostrate on the floor and prophesied that within such and such a time—I think it was three months—Bowman's congregation would fall into splinters and the righteous would forsake the worldly crowd to join his own company of Spirit-baptized souls. At the time a number of people supposedly believed this humbug. After that I was the minister of the church a few years longer but the congregation did not splinter, and even now after twenty-five years the Salem church still has not been destroyed. The fact that he must have been a lying prophet was also apparent later when he fled, perhaps to play a similar role in another place. He owed money to several of his followers which he naturally did not intend to repay.

"Test the spirits to see whether they are from God," says the Apostle John, but many people in our day seem unable to do so. Rather, they embrace them all, regardless of how many times they get burned. In this way souls forfeit their spiritual treasures to receive something they think is better. But it is exactly the opposite. A certain man in the congregation who was sickly wanted very much to be well. We prayed for him and other Christians prayed for him, but no answer seemed to come other than the answer to Paul, "My grace is sufficient for you." Eventually he came in contact with a group that proclaimed divine healing. He regained his health and ascribed it to the prayer of faith.

Now one would expect that he would become humble and brotherly even beyond what he had been before, but he did not. He became hard and judgmental against all other Christians, and the true mind of Christ seemed to disappear. What a loss. Well, let us above all walk in the fear of the Lord.

Turtle Lake, about twelve miles from Minneapolis-St. Paul, is known to our Mission people in America because many Mission Covenant pastors and other well-known people have been guests there, describing their visits in the newspapers. In the minds of our people the name is associated with Aaron Carlson in Minneapolis.

The place was discovered and became what it was by chance, just as so many other things have resulted from some insignificant occurrence. Our history at Turtle Lake goes back to the summer of 1901 when my family and I had recently moved to Minneapolis. My now departed brother-in-law, Pastor F. M. Johnson, was ill at the time and desired a quiet place somewhere in Minnesota where he could rest for a couple months during the summer. He asked me to find such a place for him, and I consulted Aaron Carlson. Carlson remembered an abandoned farm at Turtle Lake which he had never been interested in but which he now thought was a possibility. One day we met out there to look at the place, and when Mrs. Carlson saw it she too became interested. The result of our visit was that we rented the big farmhouse by the lakeshore for ten dollars a month. There Pastor F. M. Johnson's family, my own, and the Carlson family lived together for one sociable and interesting summer.

Later Carlson bought the farm, thoroughly renovated the old house, built two cottages alongside the house, and in other ways improved and tidied up the place. My family had the privilege of living in one of these cottages during each summer as long as we were in Minneapolis. In the other, S. A. Matson and his family lived for several summers while Matson was the business manager at the newspaper *Veckobladet.* Charles Wallbom, Hjalmer Sundquist, and two other families from St. Paul lived a stone's throw away on the lakeshore. What was temporarily hired for a couple months in order to give my brother-in-law the rest and quiet he needed became a summer home for families, and eventually the permanent home of the Carlsons.

The first several summers we used this place the roads were so poor that access was very difficult. It was no fun to drive back and forth with horses on roads of loose sand. The trip took from one to three hours depending on whether one was driving Maud, Nancy, or Bill. Automobiles were very rare and modern highways had not yet been built, but one could live just as well and enjoy life just as much then as now. Perhaps it was even better then. Both the adults and the children liked the lake and the shore and enjoyed rolling in the sand and climbing in the branches of the trees. Many interesting episodes from Turtle Lake spring to mind, for we had many good times there.

During the summer of 1906 I had the opportunity to visit Sweden. Because I had been troubled by insomnia for some time I needed the rest that this would give. I had had no vacation during the summers except the time I spent at Turtle Lake between Sundays while my family lived there, so when I told the congregation that I wished to visit Sweden, I was immediately given a four-month leave of absence, which I deeply appreciated. About seventeen years had passed since my last visit to my fatherland, and it was now precious to see my home province and the dear ones there at home: my parents, who have since died, and my brother. I preached a few times in my home neighborhood, and presumably at least my parents thought I spoke well. In any event, they were the best of listeners. What parents would not listen well when hearing their homecoming son preach for the first time?

Still, my greatest memory from that visit to Sweden was the Swedish Mission Covenant's Annual Meeting in Stockholm. Also present was Pastor J. Sällström, who had come directly from his trip to Palestine; we had a pleasant time together. At this conference the burning question was whether to move the Mission school from Stockholm out to Lidingö. It was discussed with vitality and heat, many seeming to oppose the move. Dr. Waldenström, who was chairing the conference, gave the gavel to his vice-chair, and in his characteristic way took part in the discussion. His presentation was spiced with humor and his arguments were clear and striking. He spoke in favor of moving the school and refuted the arguments of the opposition point by point. It was extremely interesting to follow the discussion and note the impressions that the different delegates, especially Waldenström, made on the conference. When he had spoken he took his hat and went out for fresh air, letting the voting take its course. By a great majority the delegates voted in favor of the move.

From the Sunday meetings at the great conference I have indelible memories. In the morning service the little hunchbacked Samuel Johanson preached with great power. This was the first time I had heard this noted man who, during the great revivals in Sweden, had been a select instrument in the hands of God. Dr. Waldenström was to preach after him. I wondered if it would be possible for him to sustain the spiritual warmth of the meeting which had been felt while Johanson spoke. But he was gifted to preach God's great acts with uniqueness and inspiration. God's Spirit had power with the people and we forgot everything but the message.

The missions festival was in the afternoon. Then, as well as in the forenoon, the spacious Immanuel Church was crowded with people. The missionary idea was emphasized, and when the meeting ended we all felt that we had been in the Lord's presence.

During my visit I had the undeserved privilege of living in Dr. Waldenström's home, together with Lindgren, who had accompanied Dr. Waldenström on his first visit to America. Thus I became more intimately acquainted with our respected church father whom I had known more generally through his writings and preaching. During his and Mrs. Waldenström's second visit to America I had, of course, been in their fellowship considerably, but the visit in their home was especially interesting, and I soon felt as free and relaxed as in the home of any of my friends in Minneapolis. He related many fascinating matters from the period of the break with the state church and the organization of the Covenant in Sweden. Together we visited "Skansen," of which he was especially proud, the Castle Nordiska Museum, and other places worth seeing. He even offered to obtain a promise for me to have an audience with the king, but this did not interest me sufficiently so I declined politely, and we were still just as good friends.

While in Stockholm I also became acquainted with Carl Boberg,* a poet and member of Parliament, and spent a few hours in pleasant discussion with him. He was very interested in America and in our Swedish people on this continent, but to travel here and greet his many known and unknown friends did not appeal to him.

In company with a minister named Alden, then living in Jönköping, I visited Tännforsen, the old Marby church which was now used as a museum, and Bydalen in Jämtland, all of which were of tremendous interest. I also attended the annual meeting of the Ansgar Society in Östersund where, among other things, I wrote a letter at one o'clock in the morning without any artificial light. The summer nights in Norrland are wonderful! On the way to Bydalen I saw an American flag waving from a flagpole by a villa which some American had rented. He was expressing his patriotism on the Fourth of July.

---

* author of several famous hymns, including "O Mighty God, When I Behold the Wonder"

224

Among the memories from my journey to Sweden is a visit to Fritz Peterson, who was a friend in my youth when he lived in Chicago. He is now a well-situated pastor in Sala, which has one of the most beautiful Mission churches in Sweden. I also remember the young people's meeting at Kinekulle and the great summer meetings at Vanneberga. There I first met the preacher J. Nordberg, who for some time had been harassed in the newspapers in connection with the sad death of a young servant girl. He was, however, finally acquitted from all responsibility.

The pleasant summer in Sweden sped away, and soon I had to pack my belongings and begin my journey home. I struggled through a tender farewell to the near and dear ones in Blågrindar, the place where my parents and brother now lived. Oh, those farewell moments, how painful they are. I hoped then to visit the old home settlement once more to see the familiar faces, but a quarter of a century has now passed and both Father and Mother have been buried. My brother is still living and at times the thought of another visit to my home and fatherland beckons and plays in my mind. But I am not sure that will ever take place.

Chapter Twenty-Four

Out in the Field

In October 1900, a year after I had moved to Minneapolis and begun my work as pastor in the Salem congregation, I was elected secretary of the Northwest Conference. The annual meeting that year was held in the old Salem Church and Hjalmer Sundquist, then pastor in St. Paul, was elected chairman. The conference had a large and important home mission field. Over the years much good had been accomplished, but there was still much to be done and the work lacked supervision and order. Pastor Skogsbergh had been the leading spirit from the beginning, but as pastor of a large church, president of the school, and sometimes editor of *Veckobladet* besides, he hardly had time to satisfy the needs of his congregation. He already had too many irons in the fire.

There had been a splendid awakening spirit among the people, but preachers with all sorts of angles had diligently traveled over the district splitting congregations and severing Christians from each other. We therefore needed to gather and unify the work as well as set it in order if it was to make progress.

Pastor Sundquist and I understood each other very well and cooperated for the good of the conference in the time we could spare from our churches. I felt a certain responsibility for the home missions, perhaps more than was necessary, but the common and united work interested me. I also realized what a terrible loss we would suffer if it was not taken care of better than before. At that time the Congregational Church in America was making plans to bring the Mission Friends in Minnesota into their denomination. One of their ministers wrote in the newspapers that twenty-four new preachers should be brought to this area immediately and be paid temporarily from the treasury of the American Home Mission Society. I did not believe that such a relationship to the Americans would benefit either the field or our Mission Covenant, and I saw clearly that the best way to forestall such events was for the Swedes themselves to invest more interest and energy in these missions.

Because of my interest in these needs I was away from my church more than most ministers are and more than most congregations permit. The board of the Salem church understood the situation on the field and were patient with me even though I was absent a great deal. For almost seven years I took time from the work of the congregation in order to spend time on the tasks of the conference.

It finally became clear to me that I could not go on giving more and more time to missions without harming the work at home. I thought this problem might be solved if the church called an assistant pastor, and I presented this plan to the board, who discussed the possibility but decided that it would not be useful. They therefore asked me to leave the service of the conference and devote myself wholly to the congregation. However, about the same time I was called to become full-time conference superintendent. What should I do?

Leaving the church to become full-time superintendent would entail a sacrifice for me, but perhaps an even greater one for my wife because in that position I would have to travel most of the time, leaving her alone to take care of our children and our home. When a father must be away week after week, month after month, the wife and mother must feel a heavy burden at times, but for the sake of the good cause she was willing to take on these responsibilities. After weighing the situation seriously we decided that in the Lord's name I would accept the new call.

To describe my many journeys in all directions in Minnesota and part of Wisconsin as well as side trips to North and South Dakota and even Canada would be neither possible nor interesting. Yet I want to give a clear and fairly complete picture of these three years which were so rich in experience and left such a wealth of memories with me.

I had complete freedom to organize my work as I thought best. I arranged to spend five days a month at home, but as a rule I was away every Sunday, at times preaching in two or three places, and I even had a couple of meetings on weekdays if the people could gather. On occasion I would stay in one place for a whole week and have meetings daily. When a church needed special help to achieve better order I would try to use my influence in the right direction, but usually they were so used to disorder that they distrusted any attempt to change them and bring about unity. Preachers had zealously sown suspicion against organization and denominations, and this had born a rich harvest, harming the whole field. However, little by little conditions became better and more promising.

In my travels I used all kinds of conveyances. More than once I walked six or eight miles carrying my suitcase because for some reason no one was at the station to meet me. My "apostles' horses" were younger then so I did not mind the long stretches of road. Twice I traveled short distances with oxen, but I often traveled twenty or fifty miles with horses, and a few times farther. These were not racehorses but tired work nags which in uncultivated places plodded along to make the trip more leisurely for their masters. At the end of this period I went by automobile a few times, but this was mostly in the cities, as the roads in the countryside were not made for automobiles in those days.

I was a guest in several hundred homes, from modern residences in the cities and countryside to the most pitiful small huts in new clearings in the forest. Now and then I fought all night with bedbugs and mosquitoes. Sometimes I slept in an attic where snow crept in through cracks in the walls and where hoarfrost settled on the blanket from my breath. Usually I had a bed to myself but occasionally I had to share with members of the family because there was no extra room in the crowded home, even if they had room in their hearts for the stranger.

I came into contact with people of very different cultures. Some had seen better days in their homeland and carried with them a certain refinement even among the stumps and animals. The many weathers of the passing years may have bleached much of the original breeding and culture, but enough clearly remained to bear witness to their better days, and they seemed to be refreshed by speaking to someone from the outside world. On the other hand, I also met people who had no such breeding but who were nevertheless pious and good. At times I was addressed as "pastor" even when I had implored them to discard the title. At other times I was addressed with a broad familiar *du* by young men who were not yet dry behind their ears.* But it was all interesting and I sought, with the apostle, to be content in whatever state.

On one occasion I was snowbound with a pioneer family out on the prairie. For three days a mighty blizzard raged with such biting cold that no one in the area dared to go out, and to try to gather the people for a meeting was unthinkable. Later the newspaper said that several persons had perished in the storm. To be inside day after day and hear the terrible howl of the wind around the corners of the house was a unique experience. Under the effect of it I wrote the following poem, which is included as an echo from my travels between 1907 and 1910.

A WINTER PICTURE FROM THE PRAIRIE

As angry waves on stormy sea
Strike blows against a ship
So winter wind and spraying snow
Attack my windowpane.

Like hungry howls of angry wolves
The bitter winds now sing
A threatening song at cabin's door
For old as well as young.

Boreas with his hand of ice
Is violent and bitter.
He harms, yet with his stormy whip
Will often miss his victim.

In cozy cabin's quiet fort
Are smiles and jolly fire.
Boreas there cannot invade
Wherever else he rages.

------

* The Swedish language has two forms for the second person. *Ni* is the polite form to be used with strangers. The word *du* is reserved for close friends and family only.

The boy so far from home and hearth
Through deepening drifts is plowing
With heavy steps his journey long—
His eyes betray his worry.

His poor heart full of pathos cries,
"So gray and grim the world
There is no heart still warm and kind.
I perish in the cold!"

Boreas with his lashing whip
Now answers his complaint
As if this were harsh nature's law:
To chastening, add revenge.

The little boy now stumbles, falls,
In drifts he finds his grave.
Boreas rages on and on
To obliterate the dead.

How shall we understand the storm's
Grim play with deadly arrows
Against the pale, defenseless boy
With feelings warm and tender?

Why does the bitter winter scorn
The needy children's suffering?
Can love be found in least degree
In this? We await the answer.

In this context let me bring in another sketch from 1908 which may be of interest and value to those who are concerned with the contributions of our Swedish people in America. It was published in *Veckobladet* more than twenty years ago and describes the conditions in northern Minnesota.

After I had waited for twenty hours in a miserable hamlet in the outlying countryside, the train finally came. It consisted of a little antiquated engine with a shiny tuneful bell followed by two freight cars, a baggage car, half of which was furnished for the first-class passengers, and an old discarded immigrant car to be used by smokers and lumberjacks.

We took off into the forest over bogs and swamps. The train heaved and lurched on the rough rails and poor rail bed like a ship on a stormy sea. We had to swallow our breakfasts well so as not to become ill, but we took courage because we knew that this would pass. According to the new fare and the speed of the train it cost exactly thirty cents an hour to ride—that is how slowly it moved. Three times a week the train made this run into the forest and back again.

In little clearings here and there along the railroad we saw the humble huts of the pioneers. There at the edge of the forest was a whole family waiting to see the great event, the arrival of the train from the outside world. There stood father in his patched, blanched overalls and slouch hat with a shovel in his hand. There stood mother beside him with a little one on her arm. Several other children shyly poked their curly heads from behind their parents. In front of all was the dog wagging his tail and at a distance was the cat ready to meow.

What do these settlers in the forest think about? Perhaps they remember bygone days and long for the relatives and friends they left in order to break new ground and build their own home here in the forest. Or perhaps they remember the unemployment, the lack of bread, or the doctor bills in some big city where they struggled to exist. Possibly they complain about their hard lot in the forest, but they also thank God for freedom, work, and health. However this may be, we must respect these courageous Swedes who dared the adventure of clearing the land and creating homes in the outlying areas. They are worthy of our attention.

It had rained all day, and when we came to the end of the railroad tracks, it poured. When the rain subsided a bit we continued our journey, walking under our umbrella with our suitcase in hand. In half an hour we were at our destination, a pioneer's lonely hut in which lived some old friends, pious and amicable. The cottage, about sixteen feet long and twelve feet wide, was built of big timbers and had a low door and two small windows. Inside there was only one room, which served as kitchen, dining room, bedroom, closets, and cupboards. The ceiling was about seven feet at its highest point, and both the walls and ceiling were papered with Swedish, Norwegian, and American newspapers, so that one could stand nearby and read old news in three languages.

The room was furnished with two beds, a table with two homemade chairs (one of them a common wood block), a simple cook stove, and a sewing machine. In this plain abode I was given a hearty welcome and at once felt at ease. Sophisticated civilization does not create a happy home nor does luxury and finery. We talked about old things and new, ate, drank coffee, slept, read our Bible, sang, and thanked God. I could not have had it more pleasant if I had been at the White House in Washington.

The following day I took a walk through the thick forest. My thoughtful guide let me borrow some leggings of waxed cloth so that I would be protected from the moisture on the grass and bushes, but they were about six inches too short. This inconvenience was overcome by lengthening the suspenders with a pair of hair ribbons which belonged to the little girl in the cottage. Then the big city galoshes were bound to my feet so that they would not be left behind in the clay. Thus we walked through brush, across fallen trees, and over stones and tussocks until we finally came to "the clearing" where the good-natured cow was feeding on the abundant grass, making music with her bell. Returning to the cabin, we found the little room warm and pleasant. Here the galoshes and leggings were laid aside to dry by the stove.

A few souls gathered in this forest region to hear the living Word of God. About twenty were present, a large crowd if one takes into account the "road" conditions and the distance they had to walk. No one could ride to the meetings, partly because they had no wagons and partly because there were no roads for such conveyances anyway. One was fortunate to have a path to walk on, for not long before this area had been the undisturbed home for everything wild. Now people lived here in the forest, and year by year wildlife had to retreat because the Swedes had come to cultivate the ground, build barns, and establish pleasant homes. Let us tip our hats to the industrious people who would assume such a task.

Often on my journeys, whether during this period or at other times, I thought about my family. On a trip to the southern states in the fall of 1913, while I was sitting in a hotel in New Orleans and longing for home, I wrote the following little verses to our daughter who was then fifteen years old.

TO THE FIFTEEN-YEAR-OLD

So now you are fifteen!
I hardly can believe!
It seems like yesterday
You took your first small steps.

You were a little mite,
Packed full of energy.
How we enjoyed your smile,
Your happy carefree life!

Now you're as tall as mother
And learn life's lessons well,
Your glance the same as ever.
Your heart is as before.

Remain then good and faithful
Just as in former years,
Until life's seed has ripened—
Then splendid your reward.

In the spring of 1906, before I entered the service of the conference, I published my first book, *The Revival in Wales*. It had something over one hundred pages and was a collection of stories about the wonderful spiritual movement which went through Wales and attracted great attention among Christians worldwide. The book contained nothing original, for I gleaned these stories from newspapers and periodicals and wrote them in Swedish. My intention was to awaken our people to spiritual renewal, which was needed then as now. The book was received with interest, the edition being sold out in a comparatively short time.

In the fall of 1907 the first edition of my book *The Mission Covenant in America* was published. For many years, yes, ever since my arrival in America, I had collected historical data and little anecdotes about our Swedish Mission people in America without any thought of publishing them. I had had excellent opportunities to gather such materials because I very early came in contact with Pastor C. A. Björk and others who had shared in the pioneering of the Covenant. Now and then I had looked over these historical resources but had been unable to persuade myself to shape and publish them. Yet more and more the thought matured in my mind, so I worked on the manuscript during my trip to Sweden and then in free moments after my return.

The publication of this book, a pleasant surprise for many, was warmly acknowledged by both individuals and newspapers. One of the pioneers assured me that the book was worth its weight in gold, but inasmuch as he often exaggerated, I did not consider his words entirely dependable. Since there were many orders, I saw that a new edition would be needed and began planning for it immediately. Among other preparations, I sent the book to several of our pioneers, asking them to examine it and point out errors in the recounting of events or the evaluation of the work of the Swedish Mission people in earlier days. I received a few minor corrections and took action when the facts so required, but on the whole they were very approving. The second edition was published in the fall of 1908 and has been sold out for a long time.

Chapter Twenty-Five

Another Field of Labor

Usually ministers—and other people as well—regard a call to another congregation or to some department of the denomination as a compliment, especially if it is to a larger field or a more important task. Because of this, some ministers are tempted to seek calls they do not intend to accept. This unethical conduct has its own punishment, however, for when the people discover it it brings first disdain and later an end to calls which might be welcome if not necessary for a continuing opportunity to serve as a minister.

However, circumstances arise in the experience of every pastor when he feels a special need to change the scene of his ministry. If, by God's grace and blessing, this feeling can be conquered so that he can continue in the same call with joy and success despite the hopelessness that he felt before, this is a good sign. It is a sign of weakness to long for a new field as soon as difficulties arise. Even so, a change is sometimes useful for both the minister and the congregation. Of this we have all seen clear examples.

During the seven years I served the Salem Church in Minneapolis, I received calls to the Mission churches in Omaha, Nebraska, and Rockford, Illinois. But in the face of those opportunities I was convinced that I ought to stay at Salem because there was still much to accomplish there. Later when I was called to serve the Northwest Conference it was just as clear to me that I should accept the call, even though it involved sacrifices for both my family and me, and I believe that I acted according to the will of God.

After serving the conference for three years I began to long to lead a church as pastor again. Just then an unusual thing happened. Within about two weeks I had calls to the Mission church in Boston, the Mission church in San Francisco, and the editorship of the newspaper *Veckobladet* in Minneapolis—three invitations from three different places. I had never been so rich in calls before, nor have I ever been since. One can easily get along with fewer.

Letters of call can be interesting documents for study, both in form and content. All the calls I have ever received from churches have stated that after mature deliberation and prayer the decision was made to send the call to me. That is good and beautifully done. They have also expressed the hope that I might find it in keeping with God's will to accept the call. That is also a beautiful wish. But for me it has not always been easy to decide what is the will of God.

In one letter the secretary wrote so unclearly that he actually expressed the hope that God might protect us from the unity of working together, but I accepted the call anyway and worked in unity with the congregation for several years. One of the letters I received did not say a word about salary, much less moving expenses, vacations, or other arrangements that are usually specified in calls nowadays. Another, in regard to salary, cited the words of the psalmist, "I have been young, and now am old; yet I have not seen the righteous forsaken nor his children begging bread," and Jesus's word, "The laborer deserves his wages." Leaving the question of salary unstated in a call was nothing unusual in those days, nor was it any risk for the minister to accept a call under such conditions.

Though moving west had more appeal than moving east, I was nevertheless convinced that I should accept the call to the Mission church in Boston. At the end of August 1910 we departed from Minneapolis, which had become so dear to us. Leaving the pleasant summer place at Turtle Lake and the large circle of friends with whom we had shared many blessings during ten years was not easy, but that is the lot of the minister, and he must take this into account from the beginning.

The departure was difficult for me but even more difficult for the family. Many friends gathered at the railroad station to say farewell and wave their white handkerchiefs in a last good wish to us when the train slowly rolled out into the night. Son Carl, then six years old, stared into the darkness through the car window. Then he turned to me with tear-filled eyes and stammered, "I thought it would be fun to ride on the train but it isn't." Farewell feelings stirred us all.

After a few days with relatives and friends in Chicago, hasty visits in Jamestown and Buffalo, and of course a trip to Niagara Falls, we arrived in good shape at North Station in Boston. There stood G. F. Södergren, the friendly and thoughtful chair of the congregation, and other friends waiting to meet and welcome the strangers from the west.

We were taken by automobile to 50 Woodbine Street, Roxbury, which was then the parsonage. Our familiar furniture was already there as if roguishly smiling at us. Some women in the congregation who had been there to clean and put things in order as best they could, now had a tasty meal ready for us, and when we had amply provided ourselves, we read the Word of God together and thanked him for his rich blessing and for the unseen days we were to live in Boston. It was comforting to commend ourselves into God's hand.

When the friends had left and we were alone, we found, among other things, a calling card from Dr. P. Waldenström and his wife, on which he had written some encouraging words. He had earlier visited us in Minneapolis and had baptized our youngest boy. On the return journey they had stopped in Boston and even looked in on our future home, leaving this brotherly greeting. We treasured this.

In the evening a welcome reception was held for us in the old Mission church on Ruggles Street. The church was decorated in good taste with flowers from the friend of flowers, Almborg's garden in Melrose. But the best decorations are people, and they had gathered to fill the church. About ten ministers were present, among whom were J. A. Johnson, senior and foremost, and N. E. Johnson, my good friend from Providence. They greeted us heartily and welcomed us to the ministers' fellowship of greater Boston. Chairman Södergren led the program with a sure hand and the genial rhymer of the congregation, J. E. Friberg, had strung his lyre and recited a long poem expressing his own good wishes as well as those of the congregation. One verse serves here as a sample of his greeting:

Be welcome here to spread
The Word among our people,
To comfort those who sorrow,
And make the Gospel clear,
To care for frail sheep,
And heal the lacerated.
But into sinners' wounds
Rub salt for salvation.

One of the older members of the congregation, J. A. Gustafson, wrote a lovely description of the festivities in church as well as the following poem for the first page of *Österns Veckoblad*:

The Eastern field welcomes
You heartily, our brother,
To stand where God has placed you
And do what he commands.
God give you grace and power
To seek your Master's honor,
Interpret his Law humbly,
Live pleasing to the Lord.

The friends in Boston did their best to give us a good impression and take from us any feeling of being strangers. They succeeded.

This is, of course, as it ought to be, that a congregation welcomes its new pastor heartily. If the members regard him as a gift of God, receive him as God's messenger, and respect him as his office requires, all will go well; if he is a faithful servant of the Lord, he can accomplish his work and be a blessing to the congregation.

Occasionally welcome receptions are in poor taste because of unsound or meaningless praise. In such situations one doesn't have to be a prophet to predict that the working relationship between pastor and congregation will not be what the beautiful words at the reception promised. All dishonesty and artifice should therefore be absent from such events. From the beginning we experienced every possible goodwill from the congregation.

On Sunday, September 4, I preached my installation sermons, using a text from Isaiah 61 both morning and evening. I hope my messages were not too narrow. God's word is rich, and the same text can suffice for several sermons if we have our eyes open when we study.

If anything unusual happened that first Sunday I would probably remember it, but I don't recall anything special. God's blessing rested upon us, that I can say with certainty, because it is always true according to his faithful promises of grace. Every day is a day of grace, a day of blessings.

Boston is a fascinating place for one who moves there from the west, for it is the very cradle of the United States, with many historical monuments in and around it. If one has a taste for history one is really entertained there. Bostonians generally take an interest in the historical sites and make it a point of honor to acquaint visitors with them.

Certain parts of the city remind one of Europe, especially England. One feels an atmosphere of age and permanence upon entering Boston, particularly if one arrives from some western state where youthful rush is prevalent. In Boston speed is not the most important. The narrow winding streets slow the traffic and confuse the newcomer. Yes, they almost awaken animosity. But after living there for a while one becomes used to them, finding them natural and quite interesting. At that point one has been recreated to fit into the new situation. It is fortunate that we can adapt this way to every new environment into which we are cast.

Early Boston was the center of culture, and the city still has this prestige though it is not as apparent as it once was. The following household saying now strikingly characterizes Boston, New York, and Chicago: "In Boston they ask, 'What do you know?' in New York, 'What do you own?' and in Chicago, 'What can you do?' " A well-educated person is perhaps more highly valued in Boston than anywhere else in our country.

Boston used to be especially aristocratic, too. It was the home of many wealthy and learned people whose forebears had come to America on the *Mayflower,* and they were proud of this. A considerable number of this group no doubt still live in the Boston area, but in recent decades another class of people has invaded the city and in part destroyed the old aristocracy. Immigrants from southern Europe and Ireland have streamed in. The dispersed children of Israel have also gathered there in large numbers. The Irish have taken control of politics and the Jews of business. The old Yankee stock is therefore in the minority, even in Boston.

When we lived there, Boston also had a population of Swedes, though not as many as some other U.S. cities. The different Swedish denominations and societies had a rather large attendance, and without a doubt the Mission church was one of the strongest Swedish congregations in the city, if not the strongest. The church, which had seating for somewhat over 600, was full on Sunday evenings during most of the year, but was much less crowded during the summer months when many of the servant girls who attended the church accompanied their masters and mistresses to summer homes and were therefore absent.

Sunday morning services were always poorly attended, partly because the Swedes were so scattered throughout the city that they had to take streetcars to get to church, and partly because the congregation had Sunday school work not only in the church but also in East Boston, Savin Hill, West Roxbury, and two places in Dorchester. These schools required teachers and other workers, and since the classes were held on Sunday mornings, it was impossible for these people to come to the morning worship service.

This arrangement was not ideal, but it was the best possible under the circumstances. One must be directed in the work according to conditions and do whatever serves best in each place. It does not pay to cling to old practices if the goal can be reached by changing the approach, for the goal is always the most important. It was good for the spiritual health of the believers to have this opportunity for personal work; it helped keep them warm for the cause of the Lord's kingdom.

When I came to Boston the congregation had the idiosyncracy of closing down the Sunday school and discontinuing young people's meetings during the summer months. That seemed to me a terribly dangerous habit and I could scarcely understand how my predecessor, the zealous Pastor August Erickson, could tolerate it. I told Brother Södergren that I feared this practice would cripple the church, but he comforted me by saying that there was no danger of this in Boston, however it might be in other places. When I had been there longer and had seen how this worked, I came to the same opinion as Södergren, for the situation in Boston was unlike any I had been in before.

At that time the Boston congregation also carried on a mission at North End, where we used to hold meetings on the third floor of a rented hall (I think it was at 164 Hanover Street). We brought singers and other musicians who would go out on the streets in the area inviting people to the meetings and then would participate in the service. The attendance varied between thirty and seventy or seventy-five. This was usually a ragtag audience, poor and homeless, nearly all fallen and influenced by drink. It was not difficult to persuade them to ask for prayer after the sermon; they did that willingly, at times seeming truly distressed about their sins. But most often this was only preparation for another "prayer" which they stammered forth time after time, the prayer for a coin for a night's lodging, which they really intended to use for another drink. They were more thirsty for alcohol than for peace with God, poor people who have been bound in the snares of drunkenness. But occasionally some soul was won and remained in the faith to become an active member of the congregation.

A year or so before I arrived, the Boston church had founded a home for servant girls who were without work. An old residence at 30 Savin Street was rented and furnished for this purpose, and it became a good mission which brought blessing and honor to the congregation. But the house was old and uncomfortable and almost impossible to heat in the winter. Thus we decided soon after my arrival to buy our own home for the girls, and after much looking, we purchased a residence at 169 Townsend Street. We paid $7,000 for the lot and house and about $3,000 for renovations and rebuilding. We collected $1,500 by subscriptions. After it had been furnished, we had a home fairly well adapted to its purpose in which about thirty people could live, besides service personnel. On October 15, 1912, we dedicated it. It was called "Fridhem," the Home of Peace.

Epilogue

No reasonably thoughtful reader of these memoirs can have missed in them the pathos—and the excitement—of one of history's grandest adventures: the transplantation of millions of lives from the Old World to the New within two, at most three, generations. Of Swedes alone, more than a million came, and no doubt many thousands of lonely, frightened children like the eleven-year-old Kalle, waiting in the vast confusion of Chicago to meet a relative, luckier than many to be found and given shelter.

Who among us today would permit such an enterprise in our children or grandchildren—sent halfway around the globe on a one-way ticket to a land filled with Amalekites, speaking a Babel of tongues, and following God only knows what strange corrupting customs? An eleven-year-old boy working to earn his way, ten hours daily, six days weekly, dodging for his life among saws and planers and whirring machinery belts, learning quickly to speak English and the even more confusing "Swinglish" patois used by his elder comrades in the shop.

That the boy survived, that he grew, always too long in both arm and leg for his clothes (in the shop they called him "the broomstick"), was a source of wonder to the mature man who decades later recalled the boy and told his story. We know this to be true because reliable witnesses tell us that Carl Victor Bowman was not a man to speak much of himself, but that he had a strong sense of history. He did not give us his autobiography, a few words about his origins and childhood, and then an account of his pastoral and denominational life. Just the reverse. He told the story of the boy, and felt no need to continue it when the boy had become the man. Kalle was an archetype, an experience to be preserved, perhaps never again to be repeated in quite the same way.

The conclusion of it is to be found in the poignancy of his *Julotta* experience, Christmas 1889. The boy, now nearly twenty-two, has returned after a decade to his Swedish parish for the holidays, and perhaps—to remain? Sitting in the Marbäck Parish church, "he understood at last better than ever before how Americanized he had become during his stay in America, and how powerfully that land drew his spirit. He belonged on the other side of the sea."

That last sentence invokes a primal mystery. That a peasant boy from Marbäck should be "at home" in a faraway place named (outlandishly) Chicago, that he should there, in 1885, meet his Lord, who transformed his life and ambitions in entirely unexpected and unpredictable ways, and that he should go on, in the fullness of time, to become a pastor, a Covenant leader, and the Covenant's first comprehensive historian is entirely beyond our ability to explain. And his. He has that sense of wonder, for the boy Kalle, and for the thousands of others who all unknowing made the pilgrimage to the Promised Land, "the other side of the sea."

Bowman's first letters to David Nyvall, inquiring for information about the Covenant's school in Minneapolis—its curriculum, its terms of study, its costs—reflect a peculiar completeness already present in the petitioner. The handwriting is precise, disciplined, the grammar excellent, the questions clearly phrased. Bowman will be responsible for his own costs: he owns a lot in Chicago he can sell if need be. One feels the recognizing joy in Nyvall's responses. Here indeed is a dimensional man, ready for instruction, ready for work, but keeping his own counsel and without affronting courtesy charting his own path.

Bowman put in two sessions at the Covenant school: in 1892 during Minneapolis days and in 1894-1896 after the school had moved to Chicago. He served student pastorates in Escanaba, Michigan, and Blue Island, Illinois, before assuming the pastorate of the Tabernacle congregation in Chicago during 1896.

For the next twenty-four years, Bowman served pastorates in four influential and growing Covenant congregations; the Chicago

Tabernacle (1896-1900); Salem in Minneapolis (1900-1907); Boston (1910-1917); and Edgewater in Chicago (1917-1920). During his Salem days he served for three years (1904-1907) as part-time district superintendent of the Northwest Missionary Association before receiving full-time appointment (1907-1910).

In 1920 Bowman was elected to be the first permanent secretary of the Covenant with special responsibilities for foreign missions. When E. G. Hjerpe retired in 1927, the Covenant Annual Meeting elected Bowman to succeed him as president of the church, the third since 1885, the year of its founding and of Bowman's conversion.

Both as secretary and as president, Bowman had to face formidable problems. The China fields were in uproar because of internal political instability. In the United States, conflicting ambitions and the closing off of new Swedish immigration raised basic questions of Covenant identity in the new American scene. Powerful folk leaders like Gustaf F. Johnson of the Minneapolis Tabernacle leveled attacks against North Park—and by implication the Covenant itself—as having lost its pristine devotion to Christ and the Gospel. Hardly a week passed when *Missions Vännen* did not complain about some new evidence that the faith once delivered was being washed down the drain. As dreadful example (and given the times, to many it *did* seem dreadful), Olga Lindborg declared that moving pictures could be made a powerful instrument of Christian education! Movies! Underneath it all was the deep uncertainty of an immigrant church facing the inevitable language question with all its unspoken transitional meanings, the relation of the generations to each other, and to their common traditions.

How shall a leader respond? Bowman as leader was, according to the witnesses, quiet and firm. People waited to hear his summary of the evidences, confident that he would present them fairly. That must not have been simple work given the provocative spirit of the times, nor the awful psychological tensions under which people suffered after the Great Crash of 1929 and the smashing of cultural illusions as the country slid into the gray despondency of the 1930s. But no leadership, no matter how measured and wise, could satisfy the passions of the day—or supply in honesty the simplistic solutions demanded by an insecure people or their ambitious spokesperson. Times were changing: the future was clear to no one who had the openness of mind to look objectively at the scene.

For President Bowman these stormy years were doubly painful. He suffered increasingly from a kind of inflammatory arthritis moving through his physical system, bringing unbearable pain and, finally, depriving him of the capacity to walk. There was nothing to do but resign his office in 1932. During the final five years, until his death on August 4, 1937, even the confined life of his wheelchair came to be a physical torment. We have a photo of him during these last years: sitting rigidly upright in his chair, looking grim behind his beard, a man who during all his productive years had shaven clean.

Bowman wrote well. He was careful about research, restrained and balanced in his presentation. During his Minneapolis years he wrote *Missionsvannerna i Amerika,* the first comprehensive investigation of the rootages and development of the American Covenant, published in 1907, and in an expanded second edition during 1908. (Not until 1925 was the work translated and published as *The Mission Covenant of America.*) In 1934 Bowman published *Carl August Bjork, en levnadsteckning,* translated in 1973 by Eric G. Hawkinson, presently available in typescript at the Covenant Archives. Here Bowman paid tribute to his old pastor, and his predecessor as the first president of the Covenant.

Bowman did smaller pieces on occasion. The first was *"Vackelsen i Wales"* ("The Revival in Wales," 1906, Minneapolis). Another, "On Speaking in Tongues," a balanced and judicious summary of New Testament experience of the phenomenon, has been translated from the Swedish by Vernon Westburg. Another, "On Mission Friend Principles," was translated by Eric Hawkinson and first published in *The Covenant Quarterly,* February 1971, subsequently printed in Glenn Anderson's *Covenant Roots: Sources and Affirmations,* 1980. Other articles and sermons from Bowman have appeared in books and periodicals, but as yet no comprehensive bibliography has been compiled.

We cannot leave these memoirs without asking when the boy Kalle av Marbäck became President Carl Victor Bowman. Beware, dear reader, of a simple answer. Life, as it really is, is the final astonishment.

Zenos E. Hawkinson

Family Photos

Bowman's earliest home (left), at Hembygdsgården, Marbäck

Marbäck Parish church

Bowman's parents,
August and
Johanna Skott
with his
brother Oscar

Aneby, where Bowman began his journey to America

Blågrindar (the Blue Gate), the home of Bowman's parents and brother at the time of his second trip to Sweden, 1906

Smedhemmet (the Blacksmith's Home), where Bowman was born

Klinten, where Bowman's parents were living when he made his first return trip to Sweden

Stalpet, with its mill, in the parish of Marbäck

252

The portrait taken of
Bowman his second day in
Chicago, which was sent
home to his parents

Bowman as an adolescent

253

Bowman in 1889

Bowman in 1896

C. V. and Julia Nelson Bowman's wedding picture

Bowman (left) in Minneapolis *Veckoblad* office with
G. Frykman, E. A. Skogsbergh, S. A. Matson,
and H. Sundquist

C.V. and Julia Bowman with daughter Alpha

The Bowman children, April, 1909. Left to right: Earl, Alpha, Malcolm, and Carl

Old Salem Mission Church, Minneapolis

Parsonage at 2210 Polk Street, Minneapolis

Salem Church, built in 1901

Second Bowman home in Boston, Harrishof Street

Bowman family in Boston, 1915. Left to right: Raymond, C. V., Carl, Malcolm, Alpha, Earl, and Julia

Boston years portraits

At Niagara Falls with David Nyvall (left), Aaron Carlson, and A. L. Skoog

With E. A. Skogsbergh (left)

Bowman as president

The elder Bowman

C. V. and Julia Bowman on annual
summer trip to Milwaukee

At Ridge Avenue home
in Chicago, 1930s

With Julia in Ridge Avenue home, 1932